Hjortspring

Some say a cavalry corps,
some infantry, some, again,
will maintain that the swift oars

of our fleet are the finest
sight on dark earth; but I say
that whatever one loves, is.

Sappho (c. 600 BC)

Klavs Randsborg

HJORTSPRING

WARFARE AND SACRIFICE
IN EARLY EUROPE

AARHUS UNIVERSITY PRESS

AARHUS UNIVERSITY PRESS
University of Aarhus
DK-8000 Aarhus C
Fax (+ 45) 8619 8433

73 Lime Walk
Headington, Oxford OX3 7AD
Fax (+ 44) 1865 750 079

Box 511
Oakville, Conn. 06779
Fax (+ 1) 203 945 9468

ANSI/NISO
Z39.48-1992

Contents

List of Illustrations

Introduction

Ancient warfare is an area of many and highly diverse interests. Written sources provide most of the detailed knowledge available of the politics, logistics, warriors, tactics, battles, conventions, and rituals of combat in classical antiquity. They even furnish information on affairs in Europe beyond the Mediterranean. Archaeology provides a picture of, for instance, armament and fortifications and has, furthermore, the ability to operate both outside and inside the realm of the written text (cf. Fig. 1). Nevertheless, only in a very few and unique cases are we able to observe the contours of the total material reality of ancient armies. One of these rare cases is the Hjortspring boat and weapons sacrifice, most probably the spoils of a defeated enemy army, found in a tiny bog on the island of Als, in Jylland/Jutland, in pre-Roman Iron Age Denmark: this society being remote from the Mediterranean but sharing with the south both cultural roots and elements of military and other behaviour.

The small Hjortspring army was probably made up of groups of mostly young male warriors, selected for physical, psychological and social reasons for expedition. Such a group combined, very economically, in one and the same person the warrior and sailor/rower/paddler (the wooden Hjortspring boat is, in fact, a huge canoe). Combat at sea was the exception. By contrast, in the Mediterranean during classical antiquity, a relatively small number of soldiers were transported on the warships and by a very large number of mariners and, in particular, rowers. Here combat at sea, including the ramming of enemy ships during rapid manoeuvre, was common. Larger numbers of ordinary infantry for operations on land would be transported in cargo-vessels under sail.

The Hjortspring platoons or companies of warriors were hardly identical with the total military force of a contemporaneous North European society. If fighting at home (or during migration), and especially on the defence, a community would no doubt mobilize most of its able men, who made up its social fabric, and, occasionally, perhaps even women and other individuals. The status of the

Fig. 1. The so-called Chigi-vase (found in Etruria). Corinthian work from c. 650 BC.

warrior, as of young bound closely to his comrades in arms and the local war-lords, was, throughout the first millennium BC, as well as the first millennium AD, in Northern Europe expressed in fine arms, sometimes included in burials, sometimes found as sacrifices in bogs to the forces of war, obviously closely linked with the wet subterranean domain of fertility (cf. Boyer 1981).

Thus, Hjortspring reflects not only military and social, but also religious or cultic behaviour. In fact, ancient society, seemingly, took only limited intellectual and ritual interest in its own 'economies' (Hesiod's late eighth century BC 'Works and Days', for instance, being a remarkable exception). Rather, the people of old were preoccupied with the triad of 'politics', warfare and religion (although they probably had different perceptions of them). As concepts, the three phenomena may all be grouped under the modernist heading of 'social legitimation', but can also be seen, simply, as representing the realm of fear: fear of war — a formative factor in the building of society — and fear of the unknown — a defining factor of the supernatural realm.

Structural analysis of finds, such as Hjortspring, thus probably takes us to the very centre of the self-perception of ancient society, materially (and thus archaeologically) perhaps most clearly expressed in the highly marked emphasis on, and investment in, rituals. By contrast, archaeological studies of environment, population, and production, including the pertinent social structures, are representatives of modern research culture, dominated by technology and science, also reconstructing past realities, no doubt, but on a different level of analysis.

The middle ground, or perhaps, by consequence, the supreme perspective, is occupied by systematic archaeological investigations into the style of artefacts, burials (a ritual emphasis again), sacrifices, etc., where modernist approaches of investigation might satisfactorily meet with ancient cognition (cf. Renfrew & Zubrow 1994). Even so, when it comes to interpretation, scientific study of the past material world would be compelled to take a new direction under the impact of information on actual ancient beliefs and intentions, the academic imagination thus moving from 'blind' but systematic general archaeological methodology towards ethnological and historical realities. For instance, anthropologico-scientific approaches tend to shroud the fact that Prehistoric Europe, at least since the Neolithic, is a proto-historic entity and should be studied accordingly. In the end, the academic game is not with concepts but with content, be it poisonous or not.

Throughout the study, a holistic perspective is taken, but also one in which reality has a further side to it. To quote Magritte's famous masterpiece 'Ceci n'est pas une pipe', the following is 'not' a work on an archaeological find from Denmark, in a European context. It is a study of ancient society, reflected in its material remains. In principal, the man-made material world, past or present, is unbound in space and certainly made up of features generated in temporal sequence. Since man is a highly informative being, both cultural norms and novelties have always been transmitted, even across enormous distances, and even across cultural boundaries. Thus, linkages must be sought both within regions over time and in time across regions. Finally, a particular material environment, cultural and natural, both generates and limits the pertaining social tradition, as well as ensuing historical events.

The following text embodies a triple structure. On the one hand, the North, on the other, the Mediterranean, ever the inspirator and promotor of cultural development, however indirectly, are dealt with. Thirdly, the zone of transmission, Central or trans-Alpine Europe, with adjacent regions, an entity in itself, is discussed.

A brief version of the themes of the present work runs as follows. The Hjortspring amphibious army seems to have been organized along the same lines as the classical *Hoplite phalanx* of the Mediterranean, with similarly equipped warriors, armed primarily with shield and lance and fighting in formation. What cultural contacts and European politics made this possible, and where did the Hjortspring army originate? Hjortspring is at the same time a magnificent offering. How does it fit into the picture, through time, of European sacrifices, what deities or kinds of supernatural powers did this and other types of sacrifices relate to, and how should Hjortspring be perceived in its local context?

Acknowledgements

I tourn'd the toneful Art
From sounds to things /
from Fancy to the heart
    Alexander Pope (1688-1744)

The funding in support of the readings and studies resulting in the present volume and for a portion of its costs of production, as well as correction of some of the errors of my peculiar English language, have been provided by a research professorship from the Danish ministries of research and education and a grant from the Carlsberg Foundation. For this, as for much support from both colleagues and institutions, in Denmark as well as abroad, I am most grateful indeed. This has been critical for a theme of the present scope, where pertinent information is housed in many different libraries (and in many languages). While writing the manuscript, I was also encouraged by a last — as it sadly turned out to be — conversation with the late Mogens Ørsnes on the subject of weapon sacrifices. Finally, I should perhaps, on a more general level, single out our new colleagues in eastern Europe, including the former Soviet Union, and the dialogues and collaboration ensuing.

The idea of 'Europe' is currently in the midst of a general crisis, emanating mainly from mismanagement of the dissolution of the petty Yugoslav 'empire', in the wake of the collapse of communist Eastern Europe, and from the priority of economics over human requirements within the European Union. At the same time, West European archaeology has pawned the current stage of undeniable progress to the management of national monuments, or, in short, to rescue excavations and the necessary education. Nevertheless, the search for an academic archaeology of European scope, so characteristic of the early efforts of prehistoric or (methodologically) general archaeology, nevertheless continues. It is in this, at the present time, partisan context, that the following work should be viewed.

The book came as something of a surprise, as general works perhaps often do, although drawing on accumulated knowledge of a generation's worth of active archaeology. One source of inspiration has been John Keegan's brilliant writings on warfare (for Greek Hoplite warfare, Victor D. Hanson's work). (Keegan and Hansen neglect barbarian warfare, though.) Another player, sometimes emerging like a thief of the night in the chapters of this work, has been the revelations of the power of ancient beliefs, whether in their specific economic and social contexts of investments and gifts, or, as a permeating reality of ancient culture and society. Here various authors, rather than a single few, except, perhaps, for Régis Boyer (who turned up in a bookstall in Geneva on a cold day, but who ignores archaeology), are responsible — thought most of all, the sacred finds themselves.

A potent draft, as ever, is the reading of the poetry of old and of other ancient powerful texts, reminding us of differences and similarities of human intellect and emotion, past and present. Displayed beautifully.

In writing, archaeology remains both a source of new inspiration and a daydream. In practice, however, the fascination of detail ties down the dream of things past to the realities of ancient society and culture. On the one hand, common whining about the lack of data is but the fence of laziness, on the other the concrete lack of information and libraries is a decisive factor in gaining and digesting knowledge. Grateful, I have had access to all necessary resources. Perhaps, in a future true Society of Information, such problems will vanish, making no distinction between the place of the student and the work possible. Other problems will prevail, though, in particular the deep differences in wealth and resources between archaeologists in both Europe and the world at large.

In the hot summer of 1994, this book is dedicated to my parents for their love. Both of them born during the First World War, they bridge, in the present context, the age between the long aftermath of the ages of decisive warfare (inaugurated by Greek hoplites, Roman legions and North European Hjortspring armies) and the military prevention of conflicts of the modern world. In the present age, sacrifice too has melted from the stage of exchanges. Left is modernity's sometime ignorance of tradition and beliefs as means of survival and social reproduction, sometime clouded historiscism with little content. Europe is coming of age in confusion.

PART I

_____

1. The Hjortspring Find

> Shields Bruttians threw from their doomed shoulders —
> struck by the hands of Lokrians quick in battle —
> lie in the gods' shrines, praising their bravery,
> not longing for the cowards' forearms they left.
>   Nossis (early third century BC)

The famous Hjortspring weapon and boat sacrifice from the island of Als, Jylland [Jutland] in Denmark, is one of the most conspicuous finds of the pre-Roman Iron Age. It is of European significance, and highly important to archaeology in general.

The find comes from a tiny bog at Hjortspring Kobbel, only c. 50 m east-west and 45 m north-south, or less than a mere quarter of a hectare in size. At the time the deposit was made, the bog (or rather, small lake) was hardly more than one metre deep. It is situated at a beginning of a brook, Stolbro bæk, about 40 m above sea-level and c. three kilometres from the open sea on the northern part of the very fertile island of Als (in Svenstrup parish), just off the southeastern coast of Jutland (Kaul 1989, for a recent discussion).

Unfortunately, only a few other finds from the pre-Roman Iron Age are known from the area around Hjortspring, indeed from the whole of the island of Als (cf. Appendix). This is not significant in any past social or cultural respect (relatively little research on the Iron Age has been carried out on Als). But it does mean that we have to look elsewhere, for instance to Jutland, for relevant parallels and for archaeological context, including a much better knowledge of cemeteries, other sacrifices, and, not least, settlements. One or two megalithic tombs from the Neolithic and some (Early) Bronze Age barrows are found at a distance of a kilometre

or so from the bog, but not in a number or a particular concentration that would mark out the site as especially interesting in
any way, rather the contrary.

The Hjortspring sacrifice was excavated in the early 1920s by
the technically highly skilful conservator and archaeologist, G.
Rosenberg, who also published the find in a precise, almost taciturn
text (Rosenberg 1937) (Fig. 2). In particular, his own recording of
and preservation work on the very many wooden items of the find
have attracted admiration, even today, after major re-conservation.
Significantly, the recent work on the Hjortspring boat, or huge
canoe, has not given rise to any important alteration of the reconstruction of the 1930s (cf. Rieck 1994). A new technical study of the
magnificent boat is nevertheless badly needed.

Digging for peat in the 1880s did disturb part of the Hjortspring
find before the archaeological investigation, but, on the other hand,
also reveal the existence of the find. About twenty pits for peat
were dug randomly in the bog, usually square and of 3-5 sq.m;
some were deep enough to have removed artefacts in the pit. It is
reported that numerous sharp spearheads were found, some of
bone but most of iron, which were a nuisance when the peat was
kneaded, so they were thrown away. It is supposed that the wood
found to a larger degree than the iron and bone spearheads was
left in the bog; a large plank of the boat, however, was dried and
used for firewood. In all, about half the area of the find was
disturbed, randomly, but not necessarily with fatal consequence for
the artefacts.

The boat and the other items, all housed in the National Museum, Copenhagen, have recently been put on display again after
the re-conservation and restoration process (Fig. 4). New Carbon-14
dates give the (late) fourth century BC for the sacrifice. The dating
was carried out on (1) a spear shaft: 340 BC, calibrated age 390 BC
(one standard deviation 400-260 BC); and (2) a hull rib, 290 BC,
calibrated age, 370 BC (one standard deviation 390-210 BC). Calibra-
tion for own age of the wood (20-70 years) gives, respectively, for
(1) about 370-320 BC, and, for (2) about 350-300 BC — or, on the
average, 345-325/335 BC (Tauber 1987; cf. Rieck & Crumlin-
Pedersen 1988, 74). Incidentally, a crude double seat (or thwart) of
pine-wood, perhaps resembling the ones of Hjortspring, found at
Själevad near Örnsköldsvik in northern Sweden, has recently been
Carbon-14 dated (calibrated) to around 200 BC (Jansson 1994).

Fig. 2. The Hjortspring find in 1921-22. Excavation photo (National Museum).

The Hjortspring boat was positioned directly north-south in the small bog, seemingly 'sailing' towards the north (cf. below, the position of the small deck). The boat was partly covering, partly covered and surrounded by the items listed below, including several swords and spearheads deliberately destroyed, most probably in connection with the sacrifice.

A. The Boat

The 19 m long, light and very elegant wooden boat or huge canoe, painted or tarred black, is extremely well-built, although technologically quite simple (Figs. 3-4). The major parts of the vessel were 'sewn' together (no iron or other nails being used), probably with birch-tree roots. The boat has two identical and very long double end-pieces ('prows'), the powerful design of which gives much aesthetic effect to the vessel. However, the very strong lower 'beaks' of the prows may also have been used to ram similar enemy vessels (with thin mid-boards, cf. below) amidships: push-ing, tilting, capsizing and, with luck, at least partly submerging the boat of the enemy party. (The upper 'beaks' are lighter and T-shaped in cross-section.) Furthermore, mid-ship ramming would have divided the surviving enemy crew-members into two separate groups for consecutive, thus easier, elimination.

The Hjortspring boat itself weighed only about ½ ton, loaded about 2½ tons, and was no doubt very fast. In the main, it was constructed from five long broad and thin planks (plus the prows, etc.) from lime trees 20-25 m tall with trunks at least 15-16 by about 1 m. The wood was throughout knot-free and of excellent quality. The interior measurements of the vessel are c. 13.3 by 1.9 by 0.7 m.

The construction of the boat started with the base or bottom plank, 16 m long. This plank was carved and stretched, giving the vessel its slightly curved profile. Prow-blocks with the characteristic long 'beaks' (and two free vertical connecting or supporting planks, lightly ornamented) were then fitted to the plank with the aid of a vertical plank, functionally the actual prow. Next, the two times two side planks, only two cm thick, were mounted. As seen from the side, the vessel was thus symmetrical over a vertical mid-axis. Finally, the rib-frames were put in, at one-metre intervals, on protruding knobs on the base- and side-planks.

The bottom of the boat was covered by, originally, about 85 long narrow and pointed thin walking boards (treadles), each more than one-metre in length. With the crew beached, these boards may even have seen secondary use as supporters of covers or 'tents' (perhaps made of the mantles), as a rudimentary fence, or, even, quickly established defensive pickets on a prepared battlefield, although the latter is probably less likely. Indeed, bound together at an angle and near the one end, four pairs of boards with, for instance, a couple of the below paddles as the ridge would make a decent frame for a 'tent' of a 'bench' (two men). Incidentally, the about 85 boards, thus utilized — divided by four — correspond to the size of the entire crew of the Hjortspring boat suggested below (c. 22 men, in all).

At the southern end of the boat was a small, c. 1.2 m long, trapezoid deck with ornamented fronts, seating (above one of the frames of the boat) two persons facing the centre and a third one facing an open, c. 0.8 m long, area at the very end of the boat (Rosenberg 1937, Fig. 35d) (Fig. 5). Thus described and interpreted, the end with the deck was the usual stern. A further 2 times 9 seats were found on the other frames of the vessel. Remnants of a (side) rudder was found at the stern end of the boat (with the quarter-deck); a remnant of another similar rudder lay at the other end, the usual prow. On this, traces of the tying-rope could be seen. Near this rudder, in the bog, were two (decorated) fragments of one of the two free vertical planks supporting the double 'beaks' (Rosenberg 1937, Fig. 35a-b). At this end of the boat, but in secondary position, was also found a round decorated piece of wood, perhaps part of the vertical support-plank at the stern (cf. Rosenberg 1937, Figs. 35e and 64, below).

Thus, the boat was manned by 18 ordinary paddlers (who probably rested their knees on their thwart when paddling fast) and two special persons, who may or may not have taken a part in the paddling, plus, at least, one man at the rudder and a very likely second at the alternative rudder (at the stern), probably shouting, beating, or perhaps even blowing on a flute (such was found, cf. below), the rhythm of the paddling. At the same time, this person would act as a lookout, for instance when the boat was beaching; indeed, a person at the prow is the only one who is facing the other crew-members during normal operations.

If beaching or attacking, perhaps ramming another vessel, with the quarter-deck end as the functional prow, this deck and area may have been in use as a firing or fighting platform, for up to three persons. It is also noted that the double beak stern and prow allow for a person (or more) to climb onto them and from there quickly jump to the beach or into an enemy or other vessel. Ramming with the stern end (indeed, with the lower very powerful 'beak') would also better have protected the normal prow for further navigation. When the stern was used as a prow, the person at the normal prow would of course apply his (alternative) rudder for steering the vessel.

Thus, a common crew of probably four (18%) 'commanders' and 18 (72%) ordinary warriors manned the Hjortspring boat. Most important among the crew-members was, no doubt, the 'steersman' at the narrow end of the quarter-deck. Often a larger crew is given in the literature. Incidentally, the very 'minimum' crew for normal operations is 19 (two times nine paddlers plus a steersman). Sleeping aboard is difficult (the boat may have been beached every night on expedition), but not totally impossible for parts of the

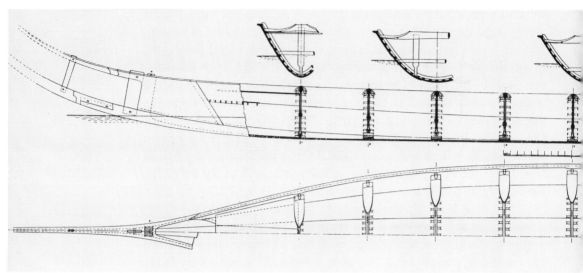

Fig. 3. Reconstruction of the Hjortspring boat in the publication (Rosenberg 1937).

crew at a time. Cooking aboard is, however, not likely. About 16 rather narrow paddles ('oars') with triangular or, perhaps, plain handles (most in fragments), possible fragments of another two paddles, plus two special paddles or punting-poles with round handles (also in fragments) were found, strikingly corresponding to the suggested number of crew. The fact that the paddles of the vessel are narrow implies a potential for high speed. It can be added that even a crude copy of the Hjortspring boat (Rieck & Crumlin-Pedersen 1988, 72; 166 (photo)) has proved relatively fast and easy to paddle and manoeuvre.

There are no real parallels to the Hjortspring boat (except for the above mentioned recent find from Själevad, northern Sweden). The similarity in profile to the Bronze Age rock carving vessels, perhaps especially the late ones, has very often been mentioned, however, but these images are not very revealing as to detail. Some heavy oak-boats from Ferriby on the River Humber in eastern England, without a keel, but, as in Hjortspring, with the planks sewn together, and with cut-out clamp blocks, are distant cousins of the Alsian boat, but lack entirely the finesse of the latter (Wright 1990) (Fig. 6). The Ferriby boats are dated to the middle Bronze Age (Scandinavian Periods II-III).

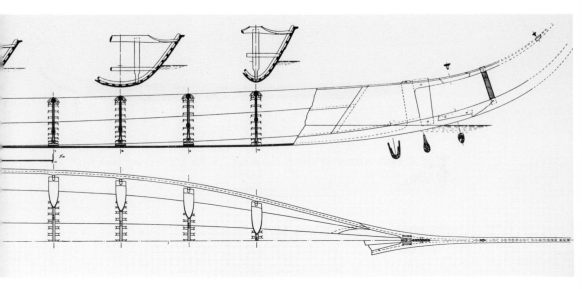

With the Hjortspring boat itself, the rudders, the paddle oars, etc. came the following weapons and other artefacts:

B. The Swords

11 single-edged swords (8 of which are complete) were found (cf. Fig. 7). The length of the blade varies between 28 and 57 cm. One specimen is a scimitar with inwardly curved edge. Some four wooden scabbards are more or less preserved.

C. The Spears

169 spearheads (138 of iron, 31 of antler/bone) plus wooden shafts of ash (the longest piece, broken at both ends, is 1.97 m long and 2½ cm thick at the middle; other shafts have diameters either slightly larger or slightly smaller) (Fig. 7). The antler spearheads are about 10 cm long; they seem to have had rather slender shafts. The iron spearheads have, according to their length, the following distribution (many are much worn): 22 are long (more than 20 cm); four of these are between 30 and 40 cm, one is more than 40 cm, 85 are of medium length (between 20 and 10 cm). 31 are short (less than 10 cm); some worn specimens are hardly more than 5 cm.

Fig. 4. New reconstruction of the profile of the Hjortspring boat (after Kaul 1988).

In terms of shape the following division applies to the iron spear-heads:

(1) 31 short broad spearheads ('javelins') with a midrib and a (very) short free socket (5-16 cm long, up to 5 cm wide, at the middle of the blade).

(2) 34 long narrow spearheads ('javelins'), usually with a high sharp midrib and a short free socket (13-29 cm, up to 3.2 cm wide, at the middle of the blade). This form seems designed with deep penetration, perhaps of mail-coats, in mind (cf. below).

(3) 8 long narrow bayonet-like spearheads ('lances') with a long (up to 12 cm) free socket ((13)-25/43.5 cm, up to 2.7/5.6 cm wide, at the base of the blade). Also this type seems designed for deep penetration.

(4) 64 powerful, broad spearheads ('lances') with a free socket of some length (12-36.5 cm, up to 6.2/7.5 cm wide, at the base of the blade). One additional specimen has no free socket, but is 30 cm long and with inlays in copper.

D. The Mail-coats

Several (10-12 (?)), perhaps torn, mail-coats. In the original publication (Rosenberg 1937) the author made a highly uncertain calculation of a total of perhaps as many as 20-24 mail-coats for the original undisturbed find, based on the extent of the excavated area with remains of mail-coats (10-12 sq.m). This calculation presupposes one mail-coat per square metre of traces of such coats. The mail-coats were far too poorly preserved for closer study, only a few rings were brought to the museum and are now preserved; the

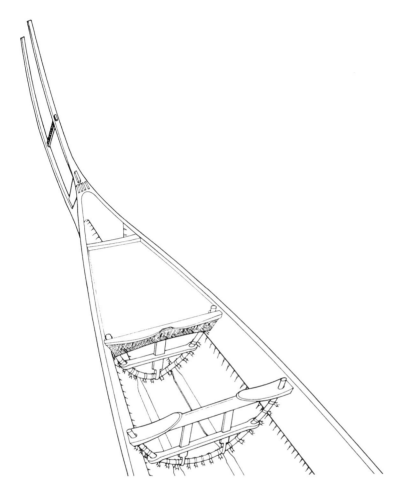

Fig. 5. The stern (with quarter-deck) of the Hjortspring boat. New reconstruction (after Jansson 1994).

diameter of the rings was usually 0.6-0.8 cm; other, smaller, rings were of 0.4 and a few larger ones of 0.9-1.0 cm.

These mail-coats are very remarkable indeed in being so plentiful and, no doubt, very costly, in fact, virtually price-less in a pre-Roman Scandinavian (or northern German) Iron Age society. They are even among the earliest mail-coats in Europe. A parallel from a princely tomb at Ciumeşti in the eastern Carpathian Basin is dated to the Celtic La Tène B period, fourth to early third century BC (Rusu 1969). This mail-coat is reckoned to be the earliest

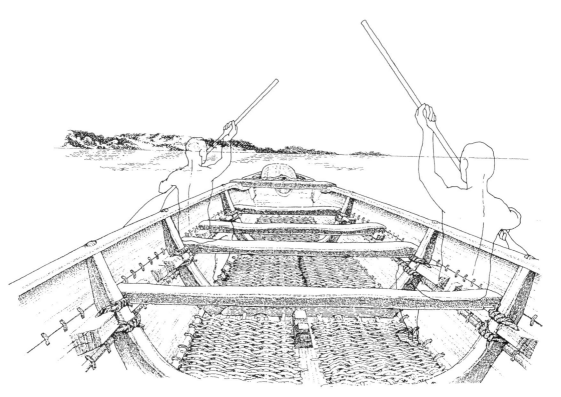

Fig. 6. Reconstruction of a Ferriby type heavy oak-boat (eastern England), length c. 15 m, from the Middle Bronze Age (Southern Scandinavian Early Bronze Age Periods II-III). Constructive details like the lack of a keel, the planks being sewn together, and cut clamp blocks make the Ferriby boats distant cousins of Hjortspring (after Wright 1990).

Central European specimen. In the third to second centuries BC mail-coats became common; they were in particular used by the Romans who, incidentally, considered them a Celtic invention.

The Hjortspring mail-coats have an interesting cultural parallel in three bizarre wooden copies of Italian/Alpine so-called Negauer-helmets (Egg 1986), which have come to light in the Uglemose bog at Birket on the island of Lolland, southern Denmark (Kaul 1995). These helmets were found near late pre-Roman Iron Age pottery and some human bones. The Uglemose helmets seemingly copy an early type of Negauer helmets, probably even earlier than Hjortspring.

One of the bronze helmets of the Žentak find at Negau/

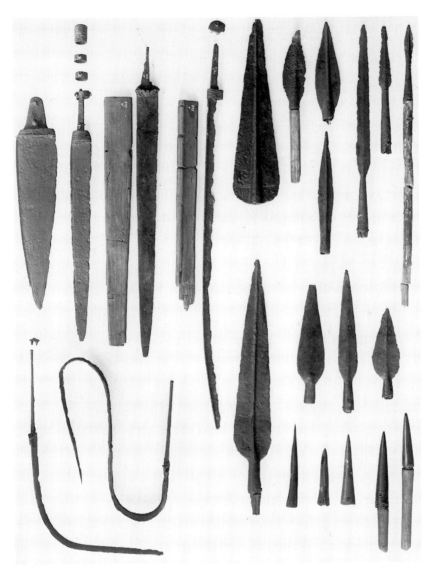

Fig. 7. Selected weapons from the Hjortspring find (National Museum photo).

Negova-Obrat (at Maribor) in Slovenia, with 26 such helmets, even
carries an inscription, HARICHASTI TEIVA HIL in the local
alphabet, perhaps (but much discussed) including the Germanic
name of *Hærgæst*, 'Army Guest', or 'Guardian', incidentally a nick-
name for the god Odin. A connection with the migrations of the
Cimbri (second century BC) has been suggested in this case, the

Cimbri probably having robbed a sanctuary and re-sacrificed the helmets according to their own customs. Earlier contacts between Slovenia and Denmark are, of course, also quite possible.

E. The Shields

64 (in the original publication (Rosenberg 1937) merely 50) rounded-square, flat and thin (on the average only about one cm thick) wooden shields, of various sub-types and, usually, of light wood, were sufficiently well preserved to allow for their lenghth and width to be approximately measured or, at least, reconstructed. To this come a number of smaller fragments, which possibly comprise parts of additional shields (cf. Fig. 8).

The shield-bosses (also wooden) are lenticular in shape and, along the longitudinal axis of the shield, divided into two halves by grooves and a moulding separating two protuberances. The length of the shields varies, according to the publication, between 0.61 and 0.88 m and the width between 0.29 and 0.52 m. About 67/69 handles for shields were found, plus 10 unfinished spares.

The handle is in the transverse axis of the shield, which thus was designed for close combat, manoeuvring and shoving rather than as a vertically held 'board' (for maximum protection against missiles and light stabs) behind which to point spears at the enemy (while 'dancing' in front of him). This observation is highly significant. Also, the particular shape of the bosses allows the shield both to slip on an enemy one and to add a punch to a shove or a blow with the shield. The more or less intact shields belong, again according to the original publication, to three groups:

(1) 9 narrow shields (the width half the length, or less; in reality only 7 shields meet this definition). Seven specimens are more than 80 cm long.

(2) 24 medium shields (the width between one half and two thirds of the length; in reality 28 shields meets this definition). Five are more than 80 cm; usually these shields are 70-75 cm long.

(3) 17 broad shields (the width two thirds, or more, of the length; in reality only 15 shields meet this definition). These shields are always less than 80 and mostly around, or less than, 70 cm long.

However, a plot of the length against the width of all shields whose main dimensions are recognizable, makes the above divi-

Fig. 8. Wooden shields etc. from the Hjortspring find, during excavation (National Museum photo). Note the two types of shield, respectively broad and narrow.

sion, solely based on arithmetic, less obvious. Using the measures and the descriptions of the shields in the excavation report (not the publication, although the general results are the same), most of the specimens (out of a total number of c. 64 shields) cluster around an average of 70-75 cm in length and c. 45 in width, the width being about two thirds of the length, whether the shield is short (down to 61 cm) or long (up to about 88 cm) (Fig. 9). However, some 11 (or 12) shields are 'narrow' (the width being half the length or less), again, whether the shield is short or long (66 to 102 cm). While the first mentioned shields, apart from protection, may have been particularly apt for shoving, the latter seem designed for manoeuvring as well; besides, they are more elegant in appearance.

F. Other Items

The various other artefacts in the rich Hjortspring find include (cf. Fig. 10): (1) a bronze pin with a so-called 'swan's neck' (the proper

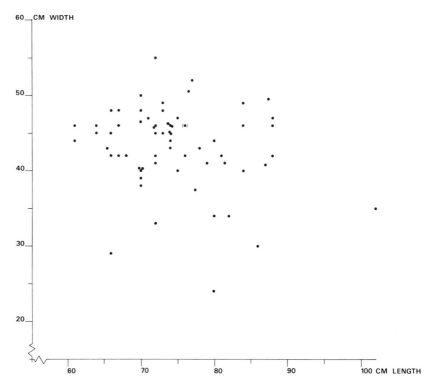

Fig. 9. Distribution of the length and the width of the well-preserved shields from the Hjortspring find (data extracted from the excavation report and supplementary information, National Museum).

head is, unfortunately, missing since antiquity), a type very often found in northern Germany in the early pre-Roman Iron Age but common in many regions; (2) a couple of small, lightly ornamented, bronze strap-tags, also with parallels in North Germany, among other regions; (3) a bronze button, softly profiled, with concentric circles (fitting into Celtic and derived ornamental language of about the fourth century BC, for instance the feet of fibulae); (4) perhaps a bronze cauldron; (5) turned, highly moulded, wooden boxes with lids (perhaps for fire-making kits, which must be kept dry); (6) other wooden boxes; (7) a small, probably also turned wooden bowl with a broad rim (in profile resembling early Pre-Roman Iron Age pottery bowls or dishes (cf. Becker 1961, Pl. 29e)); (8) wooden dishes; (9) wooden spoons; (10) wooden discs with handles, perhaps 'gongs': some (11) 'handles' found may perhaps be gong-sticks; and (12) a bone-flute.

Fig. 10. Wooden pyxides etc. from the Hjortspring find (National Museum photo).

Furthermore, several tools, probably for repair of the boat, the weapons, the clothing, and other equipment were found: (13) some axe-shafts; (14) a Y-shaped bellows tube; (15) various mallets; (16) needles; (17) a spindle; and (18) several thin ropes and strings. In addition, the following items: (19) a scoop (for emptying the vessel for water); (20) a ceramic vessel of a type with parallels in, for instance, Jutland, Holstein and Lower Saxony, dated to the early (or, in traditional chronology, the 'middle') of the pre-Roman Iron Age (cf. Becker 1948) and placed on top of a shield, thus perhaps representing a terminus ante quem for the military sacrifice); (21) an antler cheek-piece; plus several other items, including (22) a great many 5-10 cm large flint-stones, often lightly chipped, and thus, most likely, meant to be used as missiles.

G. The Pyxides

The fine turned wooden boxes (above, (5) etc.) deserve a particular note. Technologically, they are quite remarkable by being turned (normally, a much later technology in the North); in appearance they deviate from (almost) all other known vessels of the period and general region, in particular through their highly pregnant profiles.

Remarkably close, although not identical, parallels are found among Greek ceramic and other *pyxides*, for instance from Athens, a main exporter of pottery of the day (Sparkes & Talcott 1970, Pl. 42, No. 1276-84, etc.) (Fig. 12). These ceramic pyxides are all dated to the fourth century BC, those resembling the specimens in Hjortspring closely to the early part of that century. Attic pottery was common, for instance, around the northern Black Sea, in Italy and on the Adriatic, where barbarian tribal groups and individuals with connections to Central (and Northern) Europe may have encountered it. The agent might well have been the fifth to early fourth century BC Celtic expansion into northern Italy (with the famous assault on Rome), leading also, for instance, to connections with the large Greek trading town of Spina on the estuary of the Po, flourishing in the fifth and even being a prominent settlement in the early fourth century BC (cf. Aurigemma 1960 & 1965, for the cemeteries).

In the Greek, Etruscan and Roman worlds, pyxides in wood were also known. For instance, from a grave claimed to be of the fifth century BC (but probably a little later), found at the city of Olbia (northwestern Black Sea), come several turned wooden vessels (in the exibition of the Archaeological Museum at Odessa). One of these resembles, in a general way, the box(es) in Hjortspring with next to vertical sides. More important, yet another one constitutes a very close parallel indeed to the carinated Hjortspring pyxides (Rosenberg 1937, Fig. 34 below). From Palestrina (Praeneste) near Rome (Necropoli della Colombella of the early Hellenistic period; the finds now on display in the Villa Giulia museum, Rome) come small turned wooden pyxides which also resemble the Hjortspring ones, both in general and with respect to several details: for instance the specimens with straight sides, some profiles, including lids, etc. The similarities are quite intimate and hardly merely ascribable to the kinship of all small turned wooden objects.

Thus, it cannot be ruled out, although it is probably less likely, that the Hjortspring boxes, or, rather, a couple of the more significant of them, like no doubt the mail-coats, were, in fact, imported from far afield. If so, this might explain the surprisingly advanced technology applied in manufacturing the pyxides: by fast turning of the wood, a technique otherwise apparently unknown in the North for another millennium or so after Hjortspring (cf. Lønborg 1990). However, the wooden bowl mentioned above may also have

Fig. 11. Ceramic pyxis from Egebygård, Åker parish, the island of Bornholm, Denmark, cf. the wooden pyxides and boxes from the Hjortspring find in Fig. 10 (after Müller 1900).

been turned and is nevertheless of more or less the same shape as ceramic bowls (of the early pre-Roman Iron Age) commonly found in Northern Germany, as well as in Jutland.

The foreign origin of at least the type and shape of the pyxides is underlined by the fact that such were imitated in the north. Small north European ceramic vessels of the early Pre-Roman Iron Age with similar, though usually less well executed profiles (and lid) to those of the wooden boxes from Hjortspring have been found on the Baltic island of Bornholm, Denmark (Müller 1900 (Åker, one specimen)) and, in particular, in northwestern Germany (Fig. 11).

The best and, certainly, most plentiful ceramic parallels to the Hjortspring pyxides, apart from the single, though very fine, Bornholm vessel, come from cemeteries within the larger city of Hamburg (for instance, Schindler 1960, Taf. 16, 52, 54, 55 and 72) as well as immediately to south of this area (Müller-Brauel 1932) (cf. Figs. 21-22), including a few perhaps less satisfactory parallels (for

Fig. 12. Ceramic pyxides of the fourth century BC *from the Agora of Athens (after Sparkes & Talcott 1970).*

instance, Schwantes 1911, Taf. 7 (possibly also p. 6, Abb. 7); Wegewitz 1961, Taf. 4 and 23; and 1977, Taf. 49, 55 and 146). It would seem that the mentioned vessels altogether constitute the only recorded ceramic parallels to the curious Hjortspring pyxides from the northern German/Polish plains. Should this observation stand the test of time, it may sustain a Hamburg region identification of the area of origin of the unique and very exciting boat-find.

– – –

It should be stressed that the above numbers of different types of artefacts and equipment are a minimum estimate, since, as mentioned, before the archaeological excavation, cutting of peat in Hjortspring Bog during the 1880s probably destroyed an unknown number of items, including the mentioned one plank (for the boat) and 'a large number' of spearheads of 'iron and bone'. The bog is, however, very small, only c. 45 by 50 m, and was (almost) completely excavated by Rosenberg (cf. Rosenberg 1937).

Attention should also be paid to the fact that arrows and arrowheads are totally absent in Hjortspring, as is cavalry equipment (except for a lone cheek-piece). Some animals, including a horse, a dog, a puppy (dog), and a young sheep, were most probably sacrified at the same time as the boat and the weapons. These animals were placed at the perimeter of the sacrifice. In the bottom of Hjortspring bog 'wells' containing some cattle bones represent earlier sacrifices, possibly from the Bronze Age.

The Hjortspring military equipment is, functionally, of limited variety (although several sub-types of swords, certainly of spearheads and even of shields can be noted). It thus confirms the 'naked' impression of pre-Roman artefacts in Northern Europe, being almost devoid of ornamentation. Obviously, the cultural 'message' rests with the function and the shape of the items, shape allowing for some culturally specific variation. All other aspects of the artefacts were toned down, perhaps in deliberate reaction to the colourful ornamental and other art of Southern and southeastern Europe (cf. Randsborg 1994). As we shall soon see, the South is nevertheless present in Hjortspring, also beyond the single scimitar, the mail-coats and the pyxides.

2. The Warriors

> ... Only a few of them use swords or large lances: they carry spears — called frameae in their language — with short and narrow blades, but so sharp and easy to handle that they can be used, as required, either at close quarters or in long-range fighting. Their horsemen are content with a shield and a spear; but the foot-soldiers also rain javelins on their foes ...
>
> Tacitus (*Germania*, AD 98)

Large military sacrifices from the Iron Age of Southern Scandinavia, such as Hjortspring, are traditionally interpreted as the spoils from a defeated enemy army attacking the region where the find has been made. This interpretation is derived, in part, from the descriptions in classical authors of Celtic sacrifices of this kind, supported by actual archaeological finds, in part, from the cohesive nature of the finds themselves (e.g. Ilkjær 1989). Interpretations vary, though, as to many details.

A disturbing question, strangely enough apparently never asked, remains: What would the enemy have done with their spoils if they had in fact won the battle. Would they (a) have designated a sacred area and offered the weapons of the slain local force there, staying on in the region as overlords, or, would they (b) have carried the spoils home?

The simple answer to this question is that it probably never happened, due to the high and dense local populations compared to the small size of foreign expeditionary armies. Large armies of conquest, capable of expelling populations, could not be formed and supported for any longer period, unless whole tribal groups moved along too. Of such large scale population movements we have no evidence from Northern Europe. Only in Central and Southern Europe, in the late first millennium BC and during the Migration Period, accompanying the transformation of the Roman world half a millennium later, are major movements of population groups a factor in social formation.

The first military scenario to be considered in the case of

Hjortspring is thus the following, which might be termed 'spoils after a fleeing, partly destroyed enemy force'.

If each warrior of the Hjortspring army, apart from shield for protection and shoving, carried at least two spears, one heavy (lance) for close combat and one (or two) light ones, whether tipped with iron or with antler (or bone), for throwing as missiles at the beginning of combat, and threw both spears/lances in battle or in flight, the number of enemy troops would have been at least 84/85 (or a minimum of four manned boats). Counting iron-tipped spears only, we come up with a minimum of 69 warriors, a force closely matched by the number of shield handles (67/69) and, but more generally, by the number of shields (in this scenario, thrown in flight, and if so, no doubt sooner than the heavy spear and the sword). The number of swords (11) is matched by the, allegedly uncertain, number of mail-coats (10-12 (?)) and, incidentally, seems to be about equal to the number of spears with bayonet-like heads (eight). If all the warriors were equipped with a sword and a mail-coat, only the men from one boat may have been slain/caught. The rest would have reached safety after having thrown their shields and spears in the flight (and the fight). And, again, if so, perhaps only one-eighth of the entire force was lost (cf. Lønstrup 1988, argueing for the applicability of this model in the interpretation of the Danish Roman period military sacrifices).

A disturbing uncertainty about this hypothesis remains, however, for it seems highly unlikely that all the warriors would have worn the very extraordinary and costly mail-coats, some of the earliest in Europe (Rusu 1969 for the Romanian find from the La Tène B period, the fourth to early third century BC). The mail-coats, no doubt of Celtic, or even Roman, origin, were probably reserved for the 'steersmen' and the other so-called commanders, most likely also senior in age, to whom the swords (and the bayonet-spears), although not particularly costly, might also belong.

Whether the commanders carried shields is not known: On the one hand, no distinctive type of shield was found (nor, incidentally, any field-colours); on the other, the shield seems to be a general weapon. Thus, probably the rather rare narrow shields (11 or 12 specimens), apt for manoeuvring, in the Hjortspring find represent the main defensive weapon of the commanders. Furthermore, it can be argued that the commanders, depending on their role in the fighting, also held the rather splendid spears with bayonet-like heads (type (3) above) and, perhaps, the couple of very heavy lances (like the fine specimen mentioned above under type (4)). In fact, the Hjortspring *strategoi*, like their ancient Greek counterparts, may have fought alongside their men, but perhaps from the flank or rear at the onset and only at the close of the fighting in the zone of death, as the bayonet-spear and the sword, weapons of killing rather than of wounding, may imply.

For general comparison, it can be noted that on the Gundestrup cauldron, found in Jutland but manufactured in southeastern Europe as late as c. 100 BC, infantry soldiers are depicted equipped with a square shield and a spear, an infantry commander (helmet decorated by a boar crest), standing behind the foot-soldiers, has only a sword for weapon; also the cavalry on the cauldron, seemingly, wield only spears (Kaul 1991, 23). (All soldiers in this scene may be wearing mail-coats.) A similar, but earlier (late fifth century BC) representation is seen on the well-known Celtic scabbard from the Hallstatt cemetery in Austria (Moscati 1991, 131). Here the infantry carry spears and shields, the cavalry only spears, apart from one rider who also has a short sword (Fig. 66).

In fact, the numbers of different spears may be conclusive of the composition of the Hjortspring army and, by consequence, for interpreting the find as reflecting the spoils of a totally defeated enemy army (Fig. 13).

Leaving aside the antler- or bone-tipped spears, we have 64 + 1 = 65 heavy lances of type (4) (for close combat) and 31 + 34 = 65 light ones (javelins) of types (1) and (2) (for use as missiles). With the commanders equipped with mail-coats, swords and the bayonet-spears of type (3) (designed for piercing and killing), plus, probably, the couple of very heavy lances (for supreme commanders?), the iron-tipped spears are satisfactorily distributed.

We may then allow the cheaper 31 antler/bone-tipped spears to be regarded as extra missiles: after the initial throwing of the chipped flint-stones, possibly to be used at sea or in the first decent volley on land. The shields: short, average, or long, broad or narrow, can only partially be distributed in accordance with the weapon-types. Here, apparently, other factors were at work, in particular the need for a rather broad type for the common warrior. Commanders probably carried the narrow and rather elegant shields. At any rate, we must conclude that the equipment of an entire enemy army most probably was captured, gathered and

	PADDLERS/WARRIORS	COMMANDERS
Crew ratio (22 men per boat)	*18 = 82%*	*4 = 18%*
Mail-coats		10+ (?)
Swords		11
Bayonet-lances, iron-tipped		8
Lances, iron-tipped	65	
Javelins, iron-tipped	65	
– broad type	*31*	
– narrow type	*34*	
Javelins, antler/bone-tipped	31	
Shield-handles (plus 10 spares)	67/68	
Broad shields	52/53+ (82%)	
Narrow shields	.... 11/12+ (18%)	
Dogs	.... 1+	

Fig. 13. Suggested ratios of paddlers/common warriors and commanders, and distribution of the weaponry in the Hjortspring find (sanctuary).

sacrificed at Hjortspring. About the fate of the enemy warriors we can only speculate; certainly they were not found in the bog (antler- and bone-tips of spears were very well preserved), nor was any item of their clothing. Probably, these warriors were killed, possibly enslaved, perhaps even permitted to return, disarmed and humiliated, in the remaining boats, not found in the bog.

If this line of argument is at all acceptable, the weapons in the Hjortspring find may thus be of an entire army made up of a very minimum of three or four ships, each with one steersman (and a likely assistant), two other commanders — all four heavily equipped — plus some 18 common warriors with spears (and shields) only. Since the find was disturbed before excavation, the real size of the Hjortspring army must have been somewhat larger. Its maximum size, to judge from the circumstances of find and the weapons in the sacrifice, might have been six or seven boats, perhaps even eight, about 150 (130 to, perhaps, 175) probably young elite warriors along with some (c. 18%) seniors. More likely, however, there were only about 100 men, or a little more. These 100 or so warriors, may, on the other hand, well have represented a tribal group the size of perhaps 3,000 or even 5,000 people, or several hundred farmsteads (cf. Fig. 14). The island of Als (about 300 sq.km), on which the Hjortspring bog is situated, was in the pre-Roman Iron Age probably settled by a population of similar size, at any rate sufficient to sustain a militia force, that won the crucial battle with the well-equipped professional intruders.

Excursus A: Krogsbølle

Among the other major weapon-finds from the period of Hjortspring, all less well investigated, less complete, and less well preserved, is Krogsbølle (Krogsbølle parish) on northern Fyn/Fu-nen, Denmark (a few km from the coast). Here the weapons comprise only swords and spears (no mail-coats nor shields, in spite of the fact that wooden shafts of spears were preserved) found at and in a stone-built road leading across a brook in a bog. This context is normally interpreted as an actual battle-ground. Against this hypothesis is the fact that at least some of the swords were deliberately destroyed. The find, again lacking arrows, except for one (perhaps doubtful) fragment of a shaft, is made up of (cf. Fig. 15):

(A) 7(+?) swords (one double-edged, the others single-edged).

(B) 44 spearheads (25 (26?) of iron, 19(+) of bone or antler). The iron spearheads are all of Hjortspring Type 4 (lances) except for one javelin (of Type (2), or, less likely, later (cf. Becker 1948, 168 note 67)).

(C) A substantial number of various other artefacts, probably belonging to the weapon-find: a cheek-piece, a mallet, knives, perhaps axles of waggons, etc.

The ratio sword:spear(-head) is substantially higher than at Hjortspring. The ratio between iron- and bone- or antler-tipped

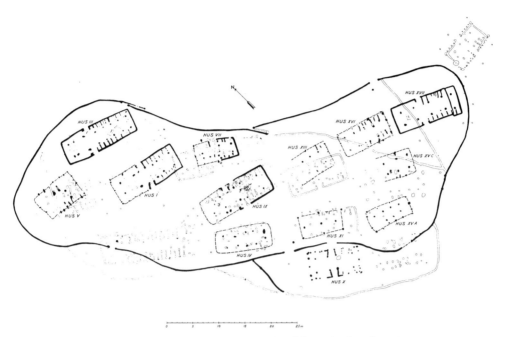

Fig. 14. Settlement from the early Pre-Roman Iron Age (about the fourth century BC) at Grøntoft, Western Jutland; first phase (after Becker 1965). Within the common cattle-fence are four larger farmsteads with stables, four somewhat smaller ones, also with stables, and four structures (farmsteads?), seemingly without stables.

spears is about equal, although there are more of iron. On the basis of the numbers of different weapons, and with a view to Hjortspring, it can be argued that each 'commander' (7+) carried a sword and, possibly, a heavy spear (lance) too, and that each common infantryman (18+) was equipped with one heavy (for close fighting) and one light bone-tipped spear (or, a lance and a javelin, respectively). The size of this enemy troop, using the same interpretation of the find as at Hjortspring, need not have exceeded two or perhaps three Hjortspring boat platoons.

The explanation of the higher number of swordsmen is, perhaps, that the Krogsbølle find represents a chronologically somewhat later event in which the sword was carried by more warriors, and the tactics, too, probably slightly different from those of Hjortspring; perhaps only two ranks were employed, the front one with common warriors, the second with 'commanders'. The

	WARRIORS	COMMANDERS
Fighter ratio	18+	7(+)
Swords (one double-edged)		7(+?)
Lances, iron-tipped	24 (25?)	
Javelins, iron-tipped	 1	
Javelins, bone-tipped	19(+)	

Fig. 15. Suggested ratio of warriors and commanders, and distribution of the weaponry in the Krogsbølle find, northern Fyn/Funen (battle-ground turned sanctuary, or just sanctuary).

ritual destruction of, in particular, the swords may be significant in this context. Still, the missing shields remain a puzzle. Were they displayed on nearby trees, for example, or were the dead warriors cremated or buried with them?

Finally, a casual find from a low hill of gravel at Tidavad in Västergötland, Sweden, with three spearheads with sockets and 14 without, may represent a parallel to both Krogsbølle and Hjortspring, but the circumstances of find are less illuminating (Salo 1962). Perhaps we here have three commanders (18%, as in Hjortspring) and 14 other warriors.

Excursus B: Bronze Age Weapon Hoards

In this Excursus, to put the pre-Roman Iron Age finds into perspective, it is explored whether the common non-burial weapon deposits of the Early Bronze Age in Denmark and neighbouring regions were militarily related sacrifices, and, to what extent they reflect the particular armament of outstanding individuals and groups of warriors of the time. Certainly, these weapon deposits or hoards (with swords, spears/lances, and axes) can only very rarely be interpreted as sacrifices of the spoils of whole defeated enemy armies (the Hjortspring model). For this, the items of the hoards are too few. Also, the weapons, in some hoards, have been found with female jewellery. In addition, the near identity of Nordic Bronze Age artefacts across rather wide distances makes it highly difficult to determine the particular place of origin of the weapons.

Nevertheless, at least some of the weapon hoards or sacrifices might still have been made up of spoils and other valuables won through war or armed conflict, plundering of sanctuaries, etc. Such a hypothesis has, it seems, never been considered, although it certainly is the main one when trying to interpret the weapons sacrifices and several other offerings of the Iron Age. Throughout, the idea among archaeologists has been that the Bronze Age sacrifices or deposits were exclusively made by peaceful local inhabitants, involving their 'own' artefacts, weapons and jewellery.

Clearly, some of the major deposits from the Early Bronze Age reflect a military structure of a kind. In addition, the relevant weapons are sometimes associated with raw materials or other indications of importation of metals, no doubt a major reason for the dispatch of trading parties, expeditions, and for armed conflict, in the Bronze Age.

(1) From the turn of the Late Neolithic comes the highly interesting Gallemose hoard from a bog at Harridslev in north-eastern Jutland (Randsborg 1991). The weight of the hoard is almost 12 kg of copper, an almost unbelievable amount for the region and period (no copper is found naturally in Southern Scandinavia). The Gallemose find consists of three ends of yokes identical to the ones used on light horse-drawn war-chariots in the Mediterranean and the Near East, probably ritual, since they are made of metal; alternatively, the pieces were for simpler vehicles (or even ritual ploughs). In addition, nine flanged axes (one very large indeed, possibly for the 'commander'), highly prestigious weapons, and nine rings (currency rings/ingots or bars) were found.

(2) Dated to Period I of the Early Bronze Age, is a bronze hoard, originally packed into a small box and deposited in a Neolithic burial complex (Becker 1964) (Fig. 16). The location is Torsted, Western Jutland; the find comprises seven flanged axes and 40 spearheads, all thus without their shafts, perhaps the weaponry of some 40(+) warriors (all with a spear/lance), including seven (18%) 'commanders' (probably, but not necessarily, with both a spear (lance- or staff-fighting) and an axe (close decisive combat)).

(3a) From later in the same period comes, among others, a bronze hoard from Valsømagle at Haraldsted, central Zealand, found by a large stone (Aner & Kersten 1976 vol. II, No. 1098 =

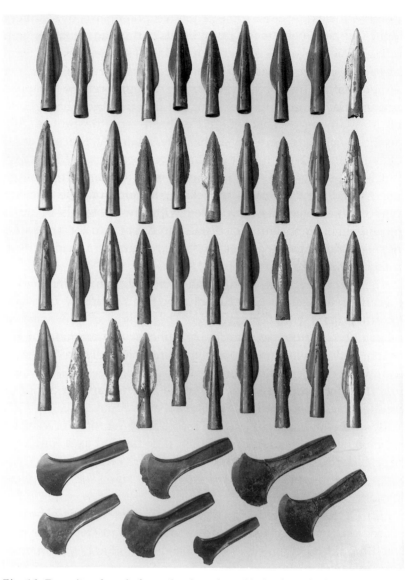

Fig. 16. Deposit or hoard of spearheads and axe-blades from the beginning of the Bronze Age (early to mid-second millennium BC/early Period I) found in a Neolithic cemetery from around 3000 BC at Torsted, Western Jylland/Jutland (after Becker 1964).

The find exemplifies the Stone Age way of fighting (bows and arrows, staves, axes, possible daggers, etc.), while at the same time introducing the novel metal-tipped spear/lance for advanced middle-range Bronze Age combat. (In theory, phalanx-techniques might have been applied too, but this is highly unlikely (lack of proper shields, etc.).)

Valsømagle II)) (Fig. 44). This find comprises a metal-hilted sword, a very large and finely decorated spearhead (lance) with fish-motifs, a smaller spearhead, a heavy battle axe, and a small pal-stave (tool?). The hoard might thus have made up the personal weaponry of an aristocrat, or perhaps, of a high aristocrat (sword, battle-axe, lance) and his junior follower (small spearhead, small axe).

(3b) Nearby, a similar find of bronzes was made (Aner & Kersten 1976, vol. II, no. 1097 = Valsømagle I). The latter hoard comprised the blade of a sword, a very large spearhead (lance), a smaller spearhead, a finely decorated battle axe (ritual?), a battle axe identical to the one in the other find from Valsømagle, a large axe with high flanges (weapon), and a big fish-hook. Again we seem to be dealing with the personal weaponry of an aristocrat (or possibly two).

The two Valsømagle hoards are related through the find spot and the close similarity of several of the items. Perhaps sacrifices of the weapons of slain enemy chiefs, possibly along with those of their followers, might explain these as well as several other 'personal' hoards. On might imagine that warring in the earliest Bronze Age involved the ritual sacrifice of the weapons of the chief opponent(s), leaving common warriors (and the means of production) largely out of the area of conflict.

By contrast, playing with a traditional, 'local', hypothesis, perhaps two generations were involved in a succession ritual. In the last-mentioned Valsømagle hoard we may thus have (a) a ritual axe, perhaps an heirloom, (b) the senior weapons of a deceased aristocrat and (c) the junior items of his heir. And, in the first-mentioned hoard, perhaps (a) the senior weapons of the latter person and (b) the junior weapons of his heir in turn. This hypothesis would fit with the, however very slight and perhaps altogether non-existent, temporal distinctions between the finds. (For the supportive arguments, cf. the Borbjerg sacrifice discussed in Chapter 7A.)

(4) A Period II hoard from Åstofte at Asnæs, northwestern Sjælland/Zealand was found in a bog or the like and made up of three full-metal hilted swords, a flange-hilted sword-blade, and two fine sword-blades with bronze pommels (Aner & Kersten 1976, vol. II, no. 771). Obviously, the supreme personal weapons of three, or perhaps six, aristocrats were sacrificed here.

(5) At Frøjk near Måbjerg in Western Jutland a contemporaneous hoard was found (on dry land) consisting of a battle axe,
a dagger blade, five spearheads (partly fragmentary), and 19 crude
palstaves (also partly fragmentary) (Broholm 1943, vol. I, 224,
M80-81). This hoard may reflect a small group of ten ordinary
warriors (armed with axes only) with their five commanders (a
high 33%): one chief with battle-axe, dagger and spear, and four
junior or lesser chiefs with axe and spear. The sequence of fighting
may have resembled that of the Smørumovre army below (no. (6)),
engaging at first the commanders, then everybody else.

(6) Finally, the exceptionally large find from Smørumovre at
Smørum, Zealand, dated to Period II is mentioned (Worsaae 1853;
Aner & Kersten 1973, vol. I, no. 354). This hoard held a high 163
items, of which 44 of the axes in the find were unfinished and may
have been currency bars or raw material in ingot form (Fig. 17).
Also the broken-off hilt of a full metal sword, a fragmentary socketed celt and flanged axe, a lump of copper, and perhaps even two
puzzling chisels may primarily be seen in terms of the 50 pieces of
raw material, or even payment, they represent.

The artefacts lay, as usual for such hoards, together in a heap,
in the present case in a bog, which certainly seems to indicate a
sacrifice, both spearheads and axes thus being without their shafts.
The spearheads refer to two types: one (ten specimens) with a short
socket (for throwing- or thrusting-spears), and one (50 specimens)
with a long free socket, fit for lance fighting (where the weapon is
in use both for thrust and as a staff in individual duels, and the
socket and lower end of the blade, more angular than on the other
type, may serve to shove an enemy weapon aside).

These weapons may thus, tentatively, be distributed among (cf.
Fig. 18): (1) ten 'commanders' (20%) with two spears (one of each
type) plus a weapon axe (or a socketed celt, having exactly the
same function); and, (2) 40 other ranks (followers and, if at sea,
paddlers too), each with one spear and one axe. Among the
artefacts are also one dress pin imported from Central Europe and
two axes of a type originating in the southeastern Baltic region, one
of these unfinished.

If correctly interpreted, the Smørumovre find provides a rare
glimpse of a larger Bronze Age force, probably a small regional
army where the common warriors, indeed everyone except the
'steersmen', were also potential paddlers of the boats used for

	COMMANDERS	COMMONERS	CURRENCY/ TOOLS
Sword			1 Fr
Dagger-blade	1		
Dress pin	1		
Spearheads			
– short free socket	10		
– long socket	10?	40?	
Celt-axes			
– ornamented	1		
– simple	1		1 Fr
Weapon palstave-axes			
– elaborate	5 (4)		
– simple	2 (3)		
Flanged axes			
– wide edge	1		2 (1 Fr, 1 Unfi)
– narrow edge		3	
'Work' palstave-axes			
– heavy		38	
– light			43 (Unfi)
Socketed chisels			2
Lump of copper			1
WARRIORS/ITEMS	c. 10	c. 40	50

Fig. 17. The Early Bronze Age (Period II) Smørumovre sacrifice, Sjælland/ Zealand (Aner & Kersten 1973, Vol. I, No. 354). Hypothetical division of the artefacts among the supposed warriors, including fragments (raw material) and ingots, plus a few tools. Note that the number of ingots (and tools) corresponds with the suggested number of warriors (payment?). Fr = Fragment, Unfi = Unfinished.

```
    c        c        c     c  C  Cs c     c        c        c
  wwwww    wwwww    wwwww    wwwww    wwwww    wwwww    wwwww    wwwww
```

*Fig. 18. Highly hypothetical order of fighting for a Smørumovre Early Bronze
Age company (c. 50 men), perhaps of two boats. The front of fighting (probably
less than 100 m wide) is up, the enemy party is not shown. The senior warriors
are in the present case grouped in the middle of the front. The tactical planning
is rudimentary: commanders are heading the charge and no concern is shown
for particular movements, either on the attack or in the defense; there is,
however, a limited potential for outflanking small enemy forces. In particular if
shields were not in use, the fighting would quickly have turned into a mêlée of
duels. Against tactically superior, even smaller, forces (cf. Hjortspring in the
below examples), the Smørumovre company could easily break if attacked in
force at its strongest point (centre). This might explain the later acceptance of
phalanx-techniques.*

*C = 'commander' or steersman (two spears: one for throwing, one lance,
axe, sword or dagger, etc.), one of the commanders is the supreme one (Cs); c
= petty 'commander' (two spears: one for throwing, one lance, axe); w =
common warrior (one spear (for lance), less exquisite axe).*

transportation at sea, of which we have representations in particular on rock carvings (cf. Randsborg 1993).

The boats employed no doubt had traits in common both with
the, albeit very heavy, English Ferriby vessels (Fig. 8), and with
Hjortspring. (On one of the ritual Rørby-swords from the period
preceeding Smørumovre we count more than 30 paddlers in one
boat alone (Aner & Kersten 1976 vol. II), No. 617.) A supreme
leader is, however, missing in the Smørumovre find, unless we
refer the (deliberately) broken sword, flanged axe and (perhaps)
celt (plus the fine, but bent, thus also 'slain' dress-pin) to him.
Indeed, this unusual find, rather than the common interpretation
as the stock of a metal worker, may, in fact, be seen as an early
parallel to the Hjortspring weapon sacrifice (as well as to the
somewhat earlier Passentin hoard from Mecklenburg in Northern
Germany, cf. Chapter 8D & below). The circumstances of find are
in all cases the same, a bog.

A troop of Smørumovre warriors may have marched up with
their 'commanders' in front, these being the only warriors of the
company to throw metal-tipped missiles at the enemy before, like

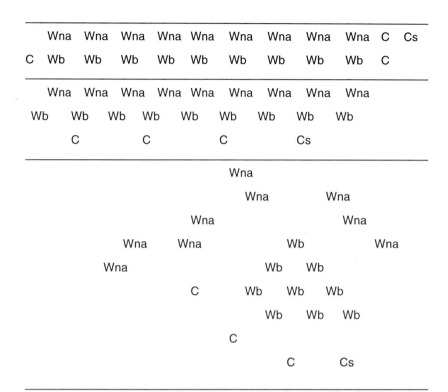

Fig. 19. TOP: Hypothetical model order of battle for a Hjortspring boat type platoon or phalanx. The width of the phalanx hardly covers more ground than 25-30 m. The front of the battle is up. The enemy party is not shown. — CENTRE: Hypothetical sequence of charges (from the front to the last rank). — BOTTOM: Hypothetical engagement (middle phase). At this stage the javelins have already been thrown, but their designations are kept in the figure for identification. No flank- or counter-attacks are experienced or foreseen in the troop-deployment (in this case).

Legend: C = 'commander' (with mail-coat, sword, bayonet-lance (or alternate), and narrow/long shield; the steersman (Cs), perhaps also with a fierce dog). W = common warrior (with lance and average shield). n = narrow iron-tipped javelin. b = broad iron-tipped javelin. a = antler/bone-tipped javelin.

eventually the rest of the company, engaging him with at first lance, then possibly with axe (Fig. 19).

Finally, in the Late Bronze Age, indeed in the whole period between c. 1300 BC (the transition between Periods II and III of the Early Bronze Age) and the sacrifices of Hjortspring and Passentin, the latter in Mecklenburg, North Germany (cf. Chapter 9D below & Schoknecht 1973), more than seven hundred years later, massed deposits of weapons (except, perhaps, for bronze shields) are highly unusual. Normally only one, or, perhaps, two weapons are sacrificed, for instance, a fine sword. Thus, there is no continuity of militarily orientated ritual between the Early Bronze Age and the age of Hjortspring. Other military sacrifices from Denmark are even later (the late Imperial Roman and the Migration periods). This is probably the reason why the Early Bronze Age finds have not been studied from a military or combat point of view.

3. The Fighting

... opposing breast to breast: that's how to fight,
with the long lance or sword-grip in your hand.
You light-armed men, wherever you can aim
from the shield-cover, pelt them with great rocks
and hurl at them your smooth-shaved javelins,
helping the armoured troops with close support.
　　　　Tyrtaios (c. 650 BC)

A. The Hjortspring Battle

The Hjortspring find evidently constitutes a unique opportunity of
gaining a close view of the size, equipment, fighting techniques,
behaviour and rituals of a pre-Roman barbarian army (and indirectly, also of its opponent). According to the Mediterranean
chronology, we find ourselves in the late Classical/early Hellenistic
period, or, in the age of Philip II of Macedonia and his son, the
famous Alexander.

In the Hjortspring battle, probably taking place somewhere on
the island of Als, the enemy force was an amphibious one, arriving
from the sea in swift vessels. Cavalry was most probably not
employed by the attacker, at least not in the initial or landing phase
of the assault. Furthermore, it seems clear that equipment was standardized and made up of one heavy spear (or lance) and one light
spear (missile). To this come, for about half the fighters, also
antler/bone-tipped javelins, plus an unspecified number of lightly
chipped flint-stones for throwing (cf. Fig. 13). A short sword was
used for close combat, but by only a few of the men. Costly mail-
coats were, no doubt, also restricted to such commanders.

The standardized weaponry indicates standardized methods of
combat, involving whole contingents of beached infantry organized
in units (platoons, or *enomotiai*, to apply an ancient Greek term) of
18 warriors under their four commanders or 'steersmen' (with mail-
coats and swords). The battle was probably opened with volleys of
stones and light (both bone- and iron-tipped) spears, followed by
fighting at close quarters between shielded spearmen or lancers

rushing to attack while maintaining 'regimental' order, since no more throwing-spears were available than what early enemy fire may have left unbroken on the battle ground. Bow and arrow, though no doubt well known by the combatants, were, interestingly enough, not employed in the fighting, at least not by the attackers, whose equipment was sacrificed in the Hjortspring bog. This absence may reflect a (probably mutual) code of combat and certainly stresses the ritual nature of combat of the age, perhaps even a kind of *rite de passage*.

The order of battle for each Hjortspring-type platoon, as well as for grouped platoons (or companies), may hence, with attack foremost in mind (and without any cavalry being involved), be drawn up in the following, albeit hypothetical, fashion, coinciding with the seating in the boat. This would draw on already established emotional links and the order of rank and seniority among the warriors, lending further credibility to the model (Fig. 19):

The commanders (except the assistant steersman) are placed on the right flank of a phalanx two warriors deep and 25 to 30 m wide. (The position to the front and right is similar to the prestigious posting of the Ancient Greek *strategos* or the Roman *centurio*; from here the Hjortspring commanders could direct the first exchange of missiles and the initial charge, if attacking.) The distribution of the javelins among the fighters is hypothetical, but one of the two main ranks, in the battle order most likely the front one, may (along with lance and shield) have held the narrow-headed, precisely aimed deep-penetration javelins and probably the antler/bone-tipped 'first volley' ones as well (especially the first-mentioned weapons require a rather high standard of spearmanship). The second rank would then (along with lance and shield) have been equipped with the broad-headed javelin.

The simple rationale behind these considerations may be applied in the form of the following scenarios (ignoring the risk of, perhaps, being considered too 'modern' in the perception of the discipline and tactics of a Hjortspring-type platoon):

Scenario A1 (attack): After having marched up, sung the battle song (cf. Tacitus, *Germania*, 3: to the German Hercules), and, possibly, performed other rites, the initial volleys of missiles would have been despatched: at the very first the chipped flint-stones, then the antler/bone-tipped javelins. The next volley, at still closer range and from behind the warriors in front, would now follow, employing the broad-headed iron-tipped spears of the second rank; like the first volleys, this one would be aimed more or less randomly at the enemy line. Shortly after this, the first rank would charge (perhaps, but not necessarily, followed by one of the commanders). The first echelon would eagerly be selecting precise targets for the piercing narrow-headed iron-tipped spears before engaging in closer combat, meant to create a weak spot in the enemy formation. Duel-like fighting is avoided as long as possible, since it slows down the advance.

The second rank would quickly follow suit. Certainly, these warriors would not want to let down their comrades and, especially, partners from the paddling thwart. Possibly, the second echelon would charge in a 'Germanic' wedge-shaped formation, mentioned by Tacitus (Tacitus, *Germania*, 6), to add to the punch, seeking to break through the enemy formation (or *phalanx*) or, at the minimum, to make it waver (broad shields for shoving and brute force seem useful here). Perhaps the second rank would (also) have been accompanied by one the commanders.

Soon after the initial stages of the battle, the (remaining) commanders, having probably already moved towards the centre, then to the point of fierce engagement, would be closing in too, perhaps seeking out their opponents in rank. The outcome of the battle would be decided a short time after that movement, if not before.

In an egalitarian military structure, and with aggressive common warriors, the benefit of using the armoured, probably senior, 'commanders' as the third, and decisive, rank probably outweighed the need to apply the same persons to direct the charges. Furthermore, it can be argued that once the battle had started, it has a certain inner logic or momentum that does not require the commanders to be present in the very front line, although they may dash there if required. With the javelins thrown, it is a simple necessity to close in quickly, and highly aggressively (or, alternatively, take to a probably even more dangerous flight).

To put the commanders at the head of the charges is also contradicted by their equipment; rather, they were in a better position to defend the flanks of the phalanx against counter-attack, especially the right one, which was not covered by shields. Thus, the commanders, tactically, both make up the reserve and the third echelon. It is possible that also the first echelon would have been attacking in a wedge-shaped formation (cf. Tacitus, 6), although this probably was less expedient and involved greater risks. The front-line of the enemy force, especially if of equal or greater strength, would have been softened only relatively lightly by the missiles and not brought in the disorder aquired for a 'wedge' to hit home.

Scenario A2 (attack): A variant of the above scenario would have the ranks reversed and the antler- or bone-tipped javelins joining the broad-bladed ones while keeping the same sequence of firing. The first to engage at close quarters, would now be the warriors with broad-bladed javelins. This procedure would, however, make it more difficult for the men of the second rank, with their narrow-headed javelins, to seek out defined targets before charging themselves. The second scenario is therefore less likely.

Scenario B (defense): The order of battle and the development of combat for a Hjortspring-type platoon or phalanx under attack may not have been too different from the above scenario, apart, perhaps, from the posting in the terrain. Here, locations commanding the high ground, and, preferably, with protection for at least one of the flanks, for instance areas near streams or bogs, narrow peninsulas, etc., may have been chosen, if time allowed. The code of honour, developed among crew members, was, no doubt, essential for keeping the military discipline under adverse conditions. Missiles would be hurled against the attackers and an attempt, perhaps by throwing the javelins with penetrating spearheads, probably followed by a restricted counter-attack, made to stop the enemy's advance before the last lines of defence. If these steps were not successful, close combat would follow, the outcome of which can only be guessed. Thus, the Hjortspring army itself may have perished. On the other hand, if judged feasible, a full counter-attack with the second rank might also have been successful in relieving the attacked.

Furthermore, against amphibious forces, a militia army on the defence would have had the benefit of applying its own cavalry, one way or another, to battle operations. The Hjortspring 'commanders' (or, at least, some of them), all dressed in costly mail-coats, a piece of highly flexible armour, probably originally invented for cavalry, may well have played this part when horses were available, as certainly 'at home'. (The single sacrified horse in the Hjortspring find was perhaps stolen by the attackers upon landing.)

Perhaps retired amphibious commanders made up the cavalry of the home forces.

Even limited cavalry forces may have decided the outcome of the fighting. For an amphibious force without cavalry a foiled infantry charge could mean annihilation. For the defender, own cavalry may harass a deploying enemy troop, attack its flanks (and rear) and, possibly, pursue the fleeing warriors. If training allowed, even a shock-effect may have been used in attack or counter-attack. Indeed, cavalry was one of the only means in antiquity, in particular before Rome, to add overall mobility to a battle between primitive phalanx armies.

An Archaic Greek source, probably even of the seventh century BC (cf. the old-fashioned chariots), in fact an inscription on a pillar at a temple in the city of Eretria mentions an army (in procession) made up of 3,000 infantry and 600 cavalry (plus 60 chariots) (quoted in Strabo, 10.1.10). Incidentally, the percentage of horsemen and charioteers here is 18%, the same as the 'commanders' in Hjortspring. The Eretria source, elaborating on the customs of war, also mentions a treaty between two neighbouring cities banning 'long-distance missile weapons', bow and arrow, sling, and, possibly, also javelin (in contrast to spear and lance). The social reason is, obviously, to reduce casualties, when settling scores, and to prevent prolonged fighting. This source thus gives a highly interesting example of the conventions and rituals of warfare that we have suggested might have been behind the conspicuous lack of bows and arrows in Hjortspring.

Finally, fierce dogs (again, cf. the sacrificed one(s) in Hjortspring) may also have been used as a true weapon, rather than for guarding and common entertainment. The dog, contrary to horses, can be brought along on amphibious expeditions composed of Hjortspring-type boats, for instance by the (supreme) commanders of the army.

In the context of Hjortspring, a rock carving from Tegneby Mellangården, Litsleby, Tanum parish, Northern Bohuslän in western Sweden, is particularly interesting (Coles 1990, 83). The representation is of a clash between two small groups of mounted warriors (respectively four and five) with spears and square shields (no swords are seen); two infantrymen, standing behind the riders and equipped in the same fashion, are also seen.

Rock-carvings are normally dated to the 'Bronze Age', but the date of the last ones is not clearly known. Riders are very rare on rock-carvings and square shields otherwise practically unknown. In the present case we may have a depiction dated to the end of the Bronze Age (Period VI) or, more likely, to judge from the shape of the shields (cf. Stary 1981), the Pre-Roman Iron Age and thus the period of Hjortspring. At any rate, the Tegneby carving is the earliest Nordic picture of potentially crucial cavalry combat.

B. Phalanx Fighting

Such battles, employing Hjortspring and possibly auxiliary forces, strikingly resemble a clash between hoplite or other *phalanx* infantry forces of the Greek Archaic and Classical periods; (thus, the slight but significant change of vocabulary from 'platoon' to 'phalanx' when referring to the Hjortspring army). This age, it has been claimed, saw the rise of 'the western way of warfare', where quick military decision was sought to avoid protracted fighting and collateral damage (Hanson 1991; Hanson (ed.) 1991; cf. Keegan 1993) (cf. Fig. 39). It is in this context that the absence at Hjortspring of bow and arrow, which may have drawn out the final decision, is particularly interesting. The small number of swords (limited in length and, besides, mostly relatively cheap) may perhaps be seen in the same light. Again, a long period of close fighting before a decision was reached is avoided. At any rate, the short swords do not permit a flowing battle, dominated by duels, as between warriors with longswords (and shields).

Phalanx warfare revolutionized combat in creating 'regiments' and in making it possible to fight proper battles. Thus, with the phalanx, political decision (and religious sanction) made it possible to estimate and plan campaigns, or operations, and to engage the warriors in tactical considerations that would, if not determine the outcome of the battle, make a desired effect a far more likely thing than both a cautious dance around the enemy, the eventual duels or a headless rush to engage would do. With the phalanx it was, in other words, possible to fight an organized battle, not merely to engage in primitive, 'ritualized' combat.

Whether a true phalanx type of combat was employed in Hjortspring, or a looser formation chosen, is, of course, in principle unknown, since we have no 'eyewitness' reports of any kind.

Above, we have opted for a mobile version of the former. The standardization of the infantry equipment, the close collaboration between warriors, organised in 'ships', speak in favour of solidarity and coherence, thus discipline, in action. On the other hand, the apparently relatively short spears and lances (2-2½ m as the maximum) and, in particular, the rather light character of the weapons employed (in particular the relatively small shield) do not permit most of the defining techniques of the heavily protected contemporary Greek Hoplite phalanx, which, with its substantial depth, may virtually 'push' its way into a breach in the enemy formation.

The warriors of the classic Greek Hoplite phalanx (ideally) wore helmet, cuirass, and greaves, and carried a very large pregnantly curved shield (the *hoplon*), all in bronze (or, in the case of the shield, bronze-covered) (e.g., Connolly 1981). Furthermore they were equipped with one, or two, rather long spears or lances (2-3 m) with pointed ferrules for killing or maiming stumbled or lightly wounded enemy soldiers (without having to turn the lance), and, a short heavy sword. In spite of the overall differences in appearance of the troops, this weaponry, dominated by shield and spear/lance, is, in fact, clearly reminiscent of Hjortspring. Even direct parallels can be found, since the 'scimitar' of the Danish find, with inwardly curving edge, most probably had a Greek, Etruscan, or other southern, prototype. However, the lack of heavy armour rather makes the Hjortspring warrior resemble the lightly armed troops of the wide Mediterranean, for instance, the Italian Samnite fighters (Warry 1980, 50, 67, & 103), or their cousin, the Greek 're-formed' light Hoplite of the late fourth century BC, whose lance was still very long, though (Warry 1980,67).

There are also perhaps quite unexpected parallels to Hjortspring, for instance, in the organisation and composition of weaponry, to the disciplined and highly manoevrable early Roman legion from around 300 BC (in fact, also earlier), with its use of three or four differently equipped tiers of warriors of different age, and, for that matter, wealth (cf. Fig. 20) (Warry 1980):

The Romans of the fourth century BC, the age of Hjortspring, positioned a rather few very young (and poor) light skirmish troops, so-called *Velites*, to their front. 'Velites' types of warriors are not present in the above-suggested Hjortspring platoon or phalanx, but were probably present when such elite units fought 'at home'.

```
v   v   v   v   v   v   v   v   v   v

H  H  H  H  H  H  H  H    H  H
H  H  H  H  H  H  H  H    H  H

P  P  P  P  P  P  P  P  P  P
P  P  P  P  P  P  P  P  P  P

t   t   t   t   t   t   t   t    t   t
```

```
HHHHHHHHHHHHHHHHHHHHHH

P  P  P  P  P  P  P  P  P  P
P  P  P  P  P  P  P  P  P  P

t   t   t   t   t   t   t   t    t   t

v   v   v   v   v   v   v   v    v   v
```

Fig. 20. TOP: Roman order of battle (for the Century units of a full Legion) at around 300 BC (or earlier). — BOTTOM: The first phase of battle. The front is up. Exhausted first line troops retreat through the gaps of the second echelon, which then lock and commence fighting (based on Warry 1980).

The size and numbers of the letters indicate the relative strength of the units of troops in question: v = very young (and poor) light Velites (skirmish troops, rather few) armed with a few short javelins, a sword, a light shield, and a helmet; H = young heavy Hastati armed with two throwing spears (pilae), a short sword (gladius), and various defensive weapons including a heavy shield and a helmet; P = mature heavy Principes armed as the Hastati; t = veteran heavy Triarii (again rather few) armed with a lance, a gladius, and various armour including a heavy shield, a helmet and perhaps even greaves and a mail-coat.

Aspiring youngsters were likely both scouting, hurling stones and, possibly, antler/bone-tipped javelins at the enemy, as well as collecting weapons for further use, including their own, from the battlefield. The equipment of the Roman Velites comprised short javelins, a sword, and a light shield.

Next, in the early Roman legions, followed three ranks of century units, of which the first and foremost was made up of young *Hastati* with rather substantial weapons, including two spears, a sword, a heavy shield, and a helmet. The following rank, of mature *Principes*, was similarly armed. The Hastati and the Principes thus resemble the common warriors of the Hjortspring platoon. (Thus, the Hjortspring 'Hastati' may, in expedition, have taken over some of the duties of the home 'Velites', cf. the above stone-throwing and use of spears not tipped by iron.)

The third rank of units of the early Republican legion was made up of a relatively few veteran so-called *Triarii*, indeed, the last resource of the army and the last to enter battle. These veteran troops were armed with a lance, a sword, and various armour including a heavy shield, helmet and perhaps even a mail-coat and greaves. Thus, they indeed resemble the above 'commanders' of the Hjortspring platoon or phalanx. The mail-coat, possibly invented in southeastern Europe during the fourth century BC as a defensive weapon for princely mounted warriors, may first have been introduced into the Roman and other Mediterranean world (though at first not applied by the Greeks) as a cavalry defensive weapon. It was, however, to become particularly characteristic of the heavy Roman infantry.

A final highly interesting issue remains in this context, namely the battlefield casualties. Above two hypothetical calculations were presented for Hjortspring. In the first one, only one-eighth (or less) of the attacking force would (potentially) have lost their lives (the persons with mail-coats and/or swords). This is actually consistent with information from Greek hoplite battles (Lazenby 1991). In the other, and, due to the supposed rarity of the mail-coats and some other factors, far more likely calculation, probably the whole army succumbed or, at least, surrendered its equipment.

The first number of casulties is probably acceptable in fighting between neighbouring groups, who must live to see each other, perhaps even collaborate, in the near future. The second number, reflecting the possible loss of an entire elite force and the potential exposure of a whole tribal group (if the losses on the battlefield were exploited by the enemy), would only seem acceptable in the case of relatively distant enemies. Below, it will be argued that this was, in fact, the case at Hjortspring. Furthermore, fighting on expedition, since revenge cannot always be meted out, may be a kind of relatively harmless piracy, a de facto rite-de-passage with the preservation of the freedom and independence, the honour of the homeland, as the main serious factor of the game (cf. Chapter 4).

Warfare or a more or less constant threat of war are strong factors both in developing and in maintaining communities.

However, when things went awry, as the evocative quote from Orosius below indicates (Chapter 5, beginning), the ferocity and cruelty of Barbarian warfare — in Central and Southern Europe in the late first millennium BC sometimes involving large armies and whole population-groups — was second to none. And the stakes must, sometimes at least, have been very high indeed.

4. The Enemy

> ... to lay waste as much as possible of the land around them and to keep it uninhabited. They hold it a proof of a people's valour to drive their neighbours from their homes, so that no one dare to settle near them, and also think that it gives them greater security by removing any fear of sudden invasion. When a tribe is attacked or intends to attack another, officers are chosen to conduct the campaign and invested with powers of life and death.
>
> Caesar (from *De Belli Gallici*, c. 52 BC)

In the above quote, Caesar leaves the impression that Germanic warfare was primarily between close neighbours and that it was almost incessant. This may well be true, although the reference sounds a bit like a standard description of barbarians and their ways. Tacitus confirms the picture, however, and even attempts to find a reason for it, by stating that 'renown is more easily won among perils', and that 'a large body of retainers cannot be kept together except by means of violence and war, since they always make demands on the generosity of their chief' (Tacitus, *Germania*, 14). Tacitus hints at a possible cause for such conflict by supposing that a party that grew strong enough would wish to seize fresh lands (Tacitus, 28).

Still, the large weapon sacrifices are relatively few, Hjortspring, for example, being unique in the pre-Roman Iron Age in Northern Europe. These finds must therefore refer to singular situations, such as a major battle between different regions or, perhaps rather, an important struggle with a dangerous intruder. The issues were certainly far more important than a trivial cattle-raid.

Tacitus also describes, however vaguely and, admittedly, for a much later period than Hjortspring, two organizational structures for campaigning Germanic forces (cf. Adler 1993, 249f). In the first one, the (supreme) leader is a picked and appointed militarily able *Dux*. He commands the (entire or militia) army with executive powers, although somewhat limited, whether he is of noble birth or not (Tacitus, 7; 30). In the second type of organization (Tacitus,

14), the elected leader, a *Princeps*, is a noble warrior commanding a group of (exclusively) young fighters, likely to be of both noble and common stock, and emotionally, as well as professionally, bound to their leader: in other words, a permanent or, rather, semi-permanent elite warrior *Comitatus* or 'Gefolgschaft'. A military organization of the latter kind was probably responsible for the Hjortspring expedition. If so, Hjortspring also provides a terminus ante quem for the introduction of élite forces in Northern Europe, indeed a division of the warriors of a community into (a) elite, *hird* or, later, guard regiments, and (b) common militia troops.

The Hjortspring find, being four hundred years earlier than Tacitus, belongs in a phase between c. 400 and the second century BC, in Greek terminology the late Classical to early Hellenistic periods. During this phase, warfare and dislocation of peoples, for instance Celtic tribes in search (in particular) of wealth, employment (as mercenaries), and new land — the latter necessary to secure subsistence abroad — occurred quite frequently in transalpine Europe and adjacent regions to the south. In the Mediterranean, this phase, seeing almost constant mobilization of military resources, makes up the transition between the early regional states, for example in the Aegean, and the later empires of the Macedonians, Romans and other peoples. Certainly, the so-called Celtic expansion must to be seen in conjunction with the general development in the southern countries. No doubt, the whole process also affected temperate and perhaps even northern Europe. Thus, perhaps, the Hjortspring battle was but a distant spin-off from southern events, taking place in the far 'Germanic' North, unknown to written history conceived in the Mediterranean and concerned with local affairs.

The question must also be raised about the 'nationality' of the Hjortspring find. Is it entirely 'Danish', as a national archaeology would want it, or does it rather reflect a battle, in Denmark, with enemies coming from, for example, present-day Germany, or even Poland? Such a simple query is not so harmless as it may sound, however, since the Hjortspring find, like so many other great discoveries from Denmark, has almost come to epitomize the cultural heritage of the country. Also, the great weapon and boat sacrifice from the Nydam bog (dated to the late Roman Imperial period), found only a short distance from Hjortspring, was, under compulsion, handed over to enemy Germans after Denmark's defeat in 1864 (a magic year, like 1945, and still not forgotten) to the allied forces of Prussia and Austria-Hungary. Indeed, archaeology is sometimes difficult to disentangle completely from the consciousness of a nation, with loyalties real or perceived, productive or even dangerous.

The Hjortspring boat is demonstrably relatively easy to paddle and manoeuvre and may have been able to cover substantial distances under favourable conditions, for instance on rivers. The mail-coats certainly point in the direction of (eastern) Central Europe and beyond (as does the 'Greek' scimitar in the find). Also the superb lime tree for the boat might have had its origin in a more southern clime than the Baltic. On the other hand, the iron weapons in Hjortspring do have close North German, Danish and Nordic parallels, as have the antler/bone spearheads. No parallels to the latter are found further away than areas bordering on the southern Baltic. Also the pottery vessel in Hjortspring, as well as, by ceramic analogies, the small, possibly turned wooden bowl or dish point to the southern Scandinavian/North German/western Baltic region. Better still, the turned wooden pyxides, although themselves perhaps imported from Central or Southern Europe, have parallels or imitations in pottery, found mainly in the larger later Hamburg region (Figs. 21-22).

If this important link with northwestern Germany holds true, perhaps even the predecessors of the Langobardi in Tacitus — 'famous because they are so few' (Tacitus, 40), come into question as the fourth century BC aggressors of the island of Als, and thus masters of the Hjortspring boat. In fact, Tacitus continues: 'Hemmed in, as they are, by many mighty peoples, they find safety, not in submission, but in facing the risks of battle.' Incidentally, to the north of the Langobardi, from the third century AD on themselves one of the great migrant tribes of history, live, again according to Tacitus, the peoples that worship Nerthus, or Mother Earth.

Why the peoples of the later greater Hamburg region would have wanted to attack the island of Als is more of a question. Possibly, expeditions were, as suggested above, part of the social life of these peoples, augmenting their military readiness and keeping the communities together. The Hjortspring tribe certainly was inspired and perhaps even trained in military affairs by the south. Perhaps easy prey was sought out, although this is less likely considering the magnitude and importance of the subsequent

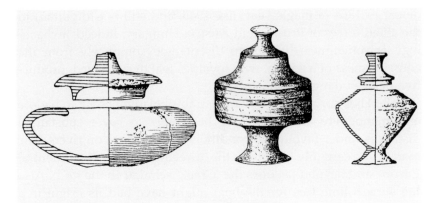

Fig. 21. Ceramic pyxides from graves of the Pre-Roman Iron Age in the Hamburg area (after Müller-Brauel 1932 & Schindler 1960).

sacrifice. Also, the wealth of these societies must have been extremely limited. Perhaps elements of revenge were a factor, or, alliances, for instance between Als (and, perhaps, the larger region of Southern Jutland) and a close neighbour of the 'Hamburg' tribe. At any rate, military power was certainly a strong factor in these pre-state societies with various ad hoc and other groups bearings arms and entering power networks.

The cultural development of the Early Iron Age in, for instance, Southern Scandinavia, displays a high degree of continuity; relatively stable 'cultural boundaries' are also noted in the region. Thus, it can be argued that the military readiness and the defensive strength of the different communities must have been high. This probably left a significant impact on both the self-perception and the 'constitutional' ideas. Attacks were a part of the military picture too, although, apparently, less successful. Indeed, the introduction and use of elite units may have been a premediated step in carrying out a campaign of conquest, involving also militia forces.

The Hjortspring boat, being so very light and manoeuvrable, even in very shallow waters, might, with ease, have been brought from the estuary of the Elbe river and the North Sea basin to the Baltic by way of the Hedeby gap, commonly used in the Viking period. Indeed, this route would, in fact, by way of the Ejder and Trene rivers, and the Sli Inlet, have taken the vessel and its

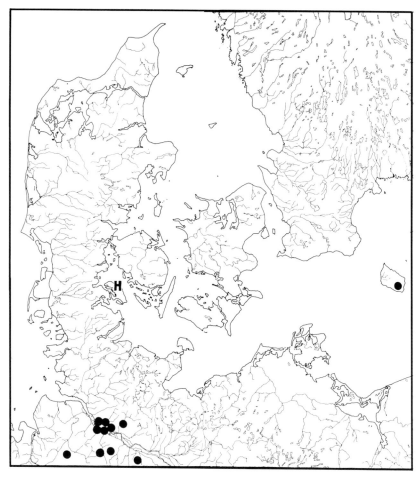

Fig. 22. Distribution map of ceramic pyxides *(in the Danish-Northern German region) of the same formal type as the wooden ones in the Hjortspring find, the latter marked with an 'H' (cf. Figs. 10-12 & 21).*

companions right to a point immediately to the south of the island of Als. Another possible route for very light vessels journeying from the lower Elbe River to the Baltic (in this case appearing at later Lübeck) would have been by way of the streams merging on the Schaal and Ratzeburg Lakes in the Holstein-Mecklenburg borderlands.

Whether the Hjortspring fleet actually made up the naval arm of a joint 'fleet-army' operation, we do not know. In the Mediterranean, and in the Near East, for instance during the Persian attacks on Greece in the early fifth century BC and Alexander's assaults on Persia in the late fourth century BC, fleets followed the coastal marches of the armies, i.a. to supply the latter. In the case of Hjortspring, supplies for the boats would more likely have come from the hypothetical land wing. Altogether, the Scandinavian and other North European military tradition seems to be one of truly amphibious forces, but the idea of a combined arms operation, a latterday 'SeaLand' campaign or battle, is an interesting one and deserves, as already indicated, to be borne in mind also in the Hjortspring case. In fact, the find itself does not necessarily speak against it, although it may only have been feasible, in the North European pre-Roman Iron Age, to keep a large army in the field for a sustained period of time by uprooting its supply base and making it truly mobile. Such may, however, under the given economic and social circumstances, have been possible only by forming a wandering tribe, in fact, a migration. By contrast, smaller elite forces may travel farther and even join a larger, friendly army outside the home-region.

Indeed, the very speed of the Hjortspring boat (despite its lack of a sail), no doubt much greater than, for instance, the clumsy Bronze Age vessels from England (cf. Fig. 6 (Wright 1990)), would have made it a near-perfect tool for complex offensive operations from a land base protected by own forces. Still, the only certain thing is, that the Hjortspring boat could land an amphibious 'commando' phalanx on far-away hostile territory. A pack of Hjortspring boats would have made a formidable enemy, perhaps only to be checked by large militia forces, preferably with a mobile cavalry arm, or with similarly equipped soldiers superior in number. Also, it is suggested (cf. below), that the Hjortspring phalanx most probably represented a novel, although not the first, wave of warfare, vis-à-vis traditional massed local militia forces of a Stone or, rather, Bronze Age kind.

The shadowy soldiers of the Hjortspring Bog force thus, according to the above, must have come from somewhere on the North German (or Polish) plains, or, from another part of Southern Scandinavia (lime in the required quality and size did not grow any futher north). The Hamburg region on the lower Elbe, at the end of a major European route of transportation and communication, emanating in eastern Central Europe, is a likely suggestion, in particular since it is sustained by finds of imitations, in pottery, of the Hjortspring type pyxides. The alternative is almost unbearable. Close neighbours, perhaps peoples from Southern Jutland or Funen, in grouped combat to the death with Alsian warriors: an Iron Age Europe in the shape of contemporary Bosnia-Herzegovina or even Rwanda.

Certainly, the mentioned area around Hamburg fulfils both the environmental, the geographical and, not least, the cultural criteria spelled out above. Finally, as to the vessel, the resemblance between the Hjortspring boat and the vessels on the Scandinavian Bronze Age rock-carvings (also seen on Late Bronze Age razors found as far south as Northern Germany) must be brought to mind, as has, in fact, often been done in archaeological literature. This observation might not allow regions further to the south to be suggested in earnest as the homeland of Hjortspring. It should be added, though, that next to nothing is known of contemporary Central European boats, which, theoretically, may have been of the same or similar design. (Perhaps less likely, since traffic on rivers and lakes probably did not require vessels with the several exact qualities of Hjortspring.)

Archaeology has, for Iron Age pre-Roman Denmark, revealed the existence of massive linear systems of multiple poles across densely settled landscapes; however, these seeming boundaries (of whatever kind they may be) do not have a defensive character proper (Becker 1982, 65 Abb. 13). The same is true of the simple palisades around contemporary farmsteads and hamlets (cf. Fig. 15). Other 'fortifications' are also, practically, absent during the pre-Roman period and even very rare during most of the first millennium AD

This cultural, economic and social landscape, without any obvious signs of warfare, is a particular property of pre-Roman (and later) Iron Age Southern Scandinavia and Northern Germany. Furthermore, in most of the the pre-Roman Iron Age, weapons are also absent from the graves, 'warrior-burials' thus being unknown in the overall region until (the second and) the first century BC (Jørgensen 1968; Nielsen 1975 (for details)). Incidentally the late weapon graves, of the close of the first millennium BC, hold a rich equipment very different from that of Hjortspring of the fourth century BC, dominated by swords (32 double-edged against 14, probably mainly early, single-edged ones), about the same number of spears (41), shields with round iron bosses (19), and, perhaps, even a few spurs. These are the weapons that the Germanic armies of the period of Caesar and Tacitus were equipped with.

Interestingly, the earliest known defensive naval barrier in Northern Europe (at Gudsø Vig in Kolding Fjord, on the coast of Eastern Jutland, some 50 km to the north of Hjortspring) has now been dated to the same general period, the latest Pre-Roman Iron Age (Tauber 1988; cf. Rieck 1991). There are two Carbon-14 samples: (1) 180 ± 75 BC, calibrated, 175 BC (with one standard deviation, 335-95 BC); (2) 30 ± 75 BC, calibrated, AD 15 (with one standard deviation 95 BC-AD 80). From these dates the so-called own age of the wood should be subtracted, which lowers the dates somewhat. Thus, Hjortspring is still substantially earlier than the, however limited, late pre-Roman Iron Age (and later) actual reflections of warfare in Denmark

Nevertheless, some, even quite sophisticated, military organization (the Hjortspring find reminds us) already existed in Northern Europe in an early phase of the pre-Roman Iron Age. Such might, as already indicated, have been made up by two elements: (a) elite forces with standardized equipment and (b) militia armies. The former (probably of the Hjortspring kind) were no doubt grouped in 'boats'. The regional armies, as much later in the Iron Age, in the Viking Age and the early Medieval Period (cf. the 'levy'), were probably based on local units. In a marine country like Denmark, or its neighbouring regions, such primarily defensive units might also have been the size of the crew of a 'ship', perhaps commanded by representatives of the regional leaders, certainly manned with their local followers.

The advanced, most probably imported, and even surprisingly early mail-coats in Hjortspring seem to belong to a level of organization much higher than that of the common local villages or group of hamlets, at most contributing members of the crew manning a single ship or boat. Also, the high-quality raw-materials, the advanced, though simple, technology and the excellent craftsmanship involved in constructing a Hjortspring boat may well have exceeded the potential of a truly local unit. In sum, political alliances and agreements, and, not least, a society existing above the military horizon, may thus have created, and secured, a degree of de facto de-militarization in other social sectors. This is not to belittle the level of conflict between these societies and individual persons, as the contemporary sacrificed bog-bodies remind us (Fischer 1979).

The North European archaeological observations stand in dramatic contrast to much of Central Europe during the mid-first millennium BC: heavily fortified with thousands of hill-forts, built and expanded ever since the Late Bronze Age. A temporary decline in construction of walled sites (all relatively modest in comparison with the huge territorial Celtic *oppida* at the close of the first millennium BC) is, however, noted for the very period of Hjort-spring. Central Europe is also very rich in warrior graves during these centuries, symbols as they may be seen, of the southern expansion of Celtic tribal groups.

The textual evidence comprises, for instance, the tales of the well-known Celtic assaults on Rome and Delphi, and the Celtic migrants into Anatolia (Randsborg 1992, 103 Fig. 6). In the Mediterranean, particularly the Aegean region, the conspicuous construcion of city walls and other fortifications, culminates, in contrast with Central Europe, during this very period between the late fifth and the early second century BC, or, the age of Hjortspring. Thus, the southern Celts and their possible, even likely, northward transmission of military knowledge, fit, as already mentioned, into the period of transition from regional states (and classic hoplite warfare) to the territorial empires of the Hellenistic period, including rising Rome, applying advanced forfication and siege techniques, along with a more complex military organization regarding the troops.

The Hjortspring find is thus a useful reminder both of the very potential and of the methodological complications of archaeology, where the finds may have several seemingly equally likely interpretations, and where burials and settlements may be silent about the kind of fierce conflict that Hjortspring reveals. However, the egalitarian ethos of phalanx infantry combat with standardized weapons (before such units were employed as regiments by the Hellenistic kingdoms) may actually be paralleled or, even mirrored, in contemporary South Scandinavian and North German society in the very many early (to middle) pre-Roman Iron Age farmsteads, none too different in size, housing single families in command of their own resources, as the individual stables reveal (Fig. 14).

Thus, in a circumstantial sort of way, the social set-up generating the petty Hjortspring army may, in structural terms, have resembled the classical Greek *polis* with its well-to-do and, legally, equal citizens, anti-aristocratic in attitude (although not in substance). These citizens manned the *Hoplite phalanx*: this fighting unit being the most evident contemporaneous model in Europe for the military organization of the Hjortspring tribes and their tiny phalanx regiments.

In the (late) second century BC, the Germanic Cimbri, perhaps from Denmark, migrated to Central and Southern Europe where they both fought and, later, joined arms with Celtic and other tribal groups. Later still, the Cimbri engaged even very large Roman armies to whom they eventually succumbed, however. The earlier developments in military structure and fighting techniques in Northern Europe, as glimpsed in Hjortspring, may well have been the main organizational factor behind the subsequent chains of events, even though the international barbarian weaponry, and, with that, no doubt other factors of fighting and warfare too, had, by then, changed.

In summary, we may conceive of two or even three basic models of early Germanic, indeed of barbarian warfare in general.

Model (I), Raids. The first scenario concerns attacks by limited elite forces of the Hjortspring type countered by large or even very large (regional) militia armies, perhaps supported by own elite forces and/or by a small cavalry force. In a field battle the larger militia army will usually win due to its defensive superiority in men and supplies (but not necessarily in military proficiency).

Model (II), Battles. In this model, the enemy is fielding the elite forces as well as the militia army (or a part thereof) with a train in the form of a tribal unit and its resources of people, animals, food, tools, etc. The enemy is met by the home militia army with its possible elite forces. Here the outcome of the ensuing battle hangs in the balance. The above 'SeaLand' variant of this scenario would have the elite forces attack from the sea, thus confusing the defenders.

Model (II) may have been the scenario of the Celtic and the Cimbri migrations as well as several of the movements of peoples in the much later Migration Period. It is also a necessity when fielding larger barbarian armies against the strong states of the Mediterranean, including Rome. In a protracted campaign the supply tribal unit will settle and start producing the necessities of army and nation, although this, for reasons of the particular mode of production, may only have been possible in regions rather similar to the home one. (To take over a Mediterranean region, a barbarian nation would have to supplant the military and the leadership while keeping the rest of the population at work.)

The introduction of the needs and demands of both smaller elite armies and, in particular, larger militia ones into the discussion of the motives for migrations is very important in understanding the history of the first millenium BC and the first millennium AD in Europe. For instance, on the basis of its remarkable cultural stability and continuity, 'Old Denmark' was probably able to maintain a clear defensive superiory throughout its later prehistory. Perhaps Model (II) was never applied by foreign peoples in their attacks on the region. Model (I), in particular attacks by elite amphibious forces, is well attested, however (cf. Chapter 11). No doubt, the 'Danes' too applied expenditionary forces.

PART II

---

5. The Sacrifice

Having gained possession of both camps and of a huge amount
of booty, the enemy seemed driven by some strange and unusual
animus. They completely destroyed everything they had captured; clothing was cut to pieces and strewn about, gold and
silver were thrown into the river, the breastplates of the men
were hacked to pieces, the trappings of the horses were ruined,
the horses themselves were drowned in whirlpools, and men,
with nooses fastened around their necks, were hanged from
trees. Thus the conqueror realized no booty, while the conquered
obtained no mercy. At Rome there was not only very great sor-
row, but also fear that the Cimbri would immediately cross the
Alps and destroy Italy.

(Orosius V.16)

A. Preliminaries

It was suggested above, with support in the analysis of the military
sacrifices of the late Roman Iron Age and the Migration Period (for
example, Lønstrup 1988), that the Hjortspring find contains the
enemy spoils from a battle with local Alsian forces. The partly
alternative hypothesis, that the offering comprises only a part of
the conquered equipment, is impossible to verify, and may be
altogether false since great effort was put into destroying the
enemy weapons and utensils. We may, for instance, refer to Orosius's famous, but not unique, account, of the victory of the Cimbri
and their allies over the Romans and their confederates, perhaps
more than 80,000 strong, near Orange in Southern Gaul in 105 BC
(cf. the above quotation).

We are also reminded of the, no doubt, humiliating scuttling of the surrendered German high sea fleet at the major British naval base of Scapa Flow in the Orkneys after the First World War, and of the destruction of indeed enormous amounts of German military equipment after the Second one: no doubt the greatest military sacrifice in world history. These acts underline the ritual and symbolic content of (used) weapons even nowadays. Enemy weapons cannot be re-used by the noble winners of battle.

In contemporary western culture, where morality has supplanted belief, no supernatural forces were thought to have been pleased by the 'sacrificing' of the German weapons of the two World Wars. In prehistoric temperate Western Europe, however, military (and many other) sacrifices were beyond doubt gifts to the supernatural forces of the earth and the underworld, perhaps linked with those of the water. Sacrifices in wet areas or rivers dominate the picture or, at least, most of our attention and imagination. Interestingly 'wet' deposits are very rare indeed in Eastern Europe where other beliefs and norms of cult obviously prevailed. In Denmark, even a celestial symbol like the famous Bronze Age Sun Chariot was deposited in a bog. Indeed, such archaeological observations impel us to make a distinction between the nature of the contents of a sacrifice and the kind of the site at which it was carried out and deposited.

In the Mediterranean, the forces to whom sacrifices were usually made seem to have occupied the heavens. The sanctuaries were preferably spectacularly placed in the landscape, for instance on mountain tops or at the interface of elements like the coast, linking heaven, land and sea. In addition, both to the north and to the south in Europe, a social pattern can be recognized whereby the holy places and sanctuaries called for repeated action. Also, sacred places were used to reinforce the social landscape by being placed, for instance, at the centre of a settlement area, in a centre itself, or on the boundary between societies (cf., in part, de Polignac 1991). In turn, societies and social landscapes may have evolved around sanctuaries.

Incidentally, in the late first millennium BC, the period following Hjortspring, the West European world strove, in its sacred philosophy and ritual landscapes, to combine the following: (A) the traditional patterns of sacrificial contact with the forces of the underworld, and (B) the official ritual world of the Mediterranean, stressing the relations with the sky. This happened, after c. 300 BC, by constructing standing sanctuaries above ground. The Celtic so-called Viereckschanzen, with their 'temples' and up to 35 m deep sacrificial shafts, are an excellent example (e.g., Buchsenschutz 1991).

B. Forces and Deities

In the case of Hjortspring (and the later military sacrifices in Denmark and adjacent areas), the notes of the classical authors on offering practices and, especially, on the particular associated deities among the Celts and the Germans are very helpful (Figs. 23-24). At the same time, the grand division of the elements and forces of the world into those relating to the sky and those to the earth, connected by those of the element of water, should be brought into mind (cf. Boyer 1981): water being present both in the sky and on the earth, on the latter, from source to river, and from bog and lake to the sea. Incidentally, in Empedoklos (c. 500-430 BC) as well as in other classical philosophers, the four basic natural elements were Earth, Air, Water, and Fire (to which come the human ones of Love and War). Fire is in the above included in the sky (the sun, etc.), and does not seem to have played an independent role among the forces and deities of Celtic, nor of Germanic, mythology.

As to the Celts, Caesar, in the mid-first century BC, gives the following list of the deities and their qualifications, using Roman names for the gods (Caesar 52 BC, Book 1-2):

(1) Mercury (who is the inventor of all arts, a guide of men upon their journeys, and the most powerful helper in trading and obtaining money) is, Caesar states, the god they revere the most and of whom they have very many images. Next in importance comes: (2) Apollo (who averts illness). (3) Mars (the lord of war to whom the Celts devote their military sacrifices in the form of captured animals and spoils). (4) Jupiter (the king of the gods). And, the female (5) Minerva (who teaches the principles of industries and handicrafts).

About the Germans, Caesar merely says that they recognize, as gods, only what they can see and by which they are benefited, such as Sun, Moon, and Fire. He also mentions that the Germans have no druids. Caesar is less well informed about the Germans than the Celts, and it is not at all clear to what extent he may simply have drawn on earlier, perhaps general ethnographic sources (cf. Lund 1993).

150 years later, Tacitus, also applying Roman names to the for
eign gods, gives the following list of deities and related information as to religious practices among the Germans (Tacitus, *Germania*, 9):

(1) Mercury, who is worshipped above all, and to whom even human sacrifices are given. (2) Hercules, to whom animal sacrifies are given, and of whom the Germans sing when they are about to engage in battle (Tacitus, 3). (3) Mars, to whom animal sacrifices are also given. (4) The female goddess Isis (worshipped by some of the Suebi tribes), who carries the symbol of a *liburna* (a fast vessel or light warship). (5) Nerthus ('Mother Earth', Tacitus is here using a latinized Germanic name for the goddess) is worshipped among the northern Germans (Tacitus, 40); she drives a waggon. On an island of the sea, Tacitus claims, is a grove with a veiled waggon. The goddess travels among her people in this waggon, which is drawn by cows; upon return, the slaves who cleanse in a lake the goddess, her chariot, and the covering cloth are drowned. Tacitus furthermore describes a Central European tribe who honoured (6) the Alcis, young men and brothers, said to be a counterpart of Castor and Pollux, the twin-gods or Dioskouroi (Tacitus, 43). These are worshipped in a sacred grove by a priest dressed up as a woman; there is no image. Finally, Tacitus mentioned an earth-born god (7) Tuisto, whose son, Mannus, is the forefather of all Germans (Tacitus, 2).

According to Tacitus, Hercules and even Odysseus visited Ger
mania, where an altar with the latter's and his father's names on it is found on the Rhine; barrows with Greek inscriptions are also said to be known from southern Germany.

It is generally noted by Tacitus that the Germans did not confine the gods within walls or portray them as human beings. Their holy places are woods and groves to which the names of the deities are applied. To Tacitus, the Germans do have priests; thus, either Caesar may have been poorly informed, which seems likely, or the Germans had acquired them in the meantime (Tacitus ,10; 40).

Interestingly, it is possible to translate these inferred deities into the gods of the Nordic Pantheon of the Viking Age, in particular documented through Snorri's retrospective writings from the high Middle Ages (Snorri c. AD 1200). However, a Nordic god at the end

CELTIC	GERMANIC	VIKING	ATTRIBUTES/Note
Mars M	Mars M	Tyr M	Mars & Tyr: Gods of war
Jupiter M	Hercules M	Tor M	Jupiter: thunderbolt, Hercules: club, Tor: hammer
	Alcis MM		Brothers; Castor & Pollux
Mercury M	Mercury M	Odin M	Mercury & Odin: Gods of knowledge, relation with death
Apollo M		?Balder M	
Minerva F			
	Isis F		Isis: Ship
	Nerthus F	Freja F	Nerthus & Freja: Waggon
		Frej M	Frej: Ship, Waggon
		Njord M	(Father of Freja & Frej)
	Tuisto M		Tuisto's son, Mannus M, is the forefather of all Germans

Fig. 23. Correlation between Roman, Celtic (Caesar (c.) 52 BC), Germanic (Tacitus AD 98), and Viking (Snorri c. 1200, etc.) gods (in part using their Mediterranean names) with their attributes and main areas of responsibility. In fact, this is merely an interpretation and translation of parts of the various pantheons, as carried out by Caesar, Tacitus, and others. The Celtic names are presented in Fig. 24. Caesar's translation and ranking of the gods is: Mercury, then Apollo, Mars, Jupiter, and Minerva, thereafter Father Dis. Tacitus' translation and ranking is: Mercury, then Hercules and Mars, thereafter Isis; Nerthus is mentioned later in Tacitus' work. A possible link between Apollo and Viking Age Balder might be suggested (see also Page 1992, 181f. for links with Bronze Age symbols). (M = Male; F = Female. The Greek names for the Roman gods are: Mars = Ares, Jupiter = Zeus, Mercury = Hermes, Apollo = the same, Minerva = Athena, and Hercules = Heracles.)

ROMAN	CELTIC	CHARACTERISTICS
Mercury M	Teutatès M	God of tribe and city, inventor of arts, director of men on journeys, helper in trading and getting money; many images, three heads; human sacrifices
Apollo M	Belénus M	God of the sun, averts illness
Mars M	Esus? M	God of war, connection with Teutatès; spoils and animal sacrifices
Jupiter M	Taran M	God of the sky, lord of the gods
Minerva F	Belisama F	Teaches industries and handicrafts
Pater Dis M		Forefather of all Celts; chronology

Fig. 24. The main Celtic gods (with attributes and characteristics) and their supposed or tentative Roman equivalents (cf. Fig. 23) (Bruneaux 1986; Hatt 1989; Roymans 1990). The names are given in French; the ranking, and the translation of the Celtic pantheon into the Roman one, is Caesar's (cf. Caesar c. 52 BC, Book 1;1). (M = Male; F = Female.)

of heathendom may well, in spite of the fellowship of name and basic characteristics, have had a different personality than that of his or her namesake a thousand years before. For instance, in late heathendom, at least in central Sweden, the mutual position and roles of two of the primary gods (Tacitus' Germanic equivalents of Mercury and Mars) were somewhat different from those a thousand years earlier in Germanic Central Europe. In fact, we are throughout dealing with a series of interpretations and translations between mythological worlds: the Roman (and Greek) one, the contemporaneous Celtic and south Germanic ones, the later Germanic, and, finally, the north Germanic or Nordic one, at the beginning of our own millennium.

Still, links have been perceived by the ancient and can be traced by latter-day research, aided by the framework of archaeology.

Among the most important clues is that of the names of weekdays, where linkages were established in the Roman-Germanic border-lands already during the imperial period: Thus, *tirsdag* (= Tyr's day)/Tuesday is the equivalent of the Roman dies Martis; *onsdag* (= Odin's day)/Wednesday the Roman dies Mercurii; and *torsdag* (= Tor's day)/Thursday the Roman dies Jovis (Fig. 23).

A Roman alter from England, erected by German auxiliary troops, was devoted to Mars Thingsus, the latter probably a latin-ized term for Tyr (Bæksted 1965, 105). Both Mars and Tyr are, of course, gods of war. Jupiter, as well as Tor, carry symbols of strength and thunder (Tor is sometimes identified with Hecules who has a very heavy club). Mercury and Odin (and, for that mat-ter, also Minerva) are gods of knowledge. For Mercury and Odin there is also a link with death.

Isis' ship is highly interesting since Frej (of the godly Vane race), the male Nordic god of fertility, also owns a ship (in the Viking Age at least), along with a horse and a golden boar. The name of the female goddess of Nerthus is etymologically very close to Njord, the father of both Frej and the female goddess of fertility, Freja (cf. 'fredag'). Finally, both Freja and Nerthus drive waggons. Archaeology provides many indications of the importance of waggons. In the present context, the famous truly magnificent West Jylland/Jutland Dejbjerg waggons from the late pre-Roman Iron Age, slightly later than Hjortspring, are particularly interesting (Petersen 1888). They also come from a bog, situated, incidentally, only a couple of kilometres to the north of a hill, 'Waggon-Hill', which at some date may have received its peculiar name from knowledge about the waggon sacrifice or, perhaps, from earlier finds of waggons.

C. Nordic Gods

A structural and parallel ordering of the above-mentioned main forces of the world and the Nordic deities of the Viking Age (but with inferred predecessors) has, tentatively, already been suggested (Boyer 1981) (cf. Fig. 65, below). Basically, this division is natural, or self-evident. The positive powers of the Sky, including, in parti-cular, the Sun (there are also random and destructive sky-powers) would thus, among others, comprise: Tyr (Mars) and Tor (Jupiter). The powers of the Earth would comprise: Njord, Frej and Freja.

Odin (with the sky-gods, of the godly Ase race) would belong with the transient but pervasive powers, both life-giving and life-taking, of the Water, although, perhaps, with at first less convincing arguments if only the late Nordic mythology were consulted and no other sources or broader conceptions; (Odin's one eye was pawned in the well of wisdom, though).

Indeed, archaeology may provide important and highly interesting additional clues, in particular for the early periods, for instance, in terms of sacrifices of 'containers', golden cups, bronze and silver cauldrons, etc., all referring to liquids and the powers of water. For the Vanes, the gods of fecundity, various sacrifices relating to fertility, offerings of female jewellery (for instance, necklaces), waggons, and, ships or boats may be significant. And, finally, for the gods of the sky, military sacrifices, horns (sounds), etc., among other things.

Using this main structural division, into sky and earth, supplemented by the third and connecting force of water, it becomes, in fact, far more acceptable that even the terrestrian Vanes were associated with water (and ships). The important qualitative distinction may be that the latter gods are related to the water of the earth (versus the sky): the rivers, the lakes and the sea, and not to water in general, or, to water as a 'principle'. For instance, even Tor, a god of the sky, is related to water, namely the rain following thunder. Still, a basic structural division of forces and deities into only (A) sky-powers and gods, and (B) earth (cum water) powers and gods, may also be an appropriate one, and is perhaps the basic structure, although not fully satisfactory in view of the given complexity.

The major methodological problem in the study of ideas about the supernatural in prehistory is, thus, the establishment of relationships between the perceived forces of the world and the personified gods. This is particularly important with regard to the recipients of the sacrifices. In the late Nordic (as well as in Classical) mythology, the personified gods behave like spoiled aristocrats with extraordinary powers. This can, perhaps, be explained by reference to the social and intellectual worlds of the latest Iron and Viking Ages, but may not quite characterize the same personalities at earlier stages of imagination. Indeed, while we can recognize a few Nordic gods and myths among the images of late prehistory (towards AD 1000), this is not, or, at least not yet, possible for earlier pictures. One main reason is the very few representations indeed from the earlier Iron Age (except for some crude wooden images of human figures with pronounced sexual organs). Furthermore, what little there is, mainly from the late Roman and Migration periods, is also different in both style and character from the Viking Age images. From the Bronze Age come very many representations, in particular the rock-carvings, but the latter are, again, very different in character.

In the case of the larger European region of 'Germania', the impact from the Mediterranean world and, in turn, from the Celtic one was, as in other cultural matters, no doubt a factor in creating the religious ideology, as Caesar's and Tacitus' interpretations and translations, in themselves, might indicate. But the actual period, in which the gods first emerged as persons, and stories (myths) were attached to them, is, unfortunately, uncertain. In the traditional evolutionary scheme of Nordic religion, personified gods are seen as late arrivals (perhaps during the Bronze Age, to judge from the emergence of statuettes, or even later, since the first representations of deities of the particular Nordic pantheon do not occur until the post-Roman period). Traditionally, the personified gods follow upon eras of worship of the so-called powers of nature, for instance, of earth and climate, supreme animals, etc.

In reality, however, there is nothing, except, perhaps, the lack of indisputable images, which definitely speaks against an even earlier occurrence of a belief in supernatural anthropomorphic beings. Such would be seen to manipulate the forces of nature and environment, thus occupying the spiritual territories of the world, being one with the power or powers they pertain to. Indeed, we may perceive the juxtapositioning of force with god as merely two different ways of communicating with the supernatural, rather than mutually exclusive systems of past beliefs.

This hypothesis may, at least in the case of the Viking Age and, it seems, the late Iron Age as well, be carried a step or two further by linking the personalities, their attributes, and the mythology of the Nordic gods with archaeological finds and phenomena. In the present context, concentrating on the gods mentioned by Tacitus, but referring explicitly to Viking Age circumstances, the following structure emerges: Tyr's role is as a general god of war; Odin's as a god of battle and death, and as a seer; he is also the owner of a famous spear, a magic golden ring which multiplies, two raven scouts, and a magic eight-footed horse. Njord is, generally, linked with the sea and with ships; his son Frej expressively owns a magic ship (and a fine horse, too). Freja, Frej's sister, owns a magnificent golden necklace, and a waggon.

The ship is no doubt both the most advanced technological feature, the central economic and political instrument, and the main carrier of armies during the late Iron and Viking Ages. Though already found in the major military sacrifices of the early Iron Age, it assumes a larger and larger role during the later first millennium AD (e.g., Randsborg 1991). The increasing role of the ship was, at first, the logical consequence of an expansion of amphibious forces, but later, in the Viking Age, also of the rise of commercialism, with tranportation of bulk goods — not merely warriors, gifts and luxury items — over long distances. The religious role of the boat is ancient, not least manifest in the Bronze Age, but did not seem to grow during the first millennium AD, except for the sector of burials, where graves in ships and stone ship-settings around graves abound in the late half of the millennium, in fact until the advent of Christianity around AD 1000. Early Christianity, a Continental religion, does not seem to harbour the symbol of the ship at all, and must have looked at it as exclusively heathen.

It has been suggested that the Roman Iron Age burials in simple expanded dugouts from the cemetery at Slusegård on the Baltic island of Bornholm, Denmark were meant for priests worshipping the fertility deities of the Vane race (Crumlin-Pedersen 1991). This particular interpretation probably goes too far, but it may be re-formulated, though still only as a hypothesis, in terms of beliefs that the dead, and their milieu, shared about the power of the ship and its place in mythology. The role of the ship in Nordic cult, in particular of fecundity, is uncontested; thus, it plays a major role in the world of the rock-carvings of the Bronze Age, incidentally, often on panels with seeping water. Among the rock-carvings, a particular finds warrants special attention.

In the huge coastal Kivik grave (from Skåne/Scania), dated to c. 1300 BC, ships, among other images, were depicted on the inner faces of the long-walls of the stone cist. The boats are positioned on the seaward side of the southern half of the cist (with man-made objects and human beings), opposite terrestrial scenes on the panels facing land (Randsborg 1993). In one panel the boats are accompanied by symbols of power, a probable tall cap (resembling Near

Eastern crowns), huge cultic axes, and swords (rather than spear-heads). At the northern half of the cist are abstract, probably celestrial symbols. This division of the motives may thus be seen to refer to the two basic dimensions of the forces and the pertaining gods: sky (sun, etc.) and earth (land-sea). The terrestrial scenes of the southern panels comprise processions, ceremonies and various display, a chariot, blowing of horns, etc.

The above-discussed 'third', or liquid, dimension may, independently, be represented by the large bronze vessel found among the grave-goods for the dead: probably a composite chief-warrior-shaman personality, almost like a Nordic Gilgamesh. In a near-contemporary grave at Skallerup (on southern Zealand) a wheeled cauldron with web-footed birds held the ashes of the dead (Aner & Kersten 1976, II, no. 1269). Indeed, the Kivik 'picture programme', the earliest well-defined and -dated representation of this kind from northern Europe, actually seems to reflect the above-hypothesized division of the perceived powers of the world.

The connection in Kivik of ships (or boats) and cultic axes is interesting, since axes are usually seen as symbols of the celestial gods (cf. the thunderbolt of Zeus/Jupiter and the hammer of the Nordic Tor). The particular representation is emblematic, though, and should probably be viewed primarily in human and only secondarily in godly terms. Nevertheless, already in the Neolithic, fine yet mundane axes are common in sacrifices deposited in bogs and in other finds which seem to relate to fertility (Reck 1979; Ebbesen 1982; 1993). Also in the early Bronze Age, axes, cultic and otherwise, as well as mundane swords (and spear-heads) are commonly found in bogs, no doubt as offerings (cf. Jensen 1993).

A shamanist structure of classic Nordic mythology, perhaps pointing to its roots in older beliefs, is, among other things, inherent in the stories of the late Odin's dream-like behaviour and travels, in animal powers, and in the giant ash at the centre of the world, where Odin may hang, pierced by a spear, as a sacrifice to himself in a bloody initiation rite. Thus, the crown of the Yggdrasil ash-tree reaches atops the heavens, while its three roots lie deep below the earth. At each of these sits one of the goddesses of respectively Fate, Being, and Necessity, or, past, present, and future. With these tales and the above observations in mind, the question should be aired whether Odin, the lord of the gods, may originally have been born out of an ancestor or hero cult.

Adam of Bremen, in his central work on the Nordic countries, renders the following information, which had been communicated to him, on the heathen Nordic sanctuary at Uppsala in remote east central Sweden (Adam of Bremen c. AD 1070, book 4): 'In this temple, entirely in gold, the people worship the images of three deities. Thus, the mightiest of them, Tor, has his place at the centre of the platform, with on his one side, Odin, and on the other, Frej. Their significance is the following: Tor, they say, reigns in the sky, governs thunder and lightning, gives clear weather and harvest. The other (the name means fury) leads the warriors and gives bravery to the men in the fight against their enemies. The third is Frej, who gives peace and pleasure to men. His image they give an enormous phallos. Odin's image is armed like our people used to represent Mars. Tor, with the sceptre, seems to be like Jupiter. They also worship human beings that have been raised to gods. ...'

Adam continues: 'All their gods have priests who present the sacrifices of the people. ... If plague and hunger threaten, they sacrifice to the image of Tor, if war threatens, to Odin's, if a wedding is to be celebrated, to Frej's. Every ninth year they celebrate a sacrificial feast at Uppsala for all the provinces of the Swedes. No one is extempted from this feast. Kings and people, together or separate, take their gifts to Uppsala ... Sacrifices are then carried out in the following way: Of every male living being they sacrifice nine ... The bodies are hung in a grove near the temple. This grove is so sacred to the heathens that they believe the single trees in it become godly by the blood or putrefaction of the sacrificed animals. ... There, dogs and horses hang along with human beings, and a Christian has told that he has seen such bodies hung together in a number of 72 ...'

Adam's tale may not be trustworthy in all details, but it seems to suggest that the main Nordic deities had changed their personal character and, in particular, their respective status (at least as far as central Sweden was concerned) since the days of their Germanic counterparts, reported on by Tacitus. In the late Viking Age, Tor had attained the supreme position (his hammer was used throughout Scandinavia for an amulet and as a heathen counter-symbol to the Christian cross), while Odin, seemingly, had taken over the role of active warrior-god, in particular with regard to battles (and death). Thus, we must throughout, also in the BC periods, expect the pan-Germanic gods to have undergone several changes and transformations, about which we can, had it not been for archaeology, but conjecture.

As to Hjortspring — with the information from Tacitus, in particular, in mind — we should, first, state that this sacrifice was clearly made to a deity of war and/or battle (to judge from the contents), and, secondly, that the terrestrial deities of fertility were somehow involved (to judge from the site of the sacrifice and the fact that the spoils were, in the main, buried). Furthermore, the ship or huge boat, although clearly an integrated part of the military equipment of the find, might also be seen as a symbol related to the fertility gods and goddesses. Other main forces and deities, ensconced in the sky as well as in 'water', may have been evoked too. Thus, reference should also be given to the linked concepts of war/battle/weapons (cf. the later Odin) and to the fact that the spoils were found in waterlogged conditions. Finally, the boat of the sacrifice 'sails' directly north in the small bog, in the direction of Hel, the Nordic Viking Age realm of death.

The place-names, always difficult to date, are of limited use in the present context, although still very interesting. 'Hjortspring' itself is a very late place-name, but only a couple of kilometres to the southeast of the weapon sacrifice, and 700 m from the open coast of the Baltic, are two critical place-names, both referring to Tyr (or, Tir), the god of war. The two localities are 'Tiskjær' (Tyr's Pond) and 'Tisbjerg' (Tyr's Hill) (Sørensen 1992). These are the only (heathen) sacral place-names not only on the whole island of Als, but, indeed, in the entire region. Place-names with heathen gods as the prefix always occur with a suffix term for a heathen (open-air) shrine or, as in the present case, a characteristic feature of the landscape. Unfortunately, the two Alsian names are almost impossible to date precisely (although certainly earlier than the tenth century AD). However, place-names with the -bjerg (-hill) suffix usually have a distinctively 'ancient' character, possibly stemming from the early (but not necessarily the pre-Roman) Iron Age. In the present context, the two place-names may even originate from, and thus indicate, the actual site of the Hjortspring battle — close to the coast.

Excursus: Smederup

In Smederup bog, Gosmer parish in Eastern Jutland a remarkable sacrifice has been found which is sharply at variance with Hjortspring, although the two are broadly contemporary, Smederup being from the fifth or the fourth century BC (Vebæk 1945). The Smederup deposit is made up of at least 373 bronze rings; no other types of artefact were found. Nearby in the bog, a well, with a fine alder tub as lining, the quality of which is reminiscent of the excellent woodwork of Hjortspring, was excavated. In the well, seemingly of sacrificial type, was, in addition to various stones, pottery of the same period as the rings.

The Smederup rings are of several types, but nearly all with narrow bodies: 32 were neck-rings and 169 bracelets (including two rings made of sheet-bronze and five very small ones). Most of the neck-rings and bracelets have a rather simple geometric decoration of strokes, multible Vs, Xs, etc. In addition 165(+) smaller rings with a loop (168, if similar rings without a loop are also counted), were found; three of these are rather large, one, with 'spokes' etc., even lavish.

Since next to nothing is known of the sets of jewellery of the period, it is not possible to group the rings with certainty. However, the almost similar numbers of bracelets and loop-rings may point to the existence of sets made up of these two types (in the graves, loop-rings occur as single specimens), perhaps indicating the participation of close to 170 women (or even more) in the sacrifice (if they each donated one set); the neck-rings may have belonged to the leaders/seniors (19%) among the women. (If, however, two bracelets and two loop-rings belonged to each person, the number of participants was only 85 and the number of 'leaders' close to one-third.) There are, of course, many other possible explanations, for instance, although highly unlikely, that loop-rings in fact belonged to the men.

Other contemporaneous sacrifices from the central parts of Eastern Jutland are of a similar nature. Thus, in a bog at Falling, only a few kilometres from Smederup, more than 271 loop-rings have been found. In a bog at Sattrup, in the same province, some 137 bracelets, 5(+) neck-rings, but only 4 loop-rings have come to light; also a rare pin with a silver-covered head, was recovered. Other finds are smaller, and the find circumstances less well illuminated, but they all originate from the same general region. For instance, from a bog at Lyngå to the north-west come 19 loop-rings, one large and spoked, 8 bracelets, 6 small rings without loops, and some potsherds. From a bog at Sal (incidentally, an ancient name for sanctuary but there may be no connection with this particular find), further to the north-west, come some 30 rings, including 16 small ones without loops, 8 loop-rings, and 6 bracelets and necklaces, all found in three bundles.

The dramatic Smederup sacrifice has a distinctive female character about it and may have been devoted to a goddess (related, probably, to earth/water). The circumstances of find are, though, the same as in Hjortspring, clearly a male find: a small otherwise anonymous bog.

The peculiar type of ring-sacrifices once more raises the important question of the existence of a correlation between the type of the sacrifice and the worshipped god or goddess, in fact, of the existence, in Northern Europe, at this age, of particular personified deities. Furthermore, a regional perspective is evoked, with the ring-sacrifices only coming from Eastern Jutland.

Thus, while Hjortspring primarily relates to a god of war and/or battle, perhaps especially worshipped in Southern Jutland, Smederup probably relates to a goddess, perhaps of fertility, in particular honoured in mid-eastern Jutland. (If such regional distribution of the finds holds true, we may, theoretically, even have had Hjortspring-type battles which did not lead to military sacrifices.)

In addition to the offerings of artefacts, sacrifices of human beings, also in bogs, were not uncommon during the Late Bronze Age and the pre-Roman Iron Age. The latter offerings comprise both adult men and women, usually found naked, hanged or with the throat cut, and unaccompanied by artefacts (cf. Fischer 1979). These 'bog-bodies' may have been sacrificed to a god of death, but there are several other, and also reasonable, explanations. Finally, from bogs (etc.) of the late pre-Roman Iron Age, come also the famous sacrifices of magnificant vessels of bronze or silver, imported from Central Europe, Thracia, Etruria and even Magna Graecia, including the princely Gundestrup cauldron, perhaps carried home by the Cimbri. In all, four distinctively different categories of pre-Roman Iron Age sacrifices can thus be demonstrated, perhaps relating to at least as many different deities. Into this, the complexity of regional preferences enters, perhaps resembling the contemporaneous Mediterranean cult communities focusing on a particular deity and temple.

In the following, archaeological dimensions of European sanctuaries will be investigated to provide a further religious, ritual and historical context to Hjortspring.

6. Sanctuaries and Societies I :
The Mediterranean

Stand there, manslaying spear; no longer drip
baneful enemies' gore around your bronze talon,
but resting against Athena's high marble temple
proclaim the prowess of Kretan Echekratidas.
    Anyte (c. 300 BC)

A. The Aegean

A sanctuary is maintained by a religious community that believes
that human activity falls within the interests of the gods. In the
case of Greece in the Archaic and Classical periods, the concept of
citizenship (of a state) implies the direct involvement of the population in the cult. Under the guidance and regulation of priests,
practically everyone, also women, could and would donate offerings to the sanctuary, where these were kept and put on display,
at least for a while. Also foreigners could relate to a region through
its sanctuaries. By contrast, non-citizens could not participate in
political life (nor could women and slaves). In addition, the
peculiar pan-Hellenic sanctuaries, for instance Olympia and Delphi,
would seem to have maintained an idea of a cultic and cultural citizenship of the entire Greek world (cf. Rolley 1983).

    In the Aegean Bronze Age the organization of cult was on a
number of counts a different one (cf. Renfrew 1981; 1985). In the
second millennium BC, in middle and late Bronze Age palaces on
Crete, both private and semi-public shrines with altars and other
ritual facilities were very common, but temples as such were not
known. In the open landscape, an interesting preference for
peak-sanctuaries, positioned like distant-relay stations for the field
of ritual activities, connecting the present and the other world, is
noted. Caves were also in common use for cultic activities, perhaps
in particular by the general populace (Rutkowski 1986). The
offerings, to judge from both representations and finds, were of
animals, even humans (Sakellarakis & Sapouna-Sakellaraki 1991,

136f), and, in particular in the elaborate shrines, of a variety of foodstuffs (and their containers), jewellery, etc. Anthropomorphic deities were worshipped and a range of aniconic symbols employed, for instance double-axes, horns, pillars, and model boats; snakes play a particular role. Also, the funerals of the period included lavish rituals and offerings of valuables.

On the Greek mainland, less emphasis was seemingly put on shrines (more so, perhaps, on funerals and ancestor-cults). Important cultic activities most probably took place in the *megara*, the main hall-buildings of the later Mycenean palaces. This may perhaps be seen as a parallel to the Minoan palace-cults which closely linked the most conspicuous and costly religious practices to the dwellings of the elite. Peak-sanctuaries are little known on the mainland, but other cult-places in the open landscape are not infrequent.

To what extent the beliefs of the second millennium BC corresponded to those of the later periods is difficult to determine. However, several names of Classical deities have, among other terms — including Potnia, 'mistress', a fertility/mother goddess, perhaps Demeter (Roman Ceres) — appeared in the, albeit primarily economic, Linear B texts from the late Bronze Age, thus, for instance (Roman names are given in brackets): Zeus (Jupiter), Hera (Juno), Hermes (Mercurius), Poseidon (Neptunus), Apollo, Artemis (Diana), Athena, Dionysos (Bacchus), seemingly Aphrodite (Venus), and perhaps Ares (Mars), etc. (Ventris & Chadwick 1956, 275f; etc.).

The Linear B tablets also contain information on rituals and sacrifices, in particular of foodstuffs. Thus, Poseidon is, at one event, but from four different contributors, the receiver of the following: one bull, four rams, 792 litres of wheat, 72 of flour, 216 of wine, 20 of honey, and four of fat (ointment), 20 cheeses, and two sheepskins (probably for ritual skirts); (the usual gift of olive-oil is missing here). The godly names speak in favour of the existence of a pantheon of gods with a link to the wellknown later deities and myths that have played such a prominent role in European ideology. However, no myths have survived from the Bronze Age, only some traditions, as is evident from Homer's epics. After the collapse of the palaces, the cult practice may have been simplified; a stress on female idols is then noted.

In the Dark Age, at the close of the second and in the first centuries of the first millennium BC, major rituals seem to have taken place in the halls of the lords, probably as a continuation of the palace-cults of the Bronze Age. In a number of important instances, altars were placed near main Dark Age structures (cf. Ainian 1988). Thus, at the Mycenean palace of Tiryns, in Late Bronze Age III C, the last Bronze Age period proper, a new structure was erected inside the walls of the former main megaron hall. The altar in front, in use from the Late Bronze Age III C period on, was transformed twice, in the middle of the eighth and in the early sixth century BC. The latter probably happened in connection with the megaron being turned into a temple, incidentally dedicated to Hera.

In western Greece, the fine Archaic pan-Aitolian sanctuary at Thermon, dedicated to Apollo, was erected on a plot with substantial late Bronze Age apsidal houses superseded by a large rectangular early Iron Age structure, which at about 700 BC was transformed into the first temple. At Zagora, the middle to late Geometric walled township (the floruit being in the (late) eighth century BC) on the Aegean island of Andros, an altar was standing in front and to the 'left' of the major building complex of the settlement. In the sixth century BC, long after the abandonment of the town, a temple was built on this very spot.

Another interesting Dark Age cult is noted at the coastal settlement of Lefkandi on Euboea. Here, a major apsidal long-house, 45 times 10 m, occupied from the end of the eleventh to the end of the ninth century BC, was probably the home of a chief. The structure's central and main room was eventually used for the burial of two persons, a man and a women with rich grave-goods, along with four horses. Upon this, the structure was destroyed and, finally, covered by a mound, thus being turned into a *heroon* (Calligas 1988). The main cemeteries (mostly of the earlier Geometric period) belonging to this settlement, abandoned altogether towards 700 BC, lie nearby.

It is significant that the earliest Greek temples of the characteristic and impressive classical tradition were not erected in the major settlements. However, from the late eighth century BC, and in particular after 700 BC, urban temples became paramount. From the sixth century BC on, temples were often constructed entirely in stone: foundations, steps, cella, pillars, gables and sometimes even the roofing. Most stone temples were erected

between 550 and 400 BC; a minor group is of the late fourth century
BC (cf. Dinsmoor 1950). In addition, sanctuaries in the open
countryside, often on conspicuous natural sites, for instance, where
elements meet, and, at the man-made frontiers between city-states,
were also common. Indeed, the early centuries of the first millennium BC see a very sharp rise indeed in ritual activities at Greek
sanctuaries, as expressed by the number of offerings (cf. below;
Snodgrass 1980) (Fig. 25). Certainly, ritual activity accompanies the
political and economical development.

For Italy, a study of the non-urban shrines and temples (underlining the strong belief in the existence of the divine in nature) in
Magna Graecia and in Etruria has demonstrated a great variety of
locations and types of ritual, in terms both of the structures
themselves and of their social function (Edlund 1987). Not least the
textual information, which has only marginally been considered
here, is highly interesting. Leaving aside the urban or 'intra-mural'
sanctuaries, a distinction can be made between shrines (1) extra-
mural (just outside the city), (2) extra-urban (technically also including type (1)), (3) political (meeting-place, for instance on
frontiers), (4) rural (usually a modest facility), and (5) 'nature' (a
shrine at a conspicuous point in the landscape).

In addition, attention must be paid to the immediate sur-
roundings of the sanctuaries. The role of water (both in the form of
the open sea, and, in particular, of a lake, of a river or stream, or
of a spring) is stressed. Usually, female gods were connected with
water on land. It is less clear, however, what water symbolizes in
the many different examples of sanctity. To a large extent the
geographical and other variation noted in Magna Graecia is re-
found in the following case-study of the island of Kephallénia in
western Greece.

In Magna Graecia there is, incidentally, also a close relationship
between the settlement patterns and the sanctuaries in 'nature',
while in Etruria, perhaps reflecting a European pattern or tradition
of selecting sacred places, nature seemingly alone determines the
position of the sanctuaries in the larger landscape (Edlund 1987,
62). In Etruria, regular temples, on the Greek model, were erected
at least from the sixth century on (Bonfante 1986).

BC	1100-900	900-800	800-700
Bronze figurines, Delphi (mainly Apollo)	–	1	152
Terracotta figurines, Olympia (Zeus/(Hera))	10	21	837

BC	1100-900	900-750	750-600
Bronze fibulae, Lindos (Athena)	–	52	1540
Bronze fibulae, Argive Heraion (Hera)	16	10	88
Bronze pins, Argive Heraion (Hera)	3	c. 250	c. 3070
Bronze fibulae, Perachora (Hera)	7	1	50+
Bronze pins, Perachora (Hera)	–	15	81

Fig. 25. Selected types of offerings at Greek sanctuaries (with names of worshipped deities), c. 1100-700/600 BC (data, Snodgrass 1980).

B. Kephallénia

The important geographical and historical circumstances concerning sanctuaries in classical antiquity in the Aegean and other Mediterranean regions may be summed up, as well as deepened, by reference, for instance, to Kephallénia (indeed, to the author's fieldwork). Thus, a certain degree of detail is necessitated in the following (cf. Fig. 26).

Kephallénia is the largest of the western Ionian Islands, marginal, yet integrated into the southern Aegean core of social, economic and cultural development before the Hellenistic period, having links in particular with Corinth and, later, with Athens. In the Hellenistic period, Kephallénia, characteristically, orientated itself towards the expanding northern part of the Aegean. Kephallénia was made up of four city-states (*poleis*), Pale (far west), Krane (south-west), Same (east) and Pronnoi (south-east), known, apart from archaeology, through sporadic references in the ancient literature, and a coin-series starting around 500 BC with emissions from Krane. (Ithaka is off same, to the northeast.) People from Pale

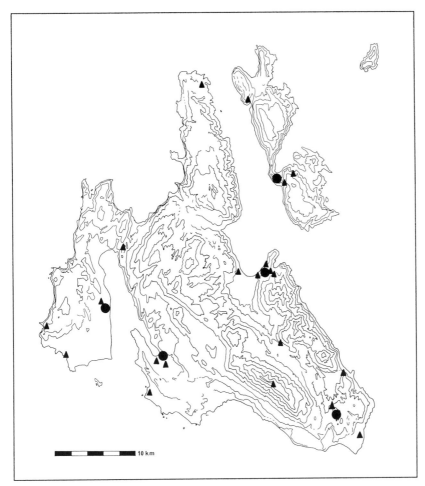

Fig. 26. Cities (poleis centres, large dot) and sanctuaries (triangles) on the island(s) of Kephallénia (and Ithaki), western Greece, in classical antiquity; the far majority of the shrines were established already in the Archaic-early Classical period (after Randsborg, forthcoming).

may have donated a statue at Olympia (Pausanias AD 175/180, Book VI), and Kephallénians were no doubt also active at Delphi (a Kephallénian won a lyre-and-song contest in the early sixth century BC) and at the religious and tribal centre of the Aitolians, Thermon (around 200 BC, shortly before the island fell to Rome, Kephallénia was a member of the Aitolian League). But primarily the sanctuaries and the ritual activities should be seen in the light of life on the island itself.

Until recently, relatively little archaeological work has been undertaken on Kephallénia, in spite of the fact that the ancient information on the island is almost exclusively material, or archaeological. The particularly fertile and, in recent and modern times, most densely populated western part of the island is, seemingly, also most disturbed by agricultural and related activities. On the other hand, deep-ploughing is not (yet) used, and the tilling of the land only rarely brings any major concentration of find to light (bulldozing of new agricultural terraces and roads are more 'effective' in that respect). Characteristically, sherds found during archaeological surveying are, compared to, for instance, Central Italy or Boeotia, usually relatively rare, small, and battered, indicating ploughing and digging over centuries at the same shallow depth of topsoil. However, flint artefacts and lithic refuse, being far more resistent to the working of the soil, are very common, suggesting that the sherds represent only a fraction of what may still be found below the top layers. Fragments of roof-tiles are plentiful too, also suggesting a rich ancient settlement. Sadly, earthquakes, including the last major one in 1953, have destroyed most of the stone architecture, fortresses, and defensive walls from antiquity. Still, a surprisingly full archaelogical picture, including sanctuaries, can be drawn.

(A) Pale city was razed for stone during the early nineteenth century, mainly by the British, who were building the nearby town of Lixouri, and no serious archaeological investigation has taken place. Most of the ancient city is today covered by houses, gardens, or small fields. Still, a few remains of a temple have been found. (B) On the akropolis of the city of Krane, fortified, at least, in the late Classical/early Hellenistic period, a sixth century BC temple has been found. Another temple, devoted to Demeter, also existed, standing near the city's harbour. (C) On the very top of the tall akropolis of the city of Pronnoi (Palaiokastro in the Medieval period) is an impressive step-altar. (D) At the city of Same, a temple (probably dating from the early Hellenistic period) stands just outside the akropolis, facing the eastern seaward approaches to the city. On the akropolis itself, a likely site for shrine (such has been claimed by old excavations), Archaic architectural terracottas have been found, at least suggesting a major sixth century BC construction. At the western approaches to the lower city, near the beach, another Archaic construction stood, most probably also a temple. Finally, a Hellenistic fountain shrine in fine ashlar (with rich offerings of golden jewellery, terracottas, etc.) is situated in the city near the harbour.

Among the rural sanctuaries of Kephallénia, the most prominent was the one devoted to Zeus, on the very top of tall Mount Ainos (1,600 m), which, at the same time, was the suggested frontier between Krane and Pronnoi, and, possibly, even Same. On or near the frontier between Same and Pronnoi, is a Mycenean fortress with a magnificent view both to Ainos and down into the valley at Same; this fortress was later turned into a shrine (drinking-cups and terracotta figurines are found on the site) with a tholos (or round-temple) of late Classical or early Hellenistic date. On the territory of Pronnoi, exactly facing the exit from the Bay of Corinth and the main western sea-lanes from the Greek mainland (including the passage to Magna Graecia and southern Italy) is a sixth century BC temple near Skala, situated on impressive geological formations on the very coast. Another sixth century BC temple was erected near Minia on the Krane beachland at the seaward entrance to Pale and Krane (the remains were destroyed during the construction of the present airport). On the coast across this bay, and on Pale territory, a sanctuary to Poseidon was erected, which seems to have existed even in Imperial Roman times.

Above the northern end of the bay leading to Pale and Krane is another sixth (possibly even seventh) century BC sanctuary, which at the same time marks the frontier between Pale and Krane, and, possibly, even Same. Here Archaic and later terracottas and fine ceramics, again including many drinking-cups, have been found; there is apparently no stone structure, not even an altar, inside the rather simple *temenos* (or enclosure) wall. To the north-west of Same, but still on farmland, is a breath-taking cobalt-blue underground lake (in fact, a river) at Mellisani, lit through the partly collapsed roof. On a peninsula in the lake is a shrine to Pan with early Hellenistic terracotta figurines. Also a cave on the territory of Pale has yielded terracotta figurines, of the Archaic to Classical period.

Finally, on the tip of the long northern peninsula of Kephallénia, on a promontory at Phiskardo, is a large late Antiquity church, positioned almost like a rural Greek temple, probably a cathedral of the entire archipelago. There are no remains to suggest that a temple was ever built here, but from behind the harbour of

Phiskardo, a rock-cut shrine from Classical antiquity with benches and a place for a statue is known.

In addition, caves and other sites throughout the island no doubt served ritual purposes. A shrine may thus have been erected on the territory of Pronnoi between the urban centre of ancient Pronnoi and the ancient harbour at present-day Poros, although the remains of terracotta columns found here may also have other explanations. At and above Poros is an antique town fortified in the late Classical/early Hellenistic period. On the highest part, perhaps an acropolis, are remnants of a monumental building in ashlar, perhaps a shrine. Below this rock, facing a narrow gap leading from the harbour to inland and to the city of Pronnoi, is a cave shrine with ceramics from the late seventh century BC on. A possible sanctuary site (where Hellenistic or Roman period graves have also been found) is in a pass-height between ancient Pronnoi and the harbour town at Poros, as one approaches from the south. In addition, rituals no doubt took place both at the old Mycenean and at contemporary cemeteries, and at the late Classical and Hellenistic farms, the Roman villas, etc., of the island.

Incidentally, on nearby Ithaki, a Geometric period sanctuary (with a later temple) was set up below the acropolis of the urban centre, or city, of Aetos, walled in the late Classical or early Hellenistic period and facing Same across the Strait of Ithaki. In the north, facing Phiskardo, a cave-shrine with very rich Geometric finds, including bronze tripods, has been excavated (a dedicatory terracotta mask of the first century AD even carries the name of 'Odysseus').

The evidence from Kephallénia (and Ithaki) thus confirms the above model of an early first millennium BC employment of both rural, extra-urban, and urban sanctuaries (in the cities of the *poleis*), a later architectural formalization of several of these sanctuaries, in particular the building of temples, and, finally, the creation of further urban and rural sanctuaries and temples.

Southern Aegean societies, like the Kephallénian poleis, from the sixth century BC on saw a commercialization of the economy, membership of demanding political and military alliances, a development of urban centres, and erection of monumental architecture, including temples. About the names of the worshipped deities, the character of the rituals, and the sacrifices at the shrines of Kephallénia, we are, however, usually, poorly informed. Probably the offerings were mostly relatively modest and mainly made up of foodstuffs, but fine imported drinking-cups must be seen in a different light, and, as mentioned, at the fountain shrine of wealthy Same, exquisite Hellenistic golden jewellery was sacrificed. Thus, Kephallénia is, indeed, in all sacred and ritual respects, a miniature representation of the Aegean.

C. Offerings

Usually, images, cultic vessels, dress-items, often minor, and, for instance, defensive armour tend to dominate among the sacrifices of the late Geometric to early Archaic/Orientalizing periods in the Aegean. These are artefacts relating either to the rituals themselves or to the supposed areas of responsibility and the appearance of the anthropomorphic Greek gods. Originally, the offerings were put on display at, or, if a structure was available, in the sanctuary, but eventually many offerings came, for lack of available space, or for other reasons, to be buried as so-called *stips votiva*, to use a Latin term. Incidentally, manufacturing of sacrificed items may also have taken place at the sanctuaries, which furthermore may have been the foci of early market exchange, along with other even more important activities, such as banquets and games (cf. Kilian 1983).

By contrast, the offerings found in the sacred groves, bogs, rivers and other sanctuaries of contemporary temperate Western Europe (to which we return below) consisted of larger artefacts, for instance weapons, usually of a 'chiefly' character. Access to the important north-Alpine shrines, where these valuables were deposited, may thus have been controlled by the leaders or aristocrats, the potential 'Heroes' of society (to apply an Aegean concept), who, in turn, represented the populace at these rituals involving valuables.

The sphere of religion and cult may be seen as a philosophical system articulating beliefs, rituals and society, and including the manipulation of sacrifices, including valuables. A highly interesting aspect of this is the correlation between beliefs and cult. The Aegean evidence, in particular, provides important linkages between the name (and area of responsibility) of the deity of a sanctuary, the character of the offerings, and the social context, in particular with respect to the area of origin of the sacrificed artefacts.

An interesting sample of non-local sacrifices (that is, of artefacts

OLYMPIA (Zeus)	Greek	Foreign
Statuettes	212	–
Bronze vessels	276	46
Weapons	72	26
Dress	23	52
Jewellery	27	7
Amulet/seal	1	1
PERACHORA (Hera)	Greek	Foreign
Statuettes	–	–
Bronze vessels	–	–
Weapons	–	–
Dress	18	16
Jewellery	14	39
Amulet/seal	3	273

Fig. 27. Sacrifices from Greek sanctuaries of the eighth and the beginning of the seventh centuries BC, excluding artefacts made in the local region. The artefacts are divided into (A) 'Greek' (i.e., other Greek) and (B) 'Foreign' (i.e, non-Greek). The sanctuaries are: (1) Olympia on the western Peloponnes, a pan-Hellenic sanctuary devoted to Zeus; also a cult for Hera. (2) Perachora at Corinth on Peloponnes, devoted to Hera. (3) Samos in the eastern Aegean, also devoted to Hera. (4) Pherai in central Greece, devoted to Artemis. (Data Kilian-Dirlmeier 1985.)

not manufactured in the region of the sanctuary) comes from important Aegean temple-sites of the eighth and the beginning of the seventh centuries BC (data, Kilian-Dirlmeier 1985). The artefacts are divided into 'other-Greek' and 'non-Greek' specimens (Fig. 27). The finds are from the following four Greek sanctuaries: (1)

SAMOS (Hera)	Greek	Foreign
Statuettes	2	64
Bronze vessels	1	11
Weapons	–	22
Dress	6	17
Jewellery	22	16
Amulet/seal	1	17

PHERAI (Artemis)	Greek	Foreign
Statuettes	1	–
Bronze vessels	–	–
Weapons	–	–
Dress	23	11
Jewellery	17	8
Amulet/seal	–	2

Fig. 27 continued.

Olympia on the western Peloponnese, the famous pan-Hellenic sanctuary devoted to Zeus, but with a cult of Hera, too; (2) Perachora near Corinth, just to the north of the Peloponnesian Isthmos, devoted to Hera; (3) Samos in the eastern Aegean, another famous sanctuary, also devoted to Hera; and (4) Pherai in central Greece (Thessaly), devoted to Artemis. Unfortunately, only at Pherai, a typical regional sanctuary with few extra-regional or even international links, has the ratio of non-local to all artefacts been established, at a low 2%.

    As to the character of the sacrifices, the following observations can be noted: (1) At Olympia, primarily devoted to the supreme male god, Zeus, a stress on images (all Greek) and cultic bronze vessels (predominantly Greek) is noted; weapons (also predominantly Greek) are common too. Even dress-items and jewellery are not infrequent. Since Hera was worshipped too, the lack of information about the particular location of the offerings is to be deplored. (2) At Perachora, worshipping Hera, the wife of Zeus, dress-items and jewellery (mainly foreign) are common, but the dominant group is of foreign amulettes. (3) At Samos, also worshipping Hera, foreign artefacts dominate, in particular among the images and cultic bronze vessels. Dress-items, jewellery and amulettes are common, but weapons (all foreign) are not rare either (this site is thus a reversed parallel to Olympia). (4) At Pherai, worshipping Artemis, the goddess of hunting, Greek artefacts are the most common. Dress-items and jewellery (Greek and foreign in the same ratio) dominate.

Thus, at the important major sanctuaries, cultic bronze vessels and statuettes are prominent. We also seem to detect differences in a male preference for weapons (Zeus) and a female one for dress items, jewellery, and the like. We may thus note a selection for items that were supposed to please a particular deity. The social dimension is, for instance, expressed in differing degrees of 'investment' (the latter not necessarily correlated to wealth, however). In addition, the many non-Greek artefacts from certain sites, for instance the Heraion of Samos, speak in favour of foreigners honouring the sanctuary. (However, Greeks too, no doubt, owned foreign articles.)

To appreciate these observations fully, a wider view of sanctuaries and the phenomenologies of cult and ritual will be taken and a line drawn back into central and adjacent regions of Europe, to the North, with Denmark, and, ultimately, again, the Hjortspring find. For reasons of argument it is most convenient to start with the North, farthest from the Mediterranean, but with equally superb archaeological data.

7. Sanctuaries and Societies II: The North

The words are stones
But the stones are also words
(Unknown, Italy)

A. Neolithic

In Northern Europe, the history of sacrifices goes back at least to the transition from the Mesolithic to the Neolithic period, around 4000 BC, involving Stone Age valuables like ornamented fine pottery, elegant polished flint-axes, amber beads, and animal or even human sacrifices. (Catchword tables of the cultural development, as well as concomitant interpretations, are given in Fig. 32 (cf. Fig. 65, below); references in various authors, for instance, in Hvass & Storgaard 1993, for data, but not necessarily interpretations.)

The whole Neolithic cultural 'package' was seemingly introduced in Southern Scandinavia at one and the same time (cf. Madsen 1986). Thus, in the early fourth millennium BC, monumental tombs were erected made up of earthen banks, so-called long-barrows, with massive timbers, 'ritual' structures, and sacrificial pits (containing pots) at the one end; the very graves, by contrast, are poor in furnishings and usually lack pottery. The early long-barrows were the first constructions which substantially altered the landscape, indeed created it. Hodder has forwarded the suggestive idea that the early Neolithic long-house of southeastern and Central Europe, in a symbolic form (as a burial monument), was applied to 'domesticate' the Northwestern territories of the Continent (Hodder 1990).

The long-barrows were the forerunners of the very common and well-known Megalithic tombs from the late fourth millennium BC: (1) dolmen chambers of large stones, mostly within an earthen boulder-framed long barrow, later often in a round one, and (2) passage graves (perhaps originally cult-houses), also in round barrows. But throughout this first phase of the Neolithic, the so-called Funnel-Beaker culture, other types of burial are also known.

Indeed, the primary Neolithic society was both complex and dynamic, although in several ways more of a Mesolithic period in disguise: man was still clad in hides and plant fibres (no woolen garments are known), and not until at the end of the fourth millennium was the traction-power of oxen used, at first for the plough, but in the early third millennium BC also for the cart, or waggon. Boats were still simple dugouts. Ordinary settlements of the period were still very small, and with small roundish structures. Only the so-called causeway camps were of a substantial size (Fig. 28). These were surrounded by palisade fences and ditches with passages and have been interpreted as 'meeting-places' (perhaps even ritual villages). The causewayed camps have very many parallels in contemporary Central Europe, in England, etc. In the ditches and in pits across the framed area, sacrificial deposits of various sorts, including fine ritual ceramics, are found (Andersen 1989). Had these impressive efforts, including the building of many thousands of Megalithic monuments, not been so de-centralized a phenomenon, some sort of petty 'theocratic' state-system, with authority, and 'monopoly of power', substituting for social 'classes' (the latter only emerging later), might even have been implied for the central areas of southern Scandinavia, from which the so-called secondary Neolithic phase (cf. below) evolved merely as a devolution.

The deposits of the period, which, most convincingly, have been interpreted as sacrifices, often come from wet areas and are primarily made up of fine pots (usually far from the shore and sometimes with common polished flint-axes for work), large, indeed often unrealistically long, finely polished flint-axes (more often near the shore), amber beads (the largest hoards may exceed 8 kg of amber or 13,000 finished beads), occasional sacrifices of animals and even of humans (Bennike & Ebbesen 1986; Ebbesen 1993; for amber finds in general, Jensen 1982).

Hoards of fine polished axes (indeed, a continuing Stone Age practice in regions with natural resources of flint), and, for instance, copper artefacts are also known from the 'dry land'. These finds may reflect practices similar to the 'wet' sacrifices in other types of location, the particular character of which is now usually lost,

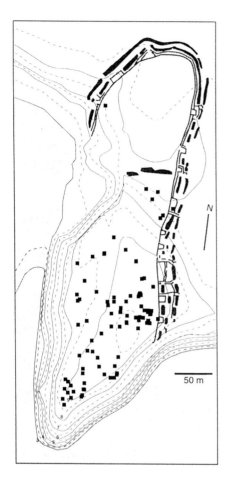

N

50 m

Fig. 28. The huge so-called causeway camp at Sarup, Fyn/Funen, Denmark in its first phase, mid-fourth millennium BC (after Andersen 1989, etc.).

perhaps except for the causeway camps. Battle-clubs and -axes, which are quite common in the Funnel-beaker culture, were also sacrificed in wet areas; when found with other artefacts, the latter are usually fine polished flint-axes and similar but equally fine so-called 'work-axes' of stone. (By the 1930s about 350 such weapons were known from the early phase of the Funnel-beaker culture, 19(+) of these from bogs, etc.; and by the 1970s about 225 from the late phase of the culture, 14 of these from bogs (Åberg 1937; Ebbesen 1975).)

Furthermore, from the composition of the sacrifices, it may be argued that the pots (with food) (and the often accompanying common flint-axe(s)) were sacrifices to the powers of fertility, at the centre of which must stand a female conception, accompanied, however, by a male one. The powers of the sky (including the sun, traditionally often a male conception) may have been related to the transparent amber (light) and the costly shining copper (through melting, fire), which mainly occurs as symbolic (though usable) axes resembling the common polished specimens of flint, but much smaller. Interestingly, amber necklaces and copper ornaments are found associated with polished flint-axes, arrowheads, etc. in burials of the primary Neolithic period and may therefore belong in the male sphere. Also, in the late fourth millennium and around 3000 BC, amber beads very often take the shape of double (battle-) axes. Indeed, the very fine, non-utilitarian, long flint-axes, appearing in separate 'one-type' hoards, may also pertain to the worship of the sky-powers.

The battle-axe, often regarded as the central symbol of the sky-powers (cf. thunder, and the later Tor, Jupiter, and even Hercules) and signalling the general status and fighting ability of the male of the species, is, as just mentioned, sometimes sacrificed in wet areas together with large flint-axes. Apparently, the depositional milieu of the sacrifice is less important, but wet finds do lend themselves naturally to fertility and perhaps a relation with fertility is inherent in all such finds. As we shall see repeatedly in the following, changing beliefs and changing emphasis on the relations with the supernatural powers may well account for a large degree of the variation in the most conspicuous part of the archaeological record, in particular, of course, the rich finds from prehistory pertaining to worship, ritual and sacrifice.

The pot sacrifices in wet areas, and, apparently, also the other most obvious sacrifices to the supernatural powers, except for the common polished flint-axes, came to a de facto halt around 3000 BC (cf. Bennike & Ebbesen 1986). In Denmark, the custom of depositing pots (with food) in bogs was not taken up again until the early Iron Age, the period of Hjortspring (Becker 1971). In their Iron Age context, such pots, sometimes found with crude wooden images of females (with their gender pronounced), but also with statues of phallic men, most probably reflect exactly a local sacrifice to the deities of fertility, both female and male, as in the later myths of the Vane-race.

In the same Neolithic period as the cessation of the pot-deposits in bogs, the construction (but not the use) of Megalithic burials also ceased. By that time, the forest agricultural resources were seemingly all seized and a Neolithic 'culture-scape', with social reference-points in the form of monumental burials, well established. The consecutive secondary Neolithic periods (of whatever cultural facies) comprise a series of novel economic and social experiments, for instance, larger settlements and house-structures and, partly, opening of the landscape (for pasture, etc.) — for instance in western Denmark — partly, a return to 'Mesolithic' practices of utilizing the resources of the wild (eastern South Scandinavia), etc.

A new series of burials, mainly under small round barrows, stressing the individual human being, presented in death with his or her own dress, jewellery, weapons and drink, belong in particular to the so-called Corded-ware facies (starting c. 2800 BC), in Denmark, 'Single-grave culture'. In these graves, the battle-axe, although well known also earlier, a fact which is often ignored (for instance in symbolic interpretation by Hodder (Hodder 1990)), is the prime male grave-gift, as it was until the introduction of the flint-dagger at the end of the third millennium BC. Amber occurs in (early) male Corded-ware graves (as large discs), but is, from now on, in particular common in female burials. The symbolic relations with the powers of the sky are seemingly reflected in the orientation of the graves, preferably east-west (within those segments of the compass defined by the summer and winter risings and settings of the sun), or, north-south (cf. Randsborg & Nybo 1984).

In the consecutive 'Dagger' or Late Neolithic period, parallel with the Early Bronze Age of Central Europe, settlements were often large and, in particular, long-house farmsteads substantial (up to 45 m). The economic prerequisites for the expansion of the Early Bronze Age in Southern Scandinavia were thus present, and direct links with various regions of Europe, supplying metal and other goods, and, not least, information, were already formed.

Symbolically (if the following elements were at all related in a straightforward fashion), we note that, during the primary Neolithic, massive graves were built (in the beginning mainly long barrows, later on also various Megalithic chambers), while man still lived in modest huts. By contrast, in the secondary Neolithic, long-houses were the norm and rather modest round barrows, among several other, all rather humble, forms of graves — often in groups or stretched out along tracks of road — were found fit for burial.

With this, an almost modern economic conception of man arose: a being tending to his or her herd and ploughed fields, clad in woolen garments, building substantial homes, driving waggons, building boats, and engaged in warring and trading. Deposits of flint-daggers, which supplanted the former hoards of flint-axes, were in turn replaced by deposits of metal axes and other coppers and bronzes, even by items of gold.

A very important group of no doubt sacred structures, so-called 'cult-houses', from the end of the fourth millennium or just around 3000 BC, rich in ritual pottery and 'killed' by burning and covering by stones after a period of use of some length, has come to light in the northern parts of Jutland (Becker 1993) (Fig. 29). These cult-houses were not 'temples' since, among other things, a central focus is lacking. Rather, they connect, with their secluded space, main elements of the Neolithic home with the Megalithic grave and ritual space. Indeed, several, perhaps all, of these small structures were erected near such graves, probably to serve the spiritual communication between the living and the dead, perhaps in connection with initiation rites, highly important events in most societies. In connection with the cult-houses we are, perhaps, also reminded of the sacrifices of pottery at the one end of the earlier long-barrows and of the important material of ceramic offerings outside the entrance to Megalithic chambers.

Finally, dated to the beginning of the third millennium BC comes an interesting group of so-called 'stone-packing graves' (also from Northern Jylland), made up of pairs of large pits next to the ends of rectangular structures (with fine but common grave-goods). These mortuary complexes are found in linear groupings across the landscape and have sometimes been interpreted as symbolic cattle-drawn carts. One of the 'carts' was found partly on top of the antechamber of a cult-house. This association is probably coincidental, since the cult-houses were 'closed' by their builders after use (contra Hodder (Hodder 1990, 212), who rather reads the observation as significant, denoting continuity in symbolic manipulation).

B. Early Bronze Age

The very fortunate (even relatively recent) finds of the dozen or so Jutlandic cult-houses from around 3000 BC demonstrate the existence of ritual structures in the Neolithic of a type that would

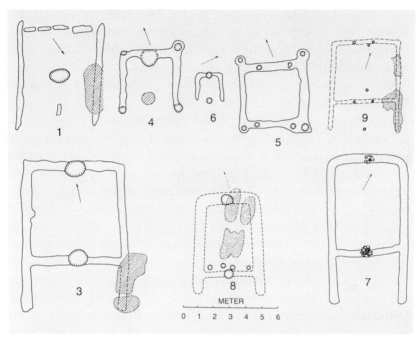

Fig. 29. Neolithic 'cult-houses' (probably related to contemporary graves) from northern Jylland/Jutland, Denmark, the end of the fourth millennium BC (after Becker 1993).

probably have escaped the eyes of most earlier field archaeologists. In studying ritual, the archaeologist must normally be content with burials and the deposits or hoards, in particular of valuables, from 'wet' locations (lakes, bogs, etc.) in particular and with similar finds on dry land. The hoards, on the other hand, make up a group of finds which occur in many periods of prehistory and across wide regions and are thus fit for comparative studies. Whether comparison of these finds is always justified from a religious or social point of view is, however, less certain. The debate often concerns the border-line to possible treasure-hoards and other non-ritual deposits. For the Bronze Age, the discussion often revolves around the supposed secular hoards of scrap-metal. The borders are indeed difficult to draw, both in terms of content and context (hoards with scrap metal have even been found in bogs), and most likely all, or nearly all, such finds are ritual. (The confusion arises from the indisputable Scandinavian treasures of gold and silver of later eras, for instance of the Viking Age, and the Migration Period.)

Archaeologically, a certain degree of similarity among the Bronze Age hoards of all of temperate Western (with Central) Europe is evident. Thus, the suggested sacrifices of valuables by the elites provide a satisfactorily common base for evaluation and further argument, just as costly grave-goods (and even the deliberate avoidance of including them) do.

For an introductory, and crucial, interpretation of the wet finds as, generally, being religious, their massive occurrence in some periods/areas and not in others is important. The occurrences are so substantial, taking place as they do over such a long time and so large an area, that an all-embracing hypothesis that the deposits merely represent hidden valuables, never recovered from times of conflict, is very unlikely, at least for prehistory. By contrast, as indicated, in the (late) first millennium AD Scandinavian silver hoards, without any obvious ritual connection or context and often found at or, rather, in settlement-sites, are abundant. In this period the burial of treasure was obviously a common practice. In Denmark, the many hoards of silverware from the years of the Swedish Wars of the seventeenth century AD, in particular from districts where the enemy had his winter-quarters and roamed unpredictibly and indiscriminately in search of food and valuables, are also a point in favour of applying even a 'war-hypothesis' to many of the late treasure-hoards (data, Lindahl 1988). Interestingly (and methodologically quite ironic), several of these treasures were hidden under water, seemingly to avoid traces of recently dug dirt, in containers possibly tied to trees or the like by strings, as a few written sources actually tell us.

However, during the mid-second millennium BC quite other deposits of exquisite bronze artefacts in wet areas (and other particular places, like big stones and burial mounds) were becoming increasingly common. These deposits included cultic bronzes for display, such as exorbitantly over-sized battle-axes, miniature waggons, like the famous Sun-chariot with its gilded disc, and other interesting items including two male statuettes copying Near Eastern deities, probably the earliest representations of such in southern Scandinavia. The latter come from a hoard, at Stockhult in Scania along with exquisite female jewellery, cultic axes, etc. (Randsborg 1993).

The typical items in these sacrifices are in the main relatively large; they comprise both major weapons and major female ornaments, while common dagger-blades, minor dress items and jewellery, the latter playing such a large role in the above-mentioned Greek sanctuaries of the Geometric period (cf. Fig. 25), are found only in graves or, as lost items, in settlements. At the same time, early Bronze Age graves, primarily from the centuries around c. 1300 BC, are lavishly equipped with the same types of swords, necklaces, belt-discs, etc. that have been found in the sacrifices. Only, the items in the hoards clearly tend to be the best executed, the largest, and thus also the costliest. The only significant difference is in gold, or gilded items, which during this particular period clearly dominate in the graves.

Among the graves of the period is a small but highly interesting group from Period III of the Early Bronze Age (c. 1300 to the eleventh century BC). This group consists of burials dug into the middle of common three-aisled long-houses which, after the funeral had taken place, were placed, precisely, within the circumference of a round mound (Boysen & Andersen 1983; Pedersen 1986). The parallel to the above-mentioned, but slightly later, 'heroon' of Lefkandi is striking (Chapter 6A). It is obvious that the dead personages involved, although not marked by particularly rich grave-goods, were buried in what was obviously a homestead, probably even their own. Early Bronze Age 'houses of dead' are squat and of a differing type (Kersten 1936, for Grünhof-Tesperhude, northernmost Germany; Lomborg 1956, for Jægerspris, Zealand, a more doubtful find). This overall phenomenon is not unique, however. The megalithic tombs in Denmark were often placed in (earlier) settlements. And, for a much later period, a large sixth century BC princely barrow at the Heuneburg fortress-town in southwestern Germany was constructed directly over a major composite farmstead, thus exactly covering the entire house-structure (Kimmig 1983).

Finally, from an Early Bronze Age (Period II, or earlier) settlement at Vadgård in northern Jutland comes what seems to be a settlement sanctuary: a stone with a rare rock-carving of a fish was the centre of a cultic structure of several surrounding rows of poles (Lomborg 1973).

C. After 1000 BC

At the middle of the Bronze Age, a new economic cycle was

initiated in Southern Scandinavia and adjacent regions, comprising agricultural intensification, large regular field-systems, probably smaller farmsteads, and new types of composite plough, tools, carts, etc. This Late Bronze Age period is, furthermore, characterized by a change in burial practices, with cremations, a pan-European practice, usually poorly equipped, supplanting inhumations, which were practically all-dominant in Southern Scandinavia until the end of the second millennium BC (in fact, till Nordic Period III, beginning c. 1300 BC). Interestingly, the earlier, strictly solar-dominated, patterns of orientation of the graves also dissolve during Period III of the Early Bronze Age. In this period, the new cremation fire and smoke both imitate the sun and reach for the sky (Randsborg & Nybo 1984).

The Late Bronze Age also represents a climax of ritual deposition of metal artefacts, in particular of bronze, though — now — not uncommonly of gold, too. Very many of the common hoards are from wet areas and characterized by fine larger female jewellery, for evident display. Thus, these deposits may, tentatively, have been related to the worship of chthonic deities of fertility: an old cult obviously revived in the Late Bronze Age, as emphasized by its very heavy 'investment' in costly bronzes. Indeed, the change from predominantly male objects in the hoards to predominantly female ones (or mixed finds) also takes place in Period III. Other sacrifices of the age were made up of large objects used in cultic rituals (cf. above, and below for further deliberations).

From the early Late Bronze Age, or Period IV, about 1000 BC or slightly later, comes a 'temple' or, perhaps rather, a cultic building (framed by a double row of stones) holding three cremation burials in huge urns placed under the floor of the structure (indeed, another *heroon*), almost 18 by 8 m (Fig. 30). The locality is Sand-agergård, Northern Zealand, Denmark (Kaul 1985). This structure, orientated north-south, had a small interior platform at the northern end, and in front of the southern facade three menhirs surrounding four slabs (up to c. 50 cm) with rock-carvings representing an arm with a hand plus four transverse stokes at the finger-tips, a symbol, perhaps, of celestial power, or of worship, hailing, possibly, the midday sun towards the very south.

This pregnant pictoral motive is also known from a series of small stone grave-cists from the northern part of Zealand and, occasionally, even further away, perhaps for worshippers from

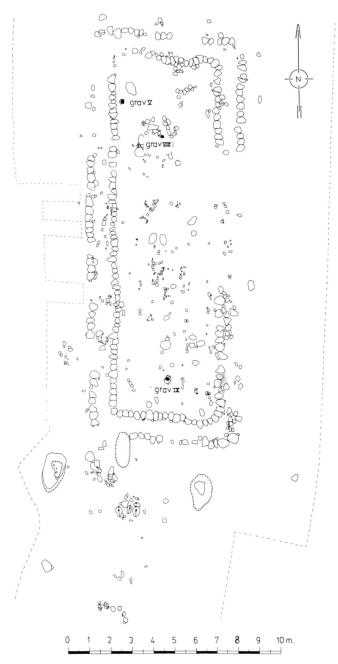

grav V

grav VIII

grav IX

0 1 2 3 4 5 6 7 8 9 10 m.

Fig. 30. Cult-structure with urn-graves from Sandagergård, northern Sjælland/Zealand, early Late Bronze Age, c. 1000 BC. In front of the building, to the south, are three menhirs and four slabs with rock-carvings of hands with arms (after Kaul 1985).

Sandagergård. In the culture layers of the 'temple' were remains from bronze-casting, but no settlement ceramics or flints were found. (A large Late Bronze Age settlement was recorded to the east of the structure, perhaps indicating a relationship between a cult structure and a central settlement, so typical of many societies.) Because of the urn-graves, the primary function of the Sandagergård structure may have been in the ancestor cult, perhaps in connection with secluded initiation rites, which might have included transmission of knowledge about bronze-working, or the production of special artefacts. Above, the same function(s) was suspected for the North Jutland Neolithic sacred structures, some two thousand years earlier. However, Sandagergård had far more space for performance of rituals than the Stone Age structures.

Parallels to Sandagergård (even with a small platform at the one end) have been unearthed in Scania, a couple of structures (43/44 m long) at a Late Bronze Age cemetery on the beach of the Baltic near the famous Kivik grave (Randsborg 1993). Finally, other, probably also ritually related structures in Denmark and Northern Germany, mainly from the Late Bronze Age, comprise groups of hundreds of cooking-pits arranged in rows, perhaps catering for whole societies gathered for special occasions (Thrane 1974; Heidelk-Schacht 1989).

– – –

The practice of sacrificing fine bronzes in bogs and at other locations continued, as mentioned, into the early first millennium BC with a larger and larger percentage of female items. These include belt-discs and tutuli, matching so-called hanging-bowls, neck-, arm-/wrist- and ankle-rings, etc. Interestingly, deposits with neck-rings but from different periods tend to occur repeatedly in the same geographical area, perhaps indicating particular sanctuaries for female deities wearing such. Throughout, similar hoards were, as earlier, often deposited on 'dry land'. Indeed, the sacrifices now dominate the find picture of valuable metal objects, richly equipped graves having mostly disappeared.

Proper cult-objects also became common in the deposits, for instance magnificent lurs (large ritual S-shaped bugles), imported bronze-vessels, including large buckets, golden drinking-cups, and thin bronze shields. Significantly, the lurs are almost only found in pairs and without any other artefacts; the latter also holds true for the shields as well as the golden cups (which may have been deposited in a large bronze vessel, though). Towards the middle of the first millennium BC (Period VI of the Late Bronze Age), neck-rings, usually in pairs and often without any other type of artefact, dominate the picture of sacrifice, distantly recalling the famous necklace of the Viking fertility goddess Freja. Again, the existence of hoards of scrap-metal poses a problem: are they (always) founders' stock or, rather, just another kind of sacrifice, perhaps to a deity also protecting the crafts, trade or acquisition, indeed a latter-day Celtic or Germanic 'Mercury'?

It is also during the Late Bronze Age (or, rather, from Period III of the Early Bronze Age, on) that we begin clearly to see a division of the sacrificial deposits into three distinct groups, probably pertaining to the three different spheres of the supernatural (earth, sky & water) discussed above (Chapter 6), rather than merely two, as previously (earth & sky). The three spheres become even more pronounced during the following Pre-Roman Iron Age. The first sphere is, as suggested, identified with the powers of the sky (including the sun), responsible for, i.a. war; to this may belong the lurs, the shields, the weapons, etc. The second sphere is the chthonic one (the land, the sea, etc.) comprising the forces of fertility (in particular a central female being); to this belong the jewellery, the neck-rings, etc. By reference to later knowledge, the ship as a symbol may also belong here. The third sphere is defined by the sacrifices of metal cups and containers (both gold and bronze) for fine liquids; these may belong to the recently introduced connecting force of water (along with mead and wine), perhaps emanating from the south-east with the fine metal vessels of, e.g., the Late Bronze Age. Web-footed bird symbols belong in the same context.

Further dimensions, in particular social ones, should also be discussed in connection with the deposits. A Late Bronze Age (Period IV) deposit from Borbjerg, northwestern Jutland, Danmark may serve to illuminate both the methodological problems and possible interpretations (Ørsnes 1958) (Fig. 31). This bronze hoard, found in a large pot at the northern base of a common burial mound, consists of a supposedly male set of weapons etc., and a female set of jewellery. The male part comprises a Central European sword (deliberately broken), a large spear-/lancehead, two light partly black-tinted spear-/lanceheads (thin-bodied and probably ceremonial), a ceremonial horn (deliberately broken), and two

Fig. 31. The Late Bronze Age (Period IV) Borbjerg deposit, western Jylland/ Jutland, Danmark (after Ørsnes 1958). This bronze hoard, found in a large pot at the northern base of a common burial mound, consists of a male set of weapons etc., and a female set of jewellery.

The male part comprises a Central European sword (deliberately broken), a large spear-/lancehead, two light, partly black-tinted spear-/lanceheads (thin-bodied and probably ceremonial), a ceremonial horn (deliberately broken), and two Central European axes with bent flanges for hafting (currency ingots?). — The female part consists of a (ceremonial) belt plate, a (ceremonial) very worn belt-box, two spiral armrings (perhaps deliberately broken), and two large (probably) cuff bracelets (ceremonial?).

Central European axes with bent flanges for hafting (currency ingots?). The female part consists of a (ceremonial) belt-plate, a (ceremonial) very worn belt-box, two spiral armrings (perhaps deliberately broken), and two large (probably) cuff bracelets (ceremonial?), or ankle-rings.

Thus, it would also seem that the Borbjerg find comprises (1) old, worn and deliberately broken both male (sword, horn) and female (belt-box, two spiral arm-rings) artefacts; and (2) new both male (three spear-/lanceheads, two axes) and female (belt plate, two cuffs) artefacts. The inherent social dimension of the deposit seems to imply both (I) personal (sword, spiral rings) and ceremonial (horn, box possibly for amulets) items of an older generation (these bronzes are even typologically older than the rest); and (II) a younger generation's items signalling wealth (axes, possibly currency ingots), status (ceremonial spearheads), and personal standing (large spearhead, belt-plate & cuffs).

If these socially related cultural observations are carried just one step further, we might, in the composition of the Borbjerg find, even see the younger generation's symbolic 'farewell' to (A) spear/lance as the main weapon of both status and fighting (and the implicit rise of the sword); and to (B) the belt-plate and cuffs as main jewellery (and the implicit taking on of the status of the belt-box (or 'hanging vessel')). A new sword, neck-rings (and fibulae) are conspicuously absent; these may be symbols of mature men and women of both rank and rights, having taken over the responsibilities of an older generation.

The social context of the Borbjerg find may thus be the exhibition of a generational rite of passage, comprising the manipulation of artefacts related to status and role. The archaeological context of the deposition (the burial mound) may merely enhance this interpretation. However, the deposit must also have been devoted to a force or a deity. Such may have been an ancestor, a force of nature or a supernatural being. (If devoted to an ancestor, he or she will probably also have been endowed with supernatural forces, thus reducing the field to the supernatural in general.) The find itself seems to give no particular clue to the problem. However, the existence of particular instruments of cult for worship of sky-powers, for instance lurs, always deposited alone, may, indirectly, point to hoards like Borbjerg being devoted to the chthonic forces of 'fertility', perhaps with a reference to ancestors. (The broken horn relates to the sky-powers in another capacity.) The deposition of the sacrifice in the ground may point in the same direction (although all archaeologically recognizable deposition in prehistoric Denmark is from below ground), as may, in fact, the common plain sickles which often accompany female jewellery, etc., in these finds.

The highly interesting custom of offering neck-rings, over time, as noted, often in the same area or even the same locality, is practically the only one from the Bronze Age surviving the transition

	SKY (M)	EARTH (F (& M))	ANCESTORS (mainly M)	GRAVES (M& F)
BC				
4000 ***				
		Bog-pots,		
	Fine flint-axes	Work-axes	Long-barrows	Pots, Amber
*	Amber, Copper	Animals &	Dolmen-chambers	Work-axes
	Causeway camps	humans	Passage graves	Stone-clubs
3000			Cult houses	
**	Flint-axes		Round barrows (continue)	Battle-axes
*	Flint-daggers			Flint-daggers
2000	Metal axes			
*	Weapon hoards			Metal weapons,
	Cult-axes			Jewellery,
	Sun Chariot	Symbol boats	Gold, Vessels	
**	Lurs	Jewellery-		Cremations
1000	(continue)	hoards	Sandagergård	(continue)

Fig. 32. Top: Suggested relationships between (1) Cults of the sky, (2) Fertility cults, (3) Ancestor cults (burial monuments, grave-goods, cult-houses, etc.), and, (4) Treatment of dead persons, during the Neolithic to the early Late Bronze Age in Denmark, and the artefacts types, monuments, structures, etc., in question. One, two or three '*' indicate (major) cultural caesura (correlating with changes in the human impact on the landscape). M = male, F = female (spheres).

Bottom: The general cultural development and other changes given in catchwords, for practical reasons within periods of approximately 200 years. (Environmental information ought only rarely be considered within such narrow periods.) A survey of Denmark's Prehistory may be consulted for the finds, for instance, Brøndsted 1957-60.

to the Iron Age, around 500 BC, and thus existing, although by then quite rare, when the Hjortspring boat and weapons sacrifice was carried out in the fourth century BC. Incidentally, the transition between the Nordic Late Bronze Age Periods V and VI (or, rather, Period VI proper) marks the decline of traditional Bronze Age chiefly society.

4000	***	Seizure of the agricultural landscape (nature to culture)
		Fertility cult, probably also worship of sky-powers
	*	From work to death: marking of interests (long-barrows)
		Emergence of social authority; cult centres; dolmens; copper
		Passage graves & ancestor worship; cult houses
3000		Economic and social changes: ploughs & waggons; (cattle & barley)
	**	Pasture lands (W) & reforestation/wild resources (E); long-houses
		The barrow and the rise/return of the individual
	*	General expansion of the agricultural area; the dagger
		Emergence of very large farmsteads; differentation at burial
2000		Direct links with the regions of Europe
	*	Social distinction; increasing role of exchange & shipping
		The traditional three-aisled longhouse; sacrifice of bronzes
		Worship of sky-powers (sun); chariots; metal vessels (worship of water)
	**	Temporal reforestation (followed by expansion of agriculture)
1000		Building of society: regions & chiefs; religion; cremation

Fig. 32 continued.

This decline, or transformation, corresponds to the emergence of the culture of the Hallstatt D period in Central Europe with its new fruitful, and in part economic, set of relationships with the Mediterranean. Taking place around 600 BC, when aristocratic powers were challenged by the Greek poleis, the period in time is noteworthy. Indeed, although rich princely graves are common in both Central Europe and Etruria in this era, the whole of the first millennium BC across Europe seems to fluctuate between egalitarian tendencies (for instance, the down-playing of personal grave-goods) and experiments with new, in particular economic, powers for the elite. In the end the latter won, as the rise of the Hellenistic empires signifies.

– – –

The settlements in Denmark during the Late Neolithic and most of the Bronze Age were dominated by large halls, from the Early Bronze Age on with three aisles (e.g. Boas 1991). The settlements of the early pre-Roman Iron Age in Jutland, the beginning of which overlaps with Hallstatt D, or the crucial sixth century BC, were, by contrast, characterized by much smaller farmsteads, probably run by single core-families, perhaps with a few additional members.

The chronology of these very small early Iron Age farmsteads, sometimes only 10 by 5 m, but still commonly with both stable and living quarters under the same roof (thus probably specifying the personal character of the ownership of the stock), is not yet finalized. Still, they may well have begun during Period VI of the Bronze Age (Becker 1982). Indeed, already at the turn of the Early Bronze Age (the very end of the second millennium BC), the farmsteads seem to start getting smaller, probably in response to changes in the social structure, most likely an intensification of the agriculture, as demonstrated by the above-mentioned new types of plough, large regular field-systems, etc.

It is no great surprise to find this important economic and social process accompanied by a re-structuring of the rituals and religious ideology. Indeed, apart from Mesolithic and earlier beliefs, Stone Age religion is only fully supplanted in the Late Bronze Age, the latter circumstances probably continuing into the late Iron Age and its well-known myths of the spoiled aristocratic Nordic gods of the Viking era.

8. Sanctuaries and Societies III: Central Europe

> Among many of the tribes, high piles of it can be seen on
> consecrated ground; and it is an almost unknown thing for
> anyone to dare, in defiance of religious law, to conceal his booty
> at home or to remove anything placed on the piles. Such a crime
> is punishable by a terrible death under torture.
>
> Caesar, c. 52 BC (*De belli gallici*, Book 1)

The circumstances in trans-Alpine temperate Europe, between the
Mediterranean and the northern lands bordering on the North Sea
and the Baltic, are from the later Neolithic on to a large extent
similar to those just outlined for the North. Ritual activities, apart
from the common events and phenomena connected with burials,
are recorded both on the household and on the settlement level
(particular deposits, special forms of ceramics, etc.) as well as on
the petty regional level involving somewhat larger groups, including their leaders, and a possible investment of costly artefacts, for
instance exquisite bronzes sacrificed in rivers. The methodological
problems of interpretation of the finds are also the same as in the
North (if not actually greater).

Only a few finds may indicate the existence of shrines in the
shape of a building before the first millennium BC, but this might
well be due to lack of sufficiently conclusive data from settlements.
A well-known example is the 'temple' (9 by 5 m) on a settlement
at Sălacea in northwestern Romania from the early second
millennium BC, perhaps around 1700 BC (Ordentlich 1972) (Fig. 33).
This building, with a frontal porch, was equipped with interior
'altar'-platforms and plaster friezes; many ceramics, including
several 'cultic' objects, were found. The structural set-up is actually
reminiscent of the above-mentioned North Jutland cult-houses from
around 3000 BC: lack of a cult statue or even a central area for worship, and, in particular, a stress on concealed activities, much as in
the Anatolian Neolithic shrines at the famous Çatal Hüyük
township, or in the *kivas* of the more recent American Southwest.

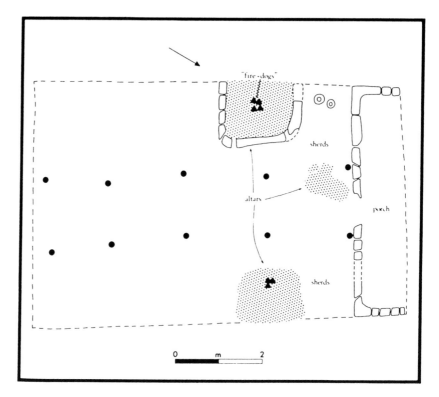

Fig. 33. Cultic structure from Sălacea, Romania, early second millennium BC (after Ordentlich 1972).

An early Bronze Age ritual well at Gánovce in Slovakia held animal and human bones, vessels with female breasts and a riveted iron dagger, possibly the earliest worked iron in Europe (Vladár 1973). Indeed, several wells with sacrifices of metal artefacts are known from Bronze Age Central Europe, both early and late.

A famous clay figurine, perhaps a female, perhaps a dressed out (male) person in cuirass armour, from Kličevac in the Banat (near Beograd) and two ceramic model waggons with four-spoked 'chariot' wheels, drawn by web-footed birds, from Dupjaja in the same general region, with similar figurines, probably males, standing under a parasol (like Aegean and Near Eastern princes), are difficult to date with certainty, but no doubt belong in the late second millennium BC, probably around 1300 BC. These fine representations are especially interesting in suggesting the existence of anthropomorphic deities in temperate Europe in the late second millennium BC, and for their Mediterranean allusions and possible introduction of southern religious ideas. Other ritual finds from the eastern part of north-Alpine Europe are less conspicuous, but they do amount to a substantial series of different activities on the level of the homestead, usually involving only less costly artefacts (cf. Coles & Harding 1979).

The East and east Central European finds from the earlier part of the Bronze Age may be contrasted with, for instance, the small ritual structure of four uprights from a bog at Bargeroosterveld in the northern Netherlands, practically in the North (Bloemers et al. 1981, 59f). In the British Isles, the last magnificent phase of Stonehenge in Southern England also belongs to the middle of the second millennium BC and marks the apogee and end of the local very long and powerful tradition of astronomically related megalithic ritual monuments. From Wilsford, in the same region, we even have an almost 33 m deep shaft with various Early Bronze Age material at the bottom (Ashbee 1963). This foreshadows the deep shafts of some, however much later, Celtic shrines from the end of the first millennium BC (Buchsenschutz 1991). In the west, ritual sites with structures are, seemingly, very rare during the Late Bronze Age.

For the Late Bronze Age in eastern Central Europe, a locality at Čakovice in Bohemia, from around 1000 BC, has revealed a likely ritual structure consisting of a ring-shaped ditch, 17 m across, with a palisade surrounding a stone stele (Soudský 1966). This structure recalls the much larger Celtic sanctuary from Libenice, also Bohemia, from around 300 BC, to which we return below (Rybová & Soudský 1962). From the turn of the Late Bronze Age come some interesting hill-top sanctuaries in southern Poland (Silesia/Schlesien), 700 m above sea-level (Gediga 1992). This, admittedly, rather meagre picture of major ritual sites of the Late Bronze Age is supplemented by homestead ritual activities like depositions of pottery in wells, pits filled with non-typical materials (for example, Müller 1964), etc. The manipulation of symbols, in particular the web-footed bird emblem and celestrial icons, is common on all levels in the Late Bronze Age, and examples are found of miniature cauldron-waggons, for instance in the princely graves at Acholshausen, western Germany (Pescheck 1972), and Milavče, western

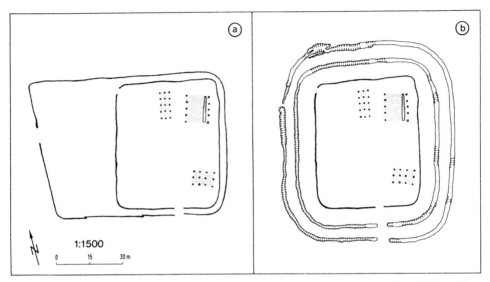

Fig. 34. Magnate farmstead at Aiterhofen, Bavaria, dated to the early Iron Age; two stages (after Christlein & Storck 1980; cf. Reichenberger 1994).

Bohemia (Kytlicová 1988, the latter supposedly with a bronze-studded leather cuirass) (Fig. 42), suggesting a particular water-cult (Pare 1989; 1992).

To obtain a level of archaeological control in both time and space, in particular a means for making comparisons, we must, again, turn to the Bronze Age offerings of metal artefacts, bearing in mind that 'wet' deposits are predominantly a West (including Central) European phenomenon. In Eastern Europe such finds are rare indeed. Furthermore, this area is one in which the archae-ological literature is comprehensive and accessible. The deposits comprise mainly bronzes, weapons, jewellery, and even tools; golden artefacts often occur alone, but not always. At Schifferstadt in Bavaria a brimmed cone of gold-foil, a ritual 'hat' or symbol of power, no doubt a display item, was found with three bronze palstave axes (Müller-Karpe 1980, Taf. 439C).

Among the sacrificed bronze-artefacts, the ones from the great rivers attract particular interest. A long-term study of Bavaria shows two peaks of such sacrifices, the first in the middle of the Bronze Age, the other, after a stand-still during the Iron Age, in the Roman Imperial period (Torbrügge 1970-71). There are also some finds from the late La Tène Iron Age period, for instance in northern Gaul, resembling the picture on the British Isles (Roymans 1990).

This overall pattern is a general one, occurring in other areas of north-Alpine Europe as well, for instance northern Bohemia. Here metal finds from the river Labe/Elbe (at impressive Porta Bohemica) are commonly from the Late Bronze Age, but (practically) not known from the Iron Age (Zápotocký 1960). Looking more closely at the chronological distributions throughout the Bronze Age, the decline in 'wet' finds is balanced by a rise in the ones from dry land, perhaps suggesting basically the same rite carried out in different regimes. The distibution of Bronze Age helmets, for instance, in various archaeological contexts gives regional information on this interesting complementation (Hencken 1971). The helmets are found in prominent burials in Italy, but in rivers, etc., in Western and in west Central Europe. In east Central Europe they occur in hoards on dry land, often with scrap metal, perhaps indicating secular functions as well. A third dimension is noted for the Rhineland. Here, sacrifices in bogs are generally earlier than those in small rivers, which in turn are generally earlier than the ones in the Rhine, the latter being mainly of a Late Bronze Age date (Zimmermann 1970, with Bradley 1990, Fig. 41; cf. Hansen 1991). This observation may actually reflect an increasing concentration of rituals on sites of major importance.

No doubt the ritual deposition of costly metal artefacts, perhaps especially in regions like Denmark without local access to relevant raw materials, represents a serious effort to placate the deities, however short-lived the period of display of the items may have been (we have no information on this, though). In the 'exhibitionist' Greek sanctuaries, major offerings were visible for ages. This implies, as has often been stressed, that the north-Alpine sacrifices had important social ramifications (cf. Bradley 1990 for an overview, which, however, lacks an appraisal of the phenomenon of sanctuary and instead chases the mirages of investment). Indeed, a tendency to see the hoards in a socio-economic light, as reflections of competition between the elites, has dominated recent research. One negative consequence of this, in other respects fruitful 'modernist' view, is the risk of confusing archaeological description with a reconstruction of society.

Belief no doubt played a decisive role in ancient societies. Indeed, the high investment in sacrifices underlines this point. But social competition, leaving aside, for the moment, the role of ancestor cults, is more likely expressed in burial goods and in the proportion of wealth that goes into these compared to other offerings (cf. Randsborg 1974). For instance, the seeming decline in depositions in Denmark at the end of the Early Bronze Age (13th and 12th centuries BC), which has even been seen as reflecting a crisis in the supply of metal, is, in fact, balanced by a larger investment of bronze and gold in the burials.

As already noted, the Iron Age in Central Europe is almost devoid of 'wet' sacrifices. However, in England the Late Bronze Age depositions in rivers, for instance the Thames above London, continue into the Iron Age, as they also do, although to a much lesser extent than in the Bronze Age, in, for instance, Denmark (Fitzpatrick 1984). Thus, the wealth connected with the rise of the new Central European early Iron Age aristocracy seems, as far as the ritual sector is concerned, mainly to have gone into the many richly furnished graves, dating from the end of the Bronze Age until about 400/(350) BC and culminating in a series of princely tombs of the sixth and fifth centuries BC (e.g., Planck et al. 1985). However, this may only be a superficial explanation. Rather, we are witnessing the start of completely different cult practices where river- and other deposits give way to proper sanctuaries. The latter are, however, still less well known.

At Antran near Poitiers in western France, a very large building at a cemetery (46 by 17 m), dated to between the seventh and the middle of the fifth century BC, has been interpreted as a 'temple' (no settlement debris was found) (Bruneaux 1986). The size, shape and location of this structure resemble those of the oblong enclosures with light constructions, like Acy-Romance in northern France, commonly found at the turn of the Bronze Age at cemeteries in northwestern Europe (e.g., Lambot 1991). A functional parallel to Sandagergård in Denmark and the long structures at Kivik might be suggested (Kaul 1985; Randsborg 1993) (Fig. 31). More to the point, on the important hill-top fortress of Danebury in southwestern England, the most extensively excavated such site, a sanctuary, albeit rather small, is situated in the middle of the settlement, at its highest point, throughout the entire existence of the fortress during most of the second half of the first millennium BC (Cunliffe 1983).

Sanctuaries of the early Iron Age are, however, still relatively few in temperate Europe (they are difficult to find in the open landscape and the archaeological situation is rarely equivocal), although found both on mountain-tops, in caves, and in settlements, for instance cultic pits in hill-top fortresses (Filip 1970). At Burkovák-Nemějice in southern Bohemia, on a 500 m high mountain, a cult site of around 500 BC revealed, apart from sherds, many hundreds of clay items, stars, rings, a few figurines, etc., all with a hole for suspension, perhaps from a frame.

The best known site of this period, but hardly a typical one and perhaps even a grave rather than a sanctuary proper (which sees repeated action), is the Býči-Skála cave in Moravia (Wankel 1882). Here large-scale human sacrifice and fires, the latter in two areas along the northern wall, the largest of which with parts of a waggon, iron ingots, etc., were connected with burned grain and costly artefacts mainly of the sixth century BC. (Perhaps the activities were not all contemporary.) The archaeological situation is very confusing, in part because of the early excavation of the find, in part due to the fact that a princely grave (in a waggon) is seemingly an essential part of the complex. Clearly ritual are parts of animals and more than forty often mutilated humans (half of them women, with jewellery (cf. Griesa 1989, 252)) in the middle of the cave (away from the fires and many of the costly artefacts). On an 'altar' lay, again in grain, the cut-off gold-ringed hands of a woman and part of a skull. Also at the cave-walls opposite the fires were finds, including a male skeleton and, in another area, various vessels (with burned grain, a human skull, etc.). Although human sacrifice is not unknown in this period, Býči-Skála is remarkable in its almost Aztec bloodiness, either the prince demanded unusual treatment or, perhaps, an elite household was exterminated. Incidentally, among the small finds are a fine bull-statuette, Italian heart-armour, and a couple of Scythian iron battle-axes. A remarkable find, indeed.

Yet another type of sanctuary, this time resembling the major Mediterranean ones, comes from the hill-top fortress of Závist near Prague, which, at the end of the first millennium BC, was turned into a large Celtic oppidum (Motyková, Drda & Rybová 1988 (and earlier, but with differing details, since the excavation is a highly complicated one)) (Fig. 35). On the 'acropolis' of the early site, almost 400 m above sea-level and surrounded by a rectangular simple palisade *temenos* wall, a sanctuary, indeed a small area also

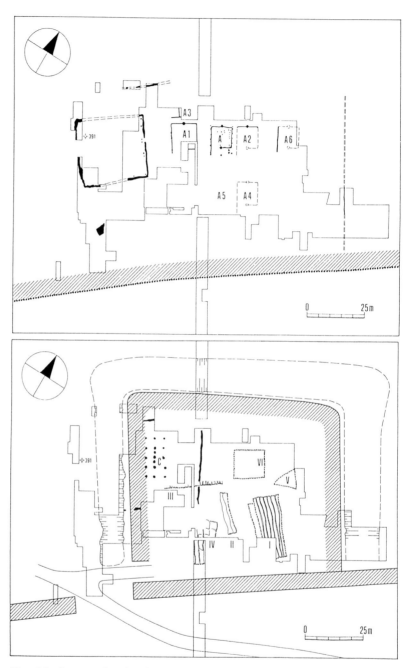

Fig. 35. *Sanctuaries dated to, respectively, (top) the middle of the sixth century* BC, *and (bottom) the fifth century* BC *from the acropolis of the hill-top settlement of Závist, Bohemia (after Motyková, Drda & Rybová 1988).*

framed by a palisade (about 30 by 27 m), was established at around the middle of the sixth century BC. Next to this structure was a row of smaller houses of the same size. (In the Mediterranean they would probably have been considered treasuries.) The basic similarity to the above Bavarian Aiterhofen-sanctuary from the eighth-seventh century BC is noted (Christlein & Stork 1980).

At the turn of the sixth century BC, the main sanctuary structure on the acropolis of Závist was a substantial two-aisled house (18 by 9 m) surrounded by a rectangular palisade. A stone-built platform was placed next to this complex, perhaps for cultic ceremonies. In the fifth century the sanctuary site was surrounded by a heavy temenos wall and ditch, enclosing an area of c. 75 by 65 m with several stone-built platforms (the largest one constructed from parallel walls, like the base of an Archaic Greek temple), including a noteworthy triangular one. On these stone platforms, wooden buildings were erected. The end of this phase of the fortress is the early fourth century BC. A final filling-in and building-up (again in parallel walls) of the entire area was never completed. Fragments of stone sculptures probably indicate that statues once stood within the sacred area (Jansová 1983). The close of the development of the sanctuary has been connected with the arrival of new Celtic tribes in the area, incidentally, only a decade or so after Celtic tribesmen conquered northern Italy and laid siege to Rome, and only a few decades, perhaps, before Hjortspring.

Constructed around 300 BC, some decades after Hjortspring, and given up or destroyed perhaps shortly after, a site at Libenice finally draws our attention in the important sequence of Bohemian sacrifices and sanctuaries (Rybová & Soudský 1962) (Fig. 36). This monument, probably only of the village level of society and cult, consists of a long oval ditch (80 by 20 m) and a figure-eight shaped pit at the one (south-eastern) end. (The ditch resembles the Late Bronze Age and Iron Age enclosures in west European cemeteries.) In the pit, with bones of children and animals and a collection of stones, stood a menhir and a couple of posts, which probably held necklaces (two such, of bronze, were found); around the pit were four wooden frames, which may all have had an astronomical significance. A proper grave for a woman (with various good jewellery) was found in the middle of the complex. The neck-rings (and the female grave) allude to the finds of neck-rings on Germanic territory during this period. Indeed, offerings of Germanic so-called

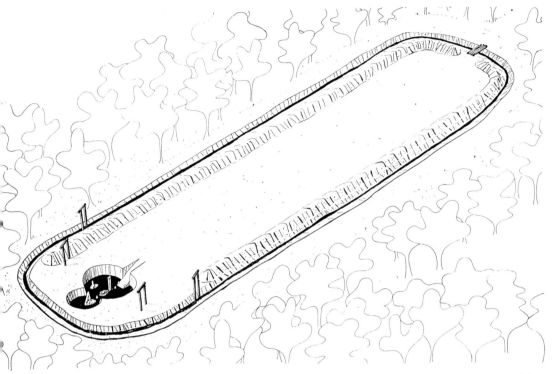

Fig. 36. Reconstruction of the sanctuary at Libenice, Bohemia; c. 300 BC (after Rybová & Soudský 1962).

Kronenhalsringe, a particularly heavy type, are distributed from Jutland to the coast of the Black Sea at Odessa (Ščukin et al. 1992).

The Bohemian sequence, and other finds, thus demonstrate the distinctive rise of sanctuaries in north-Alpine Europe at the close of the Bronze Age, and the highly varying nature of such sites. This new ritual phenomenon may also explain the disappearance of the deposits of metal artefacts, in particular in rivers. At the same time, a regionally dispersed group of princes, with richly equipped graves, made themselves manifest.

In the period of Hjortspring (and Libenice) these princes had, however, already vanished, at least archaeologically (certainly, they had lost interest in investing in rich burials), their seats mostly abandoned, and their lands dominated by militarized Celtic tribes, probably under new leadership, migrating across Europe and even into the Near East in search of new wealth, employment (as mercenaries), and new land to the base of subsistence necessary for the larger groups to maintain themselves.

From the third century BC on, new regional growth is seen, and with that, a novel series of sanctuaries, much discussed in recent archaeological literature, where wealth, in particular fine weapons, animals and humans were sacrificed. These sanctuaries are in the main western and comprise both early well-known archaeological finds of river- and lake-offerings, like La Tène in Switzerland, from around 200 BC, the so-called 'Viereckschanzen' (with deep shafts, cf. Bittel et al. 1990), and new ones like a series of French sanctuaries. Strangely enough, compared to these southern military sacrifices, Hjortspring is probably the earliest of them all, again making this find all the more remarkable.

What is particularly characteristic of this ritual development among the Celts during the last quarter of the first millennium BC is the rise of a sacred landscape with central sanctuaries at major settlement and tribal centres and a host of others in the open country, much like the Aegean in the Archaic period (and even earlier).

– – –

The sanctuary at Gournay-sur-Aronde near Compeigne in northern France has several consecutive phases and may serve as the model site in the present context (Bruneaux 1986, el al.) (Fig. 37). The cultic practices cover six or even seven hundred years, from the fourth or, rather, the third century BC to the fourth century AD, and seem to come to a halt only with the introduction of Christianity. The site is placed within the confines of a late La Tène oppidum, a tribal capital. In the central structure were found various coins, etc.; in the surrounding rectangular ditch massive amounts of weapons and sacrificed animals (and humans).

In the earliest phase, possibly around or even before 300 BC, cultic posts were erected (along axes also guiding the constructions in the following phases) within a rectangular ditched enclosure (about 45 by 40 m; an entrance is towards the east). In the late third century BC nine ritual pits were placed around a tenth in a square, open towards the east, at the centre of the enclosure. The pits have wooden linings and may have held sacrifices before these were dumped in the enclosure ditch. In this phase the enclosing ditch was also lined with wood and framed by a palisade on the

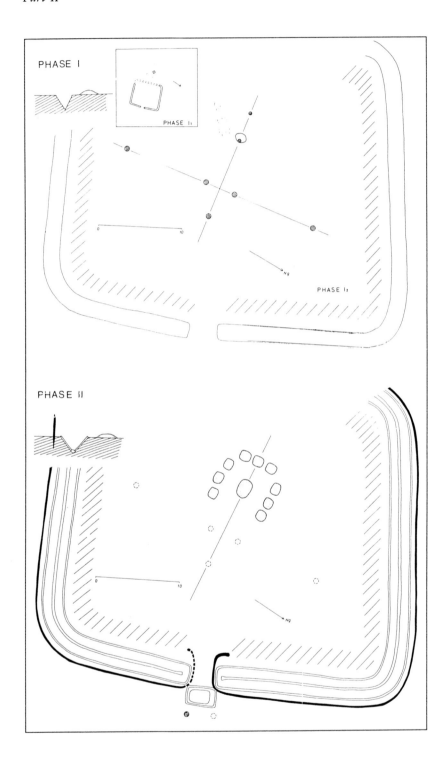

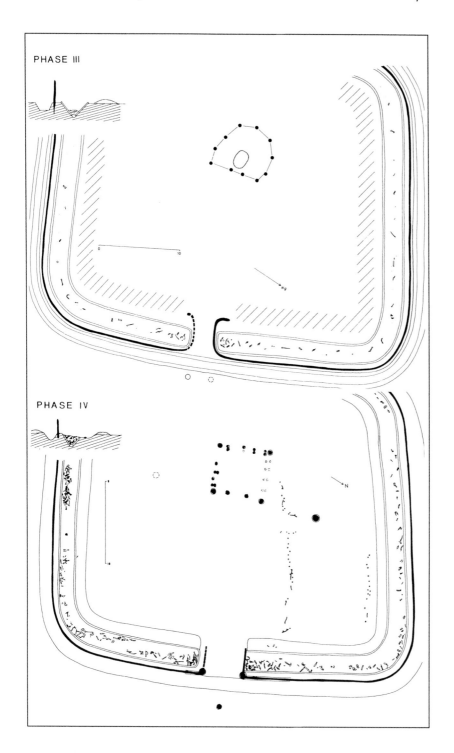

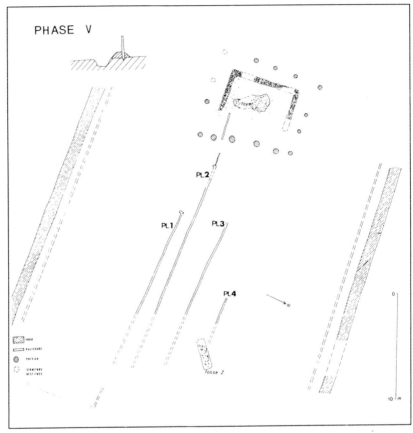

Fig. 37. The sanctuary of Gournay-sur-Aronde, northern France (after Bruneaux, Meniel & Poplin 1985): (I) Before or at 3000 BC; (II) Late third century BC, (III), Second century BC, (IV) The middle of the first century BC, (V) The end of the third century AD.

outside. In the second century BC, a light semi-oval sanctuary was erected around the central pit. At the end of the same century a new sanctuary was constructed on this very spot, now with a square plan (6 by 6 m). The square structure was burned down in the middle of the first century BC (at the time of Caesar's conquest of Gaul), but another square building or *cella*, with stone foundation and a surrounding wooden *porticus* (on the model of the later Gallo-Roman temples), replaced it. This sanctuary structure stood till the middle of the first century AD, but even after that, the site was apparently respected, and at the end of the third century AD, a final structure, a Gallo-Roman *Fanum* (temple) — a gallery around a small square cella, the base in stone — was constructed.

In the ditch of the enclosure were found, in all: 256 swords and fragments of these, 621 scabbards and furnishings, 361 furnishings for shields (including 275 bosses), 73 heads and 51 other furnishings (including sockets) for spears/lances, 125 furnishings for belts (including 88 chained iron sword-belts), 116 pieces of jewellery (including 110 fibulae), 122 rings, 76 tools, etc.; in all, 2063 items. The site also yielded a great deal of pottery. The animal bones comprise 1632 fragments of cattle (a minimum of 52 individuals, the skulls of which were deposited at the entrance to the sanctuary), 578 of sheep/goat (93 individuals), 328 of horse (eight individuals), and 212 of pig (33 individuals). There were also some 60 bone-fragments of decapitated humans, representing at least 12 individuals, some perhaps females. The human bones were deposited at the corners of the ditch.

In Gourney-sur-Aronde we may thus, as has been suggested (Bruneaux 1986; cf. Rapin 1982), encounter a shrine to the god of war, Caesar's 'Zeus' or 'Mars', while 'Mercurius', who is guiding the dead to the realm of death, may have been worshipped at a nearby sanctuary, Ribemont-sur-Ancre. In the latter were found, along with some weapons, many headless humans and a 'building' constructed from the major bones of more than 200 individuals. At Mirebeau in Bourgogne, finally, a shrine from around 300 BC on, weapons were also found, but the dominating items were pottery, jewellery and bones from sacrificed animals. Perhaps a female deity to fertility was worshipped here.

A survey of 33 pre-Roman Iron Age cult-places from northern Gaul, the general region of Gournay-sur-Aronde, demonstrates that they are almost all either from tribal centres (oppida) or from the very same site as later Gallo-Roman temples (Roymans 1990). Additional information can be extracted from the data, in particular of the Imperial Roman period. For instance, five shrines were, among other deities, devoted to Mars, three to Mercury (one of which also had an offering to Apollo), and one to Hercules. The sacrifices in these sanctuaries comprise coins, often golden, weapons, fibulae (seemingly mainly with goddesses), pottery, etc. In the Imperial period, Mars was in particular worshipped around Trier and on the Germanic left bank of the Rhine at Mainz, the major gate to Free Germany.

Also the better known truly huge Celtic oppida or tribal capitals of the end of the first millennium BC have provided finds of important shrines. At Manching in Southern Germany (380 hectares, the wall is seven kms long), some three sanctuaries with their own cultic space, including one with a remarkable polygonal structure within a square palisade fence, have been recorded (Sievers 1991); another important feature here is a gilded holy tree of bronze, no doubt of Hellenistic Greek inspiration (Maier 1990). In southernmost France stone-built shrines are found, for instance the 'Fanum' from the oppidum of Les Castels (first century BC) (Py 1990, 828 (building AXIII1)) (Fig. 38). (There are also earlier examples of stone-built shrines in the south of France.) Lastly, a huge sacred precinct with several large constructions in stone and wood at the Dacian capital of Sarmizegetusa (southwestern Romania), of the early Imperial Roman period, should be mentioned as one of the culminations of the non-Classical development of ritual or cultic structures in trans-Alpine Europe (Hoddinott 1981).

In the context of the above picture of the Central European development, Hjortspring, both chronologically and culturally, clearly belongs in the post-Bronze Age phase, where deposits of rich metal finds in often 'wet', locations, basically, had given way to sanctuaries with constructions resembling the formal Mediterranean one. The Hjortspring pond had, seemingly, already been in use for a few simple earlier offerings when the weapon deposition occurred; this may explain the particular location of the sanctuary. However, there is no indication at the site of an enclosure, structure or the like (topography may even speak against it). On the other hand, given the circumstances of find in Denmark, only excavations could, indeed should, test such propositions. The most interesting factor is, perhaps, that Hjortspring seems to be as early as or even earlier than the large Celtic weapon-finds at formal sanctuaries such as Gournay-sur-Aronde. For phenomenological reasons, a parallel to the late 'nature' deposits, such as La Tène in Switzerland, should be seen, but also these are generally later than (or, at most, contemporary with) Hjortspring (cf. Duval 1990, for Tronoen). Thus, Hjortspring remains a truly unique find, even on the European level.

– – –

Finally, connecting north-Alpine Europe with the Mediterranean by

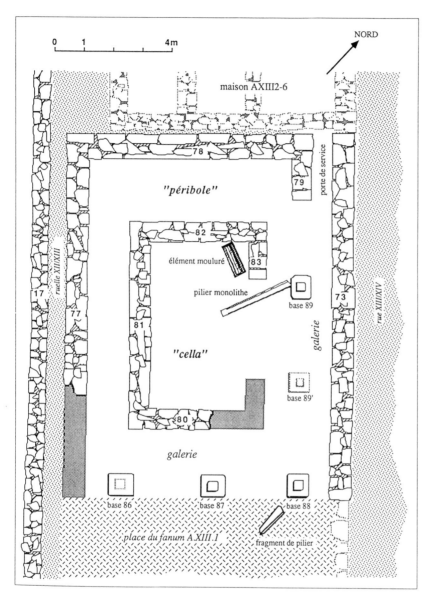

Fig. 38. Fanum ('temple') at the fortified town of Les Castels, South of France; first century BC *(after Py 1990).*

way of Italy, which no doubt was the main link, stone-built shines occur in Etruria at least from the Archaic period on (Bonfante 1986). Although the Mediterranean impact was doubtless important, we should not view the common and well-documented creation of sacred structures and formalized permanent sanctuaries in temperate Europe at the end of the first millennium BC solely in terms of the then massive impact from the Mediterranean during the Hellenistic period. (Possibly, the Mediterranean impact also led to the powerful institution of the Celtic Druids that Caesar describes.) The tradition of a sanctuary with particular features is a much longer one in Central Europe, as described above, manifest from the beginning of the Iron Age. The formal sanctuary, to judge from the abrupt disappearance of deposits of metal artefacts at the time of its introduction, most probably implied new cultic practices, perhaps also with Mediterranean inspiration, but with little, if any, of the Mediterranean, in casu Creek (or Etruscan) architectural language of sanctuary and temple.

Nevertheless, these were not the earliest sacred sites with a structure to the north of the Alps. In Denmark, for instance, small cult-houses from around 3000 BC are examples of such very early consecrated buildings (Fig. 29). These either seem to represent an independent development or, perhaps, very early contacts with the south, resulting in the construction of sacred facilities differing from common 'open-air' sanctuaries. The idea obviously was to create a small secluded and intimate room, like a house or a grave. This is quite the reverse of the supposed (or potentially) 'public' displays and sacrifices at, for instance, the holy bogs of Southern Scandinavia or, in 3000 BC, for instance, the ritual causeway camp enclosures (Fig. 28).

With the Neolithic cave-like passage graves in mind, communication between the dead and the living may be the rationale behind the cult-houses, perhaps involving initiation rites. The same may also be the case in Nordic Bronze Age finds like Sandagergård and the long structures at Kivik (Fig. 30) (Kaul 1985; Randsborg 1993). In a Romanian case, Sălacea (Ordentlich 1972), Aegean Middle Bronze Age rooms (in houses and palaces) or buildings with cultic facilities might be the parallels (Fig. 33). But also here the functional purpose of the structure may have been an ancestor-cult and/or shamanistic rituals, initiation rites, etc., probably quite different from the worship of the Mediterranean. In fact, in the Aegean, names of later Greek gods appear, at least from the Late Bronze Age on, although 'healers' and shamans, in one kind or another, most likely existed in the Aegean, too.

Thus, the rise of post-Bronze Age sanctuaries in temperate

Europe is rather connected with the institutionalized and elite-led worship of a pantheon of anthropomophic gods. Certainly, the many constructions after c. 300 BC, and the written texts from the end of the millennium, set a terminus ante quem for the arrival of this kind of beliefs and worship in trans-Alpine Europe. But probably, indeed, most likely, it was introduced or generated much earlier, at least in rudimentary forms.

Thus, Hjortspring and similar 'one-dimensional' sacrifices from the latest Bronze Age and the pre-Roman Iron Age in Northern Europe were probably also to specified anthropomorphic deities. Through the different classes of archaeologically defined deposits and sacrifices of valuables, we may even suggest that these structural ritual traditions reached back into the Early Neolithic of the fourth millennium BC, whether or not they already then had a specified anthropomorphic frame of reference attached to them.

The basic forces identified are the chthonic ones, the fertility gods. But also the forces of the sky must have been worshipped in an early period, indeed, possibly, already during the remote Mesolithic, to judge by the orientation of the graves of such hunting communities in Southern Scandinavia. The burials were, in fact, all positioned within the compass segment of summer and winter sunrise or sunset, or, on the north-south axis, of the powerful midday position of the supreme celestial body (Randsborg & Nybo 1984).

PART III

---

9. Early Warfare

> Gilgamesh took the axe, he slung the quiver from his shoulder,
> and the bow of Anshan (district), and buckled the sword (dirk)
> to his belt; and so they were armed ...
> From 'The Epic of Gilgamesh' (third millennium BC)

A. The Mid-first Millennium BC

The weaponry and tactics of the Greek hoplite infantryman, the
central conception in the present military context, found their final
form no later than c. 650 BC (cf. Fig. 1). However, the particular
style of hoplite combat may be slightly earlier, as simple phalanx
infantry tactics certainly were. The hoplite spear/lance is a much
cheaper weapon than the aristocratic sword, but the heavy armour
(apart from the shield) represents a substantial investment for the
warrior. (Near Eastern armies, in particular Neo-Assyrian Spearmen, may have provided some of the inspiration for hoplite
weaponry and tactics.)

On Greek vases of the later Geometric period (c. 850-700 BC)
swords make up almost half the weapons depicted in action, spears
(lances) only one quarter (van Wees 1994) (Fig. 39). On proto-
Corinthian vases (700-650 BC), by contrast, spears/lances make up
almost 90% of the weapons shown in use. Interestingly, the combat
weapons mentioned in Homer's Iliad are also mainly spears/lances
(about 80%). Homer is no doubt describing the military tactics of
his own period, while making allusions to traditional knowledge
of Bronze Age weaponry, etc.

Hoplite tactics may have made an impact on Central Europe,
most likely by way of Etruria and northeastern Italy, alternatively

BC	850-750	750-700	700-650	ILIAD
Sword	9 (53%)	20 (41%)	2 (5%)	19 (9%)
Spear/lance	4 (24%)	12 (24%)	34 (87%)	166 (81%)
Arrow	4 (24%)	17 (35%)	3 (8%)	21 (10%)

Fig. 39. Weapons wielded on Greek vase paintings, and weapons used in battles mentioned in Homer's Iliad (based on van Wees 1994). Of the 166 spear/lances in The Iliad, 87 were thrown (spears or javelins) and an about equal number, 79, thrusted (lances). (The percentages of the period 850-750 BC are only indicative.)

A marked change in weaponry is noted around 700 BC with a sharp decline in the number of swords and (bows &) arrows, and an almost total dominance of spear/lance in the early seventh century. Furthermore, the type of combat described in Homer is clearly the contemporary one with spear/lance as the main weapon (phalanx).

by the difficult route across the Balkans, from about the beginning of the late early Iron Age, the so-called Hallstatt D period (the sixth century BC). However, the particular heavy standardized armour and huge round shield (for protection as well as shoving) of the hoplite were not introduced into Central Europe. In fact, the oval shield, originally an Italian so-called Villanova Culture, or, Early Iron Age/Central European Late Bronze Age, invention, was preferred from the seventh century BC on (Stary 1981b) (Fig. 59). What seems certain is merely the existence of an inspiration from infantry phalanx warfare in general, redefined to serve aristocratic purposes, with lance (as the main offensive weapon), supposedly shield, and, if wealth allowed, helmet and possibly cuirass.

Depending on the absolute chronology, perhaps already in the eighth, but certainly in the seventh century BC, a preference for spear/lance (very often more than one) and axe weapons was shared between the northern parts of Italy and the eastern Alpine regions, previously dominated, in particular, by long swords (cf. Stary 1982) (cf. Figs. 54 & 58). This is exactly the period when Etruria was strongly influenced by Near Eastern weapons, including heavy daggers, heart armour and round ornamented shields, in use along with the common spear/lance. The iron dagger was particularly common in Italy in the (early) seventh century BC. Indeed, it linked wide regions of the Mediterranean between the Near East, Italy and Iberia (Schüle 1969).

The popularity of the heavy dagger probably stemmed from its use as a main weapon by the powerful Neo-Assyrian armies. However, from the late seventh century BC on, the Greek impact on the Etruscan weaponry, involving hoplite equipment, quickly became highly marked; in the sixth century BC even modified hoplite tactics were, apparently, adopted (Stary 1979). Significantly, at first the heavy dagger and then the axe went out of use following the introduction of the Greek-style weaponry.

In the western Alpine and adjacent regions, the long bronze and iron swords of the Hallstatt C period, usually found in graves as the main or single weapon (cf. Gerdsen 1986), were in the subsequent Hallstatt D period abruptly replaced by the heavy iron dagger, now, ironically, going out of fashion in Etruria. The long sword first appeared in temperate Europe (probably from the Aegean) at the beginning of the Middle Bronze Age and remained for a thousand years, all the way through the Late Bronze Age and the first phase of the Iron Age (Hallstatt C), the single most prestigious weapon in western Central Europe (as in the North).

Furthermore, the sixth century BC is the period of substantial Etruscan, Greek, and other exportation, in particular from Marseilles, and by way of the Rhône River, of luxuries for the regional trading princes of western Central Europe. In chambered graves from huge mounds around fortified centres, fine furniture, four-wheeled parade waggons or chariots, cauldrons (including the famous huge Archaic Greek one from Vix, eastern France), noble dresses, etc. (but almost no weapons, except for the personal dagger and the bow and arrow for hunting) have been found. Even the Greek style of brick (or pisé) fortification walls with bastions, on stone foundations, was put into use in moist Central Europe, as at the archaeologically renowned Heuneburg hill-fort on the upper Danube in southwestern Germany.

From southeastern Austria and Slovenia, along the upper Drau/Drava river, come a limited number of seventh and sixth century BC graves with fine cuirasses and/or helmets. These, along with other more humble burials, all dominated by axes, are frequently equipped with one or, usually, more spears/lances. Most interesting in the military context are the depictions on the famous both contemporary and slightly later situla (from princely graves mainly in northeasternmost Italy and Slovenia (cf. above)) of marching, almost uniformly equipped and dressed infantrymen. These most probably fought in phalanges, in particular because they are carrying Hjortspring-like shields, lances (sometimes two), and axes (for close combat), and wearing different kinds of helmets (sometimes with a feathered crest); also light cavalry is common in situla art (for example, Frey 1969). The Slovenian princes also owned, for instance, ceremonial waggons — here, as in Italy, with only two wheels — although these were not placed in the graves, as was commonly the case in the old Celtic lands in the west (as well as in Bohemia) (Pare 1992; Parzinger & Stegmann-Rajtár 1988).

Further to the north, for instance at Smolenice in southwestern Slovakia, southern luxuries and impacts are fewer, and the social milieu seemingly less wealthy, although Italian imports are not unknown in the general region.

Thus, approaching the age of Hjortspring (fourth century BC), we might soon have jumped to Northern Europe. However, to put the Hjortspring sacrifice into both international and regional perspective, a longer view is at first taken.

B. The Stone Age

The history of regulated, whether ritualized or otherwise organized, combat in Europe to the north of the Mediterranean did, however, not start in the sixth century BC. In fact, already in the Early Neolithic in Denmark (fourth millennium BC) battle-axes with shaft-holes and mace-heads, both of elaborate shapes, were common, indicating, although hardly surprising to anthropologists, the existence of close fighting with items designed as weapons (for instance, Gardner & Heider 1968 for Stone Age warfare in near-contemporary New Guinea). Violence as such is, of course, a much earlier phenomenon, as finds from the Mesolithic period in Denmark of bodies, shot by bow and arrow or stabbed by bone- or antler-pointed hunting and fishing spears, reveal (Albrethsen & Petersen 1976). Indeed, hunting weapons are equally suitable for killing animals and humans.

Interestingly, these very first finely polished battle-axes in stone from Denmark, as well as most other similar, indeed, often quite identical specimens from Central or other parts of Europe, may, directly or indirectly, have been inspired by battle-axes in copper in Southeastern Europe. The very earliest shaft-hole axes in copper in southeastern Europe are probably, although archaeological contexts are very rare, even from the late fifth millennium BC (cf. Whittle 1985; Západocký 1991; generally, Lichardus 1991; 1992). The production of the latter items was a highly significant and very advanced metallurgical accomplishment, in particular the casting of items with holes and of 'three-dimensional' shape, not flat, like simple axes, for instance.

Metal lends itself easily to the dimensions of prestige and status connected with primitive warfare. Originally, however, the copper battle-axe must have taken its own form from crude perforated axes of stone or antler/bone. In the same way, the far more common, and quite early, flat axe of copper took its shape from polished axe-blades of stone or flint. Incidentally, the Neolithic way of fighting (with bow and arrow, and axe or mace-head) is also reflected in the many trepanations of the period, seemingly mainly carried out to mend combat wounds. These trepanations are almost always on the left side of the skull, where blows from battle-axes and clubs or mace-heads (by right-handed opponents) are received (cf. Bennike 1985, for Denmark).

In the third millennium BC, the dagger — accompanied by the halberd and, in particular, the increasingly common flat metal axe — is the dominating personal or 'dress' weapon, whether manu-factured in flint or copper. The copper daggers are the likely pre-cise prototypes for those in flint. (Again, the very first crude dag-gers were no doubt in bone or antler.) At the very end of the third millennium BC, the first daggers in bronze occur. Metal daggers are even included in graves, only rarely holding the heavier (thus, more costly) metal axes (e.g., Krause 1988, for southwestern Germany).

Although the copper shaft-hole axe and, later, the copper dag-ger and halberd probably did not revolutionize Stone Age warfare, they were true weapons, and not, like the flat copper axe — along with jewellery the first metal artefact in history — merely a metal edition of a tool (cum weapon). Furthermore, while the intro-duction of the dagger and the halberd was no doubt conditioned by new developments in Stone Age metallurgy (for example, casting in double-moulds), socially and symbolically, the agent was

an increasing need for underlining the status of particular personalities through conspicuous consumption of luxuries.

The recent, already world-renowned find of the extraordinarily
well-preserved 'Ice-man', from about 3300 BC, found in the Simi-
laun glacier in the high Ötztaler Alps on the Austrian/Italian frontier, highlights the tools/weapons of the late Stone Age man equipped for hunting and fighting (Höpfel et al. 1992). The weapons consisted of a long-bow and a large leather quiver with arrows, a
copper-axe, slightly flanged, in a bent wooden shaft, and a short
flint-dagger/knife in a braided grass-scabbard with a marble bead.
Incidentally, the Ice-man also carried two birch-bark boxes (the one
for carrying burning charcoal) and a leather rucksack with a
wooden frame. The highly interesting layered clothing (woolen tex-
tiles were not yet in use) consisted of a leather belt cum purse
containing, among other things, three flint artefacts, a bone awl,
tinder for fire-making and a blackthorn. Fur-leggings were attached
to garters in the belt; the loin-cloth and the grass-lined tied shoes
were of leather. The coat and the cap (with chin-straps) were of fur
and, finally, the mantle was of grass.

Unlike the copper shaft-hole axe, which, it would seem, is a
European patent, the development and particular status (if not the
invention) of the dagger and the halberd were no doubt inspired,
however indirectly, by the weaponry of the armies of the early
states and civilizations of the Near East of the late fourth and, in
particular, the third millennium BC (cf. the above Gilgamesh
quotation). These warriors were equipped with daggers, axes or
clubs, halberds (or, rather, edged clubs), spears and light shields
plus bows and arrows. Indeed, the Egyptian armies maintained
much of this Stone Age ethos of combat and battle, represented by
simply and lightly equipped troops, until well into the first
millennium BC (the Iron Age is a remarkably late introduction in
Egypt). For instance, armour and helmets were not worn, and the
shield remained light.

The dagger, the flat metal axe (now clearly flanged), and the
halberd were also the prime weapons of the Early Bronze Age in
Central Europe, of the late third to early second millennium BC
(parallel with the Late Neolithic in Denmark). Towards the middle
of the second millennium BC, however, both the bronze sword and
the bronze socketed spearhead (to judge from its shape and size

mainly for lances, in duels no doubt also used as metal-tipped fighting-staves) were introduced in both Central and Northern Europe. (Long daggers or dirks were known somewhat earlier in both Greece and Spain.)

This remarkable development indicates that a major step was now taken away from the Stone Age kind of either distant (bow and arrow, and stone missiles) or very close, thus personalized combat, in fact duels at close quarters with much bodily contact (axe, dagger, etc.), towards middle-range tactics, paving the way for mobile infantry and other later tactics. While the metal-tipped spear and/or lance were perhaps the most important innovations, in use throughout among both high and low, the costly sword came to signify the highly personal, almost mystical and often very well-made weapon with an aristocratic air about it. The sword was, for many centuries to come, to symbolize personal standing, while the lance was rather a symbol of adulthood and authority (cf. earlier the axe).

C. The Bronze Age

In the Near East, the introduction of the light and, in particular, very fast horse-drawn chariot (with two, usually four- or six-spoked, wheels) manned by a driver and, for instance, a bowman, revolutionized warfare in the period after (perhaps even around) 2000 BC (e.g. Shaw 1991). (Related vehicles may be a full millennium earlier on the Steppes.) The same did the invention, probably slightly later, of the strong composite bow with its enormous range. This bow, requiring high and particular skills, was never much used to the west of the Steppes, perhaps because of battle conventions, but more likely due to the limited employment of mounted bowmen in most of Europe throughout its later history. The light chariot appeared in the Aegean at about the same time as in the Near East (or, rather, a little later) and was already known in Scandinavia before 1300 BC. In Central Europe (the eastern parts) and in Scandinavia it was certainly not used as a massed weapon of manouevre battle, but rather for aristocratic ceremonial and ritual purposes, although such may also apply in war (Pare 1992, 12f). In the Aegean, war-chariots may have been used to ferry the commanders around on the battle-field and to provide mobility and shock (van Wees 1994).

A long debate, inspired by Homer's epics, about the nature of Bronze Age warfare, has given rise to the idea that fighting primarily took the form of duels between high-ranking opponents, the role of the commoners being mainly that of bystanders (and guards) (cf. van Wees 1994, with references). This interpretation is probably wrong; certainly the chariots, however few, were not merely 'taxis' to the battle-field for the heroes and aristocrats, but in use as a cavalry before true cavalry. (Regular cavalry was hardly employed before the Iron Age, or, in the early first millennium BC.) In the Aegean, Late Bronze Age weaponry, apart from bows and arrows, was dominated by long piercing metal weapons, whether swords or lances, which may have been handled from chariots too (Fig. 40). The pictorial representations of fighting are rather of combat between ranks of infantry with spears (lances), swords, helmets, and, truly huge shields of organic materials for protection only (not for shoving), but no axes (Doumas 1992, 45f; Marinatos (et al.) 1960, Pl. XXXVI: a hunt, though); sometimes, heavy metal (and quite primitive) body-armour was also used. Seemingly, fighting was not overly dangerous to the participants.

Larger contingents of warriors, in particular sailors, must have been employed in naval campaigns, of which the legendary expedition to Troy is a much exaggerated example. Homer's total forces against Troy (Iliad II, the so-called Catalogue of Ships) were 1,186 ships from 29 kingdoms or realms in southern and central Greece (ironically, in the light of current nationalistic debate, northern Greece, Macedonia and Thrace, and western Asia Minor, sided with Troy). These ships were, supposedly, each manned by from 30 to 120 men (in all, perhaps 100,000 men). The logistics needed to keep such forces in the field for years on end are even beyond the ability of most modern nations. Still, the existence of naval expeditions in the Aegean Bronze Age is not in doubt, some are even depicted in art, and in great detail, including the famous miniature frescos of the West House of Akrotiri, Thera (Doumas 1992, 45f).

To some extent this picture of Aegean combat in the mid- to late second millennium BC can also be applied to Central and Northern Europe. Swords and spears (lances) were widespread, axes and daggers very common too. In the North, very thick woolen felt-caps were worn for helmets, and heavy mantles, as carried over the one arm, may have been in use for 'shields' and

	Sword	Dagger	Lance	Axe	Knife	Arrow	Helmet	Armour
MYCENAE	14	14	7	–	8	1	2(+)	–
LATER	7	10	7	2	8	3	4	2

Fig. 40. Numbers of graves with different types of weapon (very often several specimens of the same kind of weapon in each burial) in: (A) the two princely shaft-grave circles at Mycenae, Greece (early to mid-second millennium BC); and (B) among princely graves from the mid- to late second millennium BC in Greece (source Kilian-Dirlmeier 1986). In two of the late graves with knifes, the specimens are very heavy.

The weaponry is clearly of pre-phalanx type, sword and dagger dominating, lance only playing a secondary role.

other protection. Metal or metal-covered shields were not yet in use. In Central Europe, some metal studs, perhaps from small round wooden shields, are recorded from (about) the 14th century bc on (Schauer 1980; Stary 1980) (cf. Fig. 41); in the North, both a few such studs are known and some gold-foil discs (from graves) which may have been symbolic small round shields (Randsborg 1967 (re-interpretation); 1993). Nevertheless, the seeming (or near) lack of proper shields would have made fighting both relatively mobile and quite dangerous, especially against opponents with swords and spears. Certainly, this would have implied the use of middle-range battle-techniques (rather than close-range ones). Perhaps, fighting was even ritualized and carried out, at least at some stage, as single or massed duels.

A sample of so-called chiefly graves from southern Germany and adjacent areas, defined by the presence of swords (etc.), is available for the periods between Middle Bronze Age C 1 and Late Bronze Age Period Hallstatt A 2 (Stary 1980) (cf. Fig. 43, with Figs. 41-42). We note that axes and daggers, manisfesting Stone Age fighting techniques, were still accompanying the sword in the early periods. Lances, few as they may be, because of the cremation rites of the late periods, constitute, with the sword (and the powerful so-called hunting-knife), the standard aristocratic weaponry of the Late Bronze Age, as well as of the earliest Iron Age in these regions. We are, unfortunately, less well informed about the common combatants, since weapons, on the whole, are rare in graves and

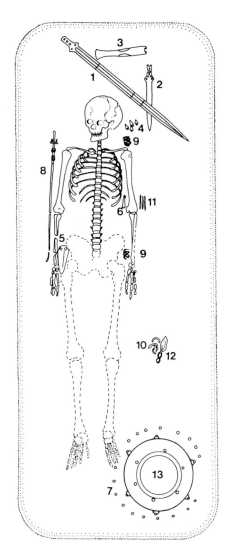

Fig. 41. Richly equipped grave from Hagenau at Regenstauf, Kreis Regensburg in Southern Germany; c. 1300 BC (after Stary 1980). The bronze bosses may have ornated a small wooden shield.

practically confined to the supposed aristocratic ones. Probably the axe, and in the early phase also the dagger, and the staff/lance plus, of course, the bow and arrow were the main weapons of ordinary warriors.

To judge from contemporary representations of boats, for instance from Denmark, vessels existed in the Bronze Age that were at least the size of Hjortspring. These boats had crews which, if properly armed, would have constituted small armies (the boat

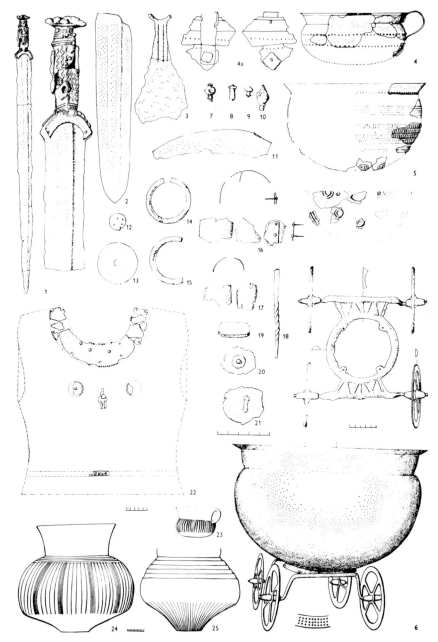

Fig. 42. Richly equipped grave from Milavče, Domazlice Cechy district, western Bohemia; 13th century BC (after Kytlicová 1988). Note the supposed leather cuirass.

GRAVES		Sword	Dagger	Axe	Lance	Knife	Arrow	Gold	Waggon
C1	(26)	26	18	22	–	–	(5)	(10)	–
C2	(28)	27	9/10	11	1	1	(9)	(6)	–
D	(33)	32	3	–	8	7	(2)	(1)	–
HaA1	(24)	23	1	–	3	17	(5)	(2)	3
HaA2	(18)	18	–	–	2	12	(3)	(-)	–

Fig. 43. Chiefly graves (so-called; as defined by the presence of swords, etc.), from Southern Germany and adjacent regions, including Bohemia, between the Middle Bronze Age period (Reinecke) C 1 (c. 1400 BC/Nordic Period II) and the Late Bronze Age period Hallstatt (Ha) A 2 (1100/1000 BC/Nordic early Period IV). The numbers of different items are listed, except for bronze arrows and golden artefacts where only the number of graves with such are indicated (in brackets). The number of graves in each period is also listed (in brackets).

The diagram reflects the very end of Stone Age fighting techniques for Central European Bronze Age commanders (dagger and axe accompanying the sword) and the rise of the Late Bronze Age set of weapons comprising sword, lance, and knife. In the Hallstatt A phases, dominated by cremation, the burial goods tend to be scarce. Note the transition from axe to lance (as the main weapon during the early stages of combat before recourse is taken to the sword) between Periods C2 and D, or, about 1300 BC. (Data are extracted from Stary 1980.)

depicted on the Early Bronze Age Rørby-sword (Aner & Kersten 1976, No. 617), for instance, has a crew of more than 30). In fact, the Hjortspring boat represents the likely last of a long line of 'Bronze Age' double-prowed vessels, well known from the rock-carvings. With a slight change of the character of crew it can actually be brought to represent one of the models of proposed Bronze Age fighting, the duels, perhaps ritualized, between aristocrats and their followers (rather than phalanx-warfare) (cf. Fig. 19).

The commanders on the small decorated deck are in this narrative the aristocrats; normally they do not participate in the paddling. The ordinary warriors are paddlers (on land retainers, bodyguards, and, eventually, fighters); the steersman or -men merely captain(s) of the vessel. Indeed, the very large sacrifice from a bog at Smørumovre, Zealand, dated to Period II of the Early

Bronze Age, may represent a weapon sacrifice pertaining to such a force (Aner & Kersten 1973, No. 354) (Fig. 18). A parallel to the naval frescos of Akrotiri is also noted (Doumas 1992). Here armed aristocrats are ferried by paddlers and a steersman.

Bronze Age bands of combatants would have been led by warriors whose splendid swords and other equipment are found in the thousands of graves from Denmark and neigbouring regions dating to the late first millennium BC. In these individual graves, the prime weapon is the sword in a variety of forms, from a simple dirk with a bone handle to a long flange-handled blade with plates of bone or a full metal-hilted cut-and-thrust sword. Daggers occur (with men and, notably, with women too), and light battle-axes, in some cases as an adjunct to the sword (or dagger). Spears (lances) are rare in the graves, but, like the axes, common in hoards. Arrowheads, interestingly, are also rare, and here the size of the weapon cannot have been a factor. Also a number of the deposits or hoards of the Early Bronze Age seems to reflect the personal weaponry of prominent persons, for instance the exquisite Valsø-magle hoard (Hoard II) from Zealand (Fig. 44).

Furthermore, there is no standardization in the type of equipment, which seems to vary substantially, not least in weight of metal (thus, value). High skills and much energy were invested in embellishing these weapons (as in the appearance of the other bronzes of the Early and Late Nordic Bronze Age), which, aesthetically, are very fine pieces. It is obvious that display played a very important role in Bronze Age warfare.

A summary study of the finds from most of the second millennium on the Danish islands, and in present-day Southern Sweden, specifies the Nordic development in weaponry from the Late Stone Age to the beginning of the Late Bronze Age (Willroth 1985) (Fig. 45). Spears (lances) are at first far more common than the costly swords (even if the latter are supplemented by the daggers). By the middle of the Early Bronze Age (Period II), the sword is, seemingly, the more important weapon of the two. Discounting the hundreds of swords from graves (where spears are practically unknown due to their size), however, the picture is a somewhat more balanced one. In Period III, swords even outrank spears in the hoards and the stray deposits, perhaps indicating the beginning of a phase where 'aristocratic' duels were particularly common. The (battle) axe remains a major weapon/tool till the beginning of the

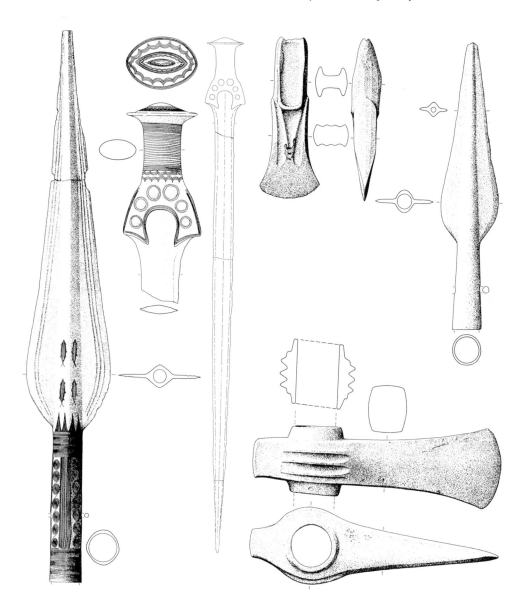

Fig. 44. Deposition or hoard from the Early Bronze Age Period I (late) on dry land (at a boulder) in Valsømagle (Valsømagle hoard II), central Sjælland/ Zealand (after Aner & Kersten 1976, vol. II).

last phase of the Early Bronze Age (Period III), when it practically disappears.

Furthermore, a close correlation has been noted between the

	Halberd	Axe	Palstave	Celt	Dagger	Sword	Spear
NEOLITHIC							
Graves		1					
Hoards	20	115			1		
All finds	23	191			2		
PER. I							
Graves		2					1
Hoards		113			1	11	47
All finds		228			4	13	82
PER. I/II							
Graves		10	2		10	6	4
Hoards		116	42		4	9	30
All finds		228	65		17	17	52
PERIOD II							
Graves		4	70 (54)	2	164	236	20
Hoards		4	293 (35)	10	24	61	84
All finds		12	563 (116)	21	254	413	136
PERIOD III							
Graves					94	245	9
Hoards		1		22	31	37	21
All finds		10		30	192	381	57

Fig. 45. Distribution of selected types of weapons and weapons/tools (axes, palstaves and celts) in different categories of find from the Late Stone Age and Early Bronze Age on the Danish Islands and in Southern Sweden (data, Willroth 1985). Shaft-hole axes (probably mainly ritual) are omitted; they are most common in Period I. The 'All finds' is the total number of a particular type of artefact in all categories of find, including stray-finds. The dating by Willroth of many early items and some later ones is not wholly satisfactory, but the general pattern is reliable. The number of (weapon) Palstaves is indicated in brackets.

The Axes before Period III are all flanged, in Period III they are all winged. (Celts are socketed axes; Palstaves are thick narrow axes with flanges on the upper body.)

At the beginning of the sequence, the investment of metal weapons in burials is highly limited. Later on, personal weapons are included, at first mainly daggers, then swords. Spears (lances) are rare in graves, probably because of the long shaft. Axes dominate the early periods and are, due to the invention of the Palstave, even very common in Period II. Axes are rare in Period III. Apart from the weapon Palstaves, axes are more common in hoards than in graves. In proportion to Spears (lances), Swords become more important over time.

numbers of single axes (67%), swords/daggers (16%) and spears (16%) from the hoards of the Early Bronze Age, and the numbers of the same artefact types (all single, not in use) depicted on Scandinavian rock-carvings (68%, 16%, and 15% respectively) (Willroth 1984). What makes this correlation surprising at first is that rock-carvings in general belong to both the Early and (in particular) the Late Bronze Age. Thus, this observation might, firstly, imply that rock-carving pictures of various items were, in fact, 'offerings', and secondly, that hoard depositions make up the most precise reflection of the contents of an average Nordic Bronze Age armoury. However, the pictures of weapons almost exclusively belong with the rock-carvings in Skåne/Scania (eastern Southern Scandinavia) and in Östergötland (in Eastern Sweden), and may, primarily, be an Early Bronze Age phenomenon (cf. Randsborg 1993).

Further temporal variation among the numbers of weapons in the hoards is noted when the Late Bronze Age is included. The finds of all of Denmark (data in Broholm 1940f; cf. Levy 1984) show that spears were, in fact, far more common than swords in the Early Bronze Age, in Period II thus a high 82% versus 18% (without the huge Smørumovre find (cf. Chapter 2, Excursus B), 70% versus 30%). In Period IV of the Late Bronze Age, however, there are almost twice as many swords (although very costly) as spearheads. As indicated above, the latter Period, with Period III, perhaps constitutes a phase, during the late second millennium and around 1000 BC, dominated by aristocratic duels.

In Period V the numbers of the two main weapons are about equal, perhaps indicating a novel standardization in terms of full aristocratic equipment, incidentally supplemented by rare thin metal shields and helmets (for commanders), among the latter are, for instance, the famous horned and feathered helmets from Viksø, Sjælland/Zealand. These new costly defensive weapons, and especially the shields, may merely represent aristocratic parade or ritual versions of commen wooden or wooden/leather shields and leather helmets, body-armour, etc. However, this is not to say that the metal shields and helmets were not worn in battle, too. The need for the conspicuous is never so critical as in conflict and among the leaders of men in battle. At any rate, such shields are for protection, not for shoving, as in hoplite battles.

Continental Late Bronze Age hoards and other deposits usually also point to an almost equal ratio between swords and spears, for instance the truly huge Vénet hoard from southwestern France (contemporary with Nordic Period V), artefact types in question incidentally having a range of distribution from Denmark and England to Portugal and Sicily (Coffyn et al. 1981). In the German Rhein-Main area, swords and spears from the prestigious ('aristo-cratic') river finds of the Urnfield Culture (parallel with Nordic Periods III to V), the majority of which are late, occur in equal numbers (Hansen 1991, 173). The Swiss lakeside settlements yield roughly the same ratio, lances perhaps even slightly outnumbering swords (Rychner 1979 (for Auvernier) & Bernatzky-Goetze 1987 (for Möringen); both finds are relative late). In the Late Bronze Age hoards of Transylvania (central Romania), the number of swords also seems to be about the same as of spears, although the, albeit relatively early, colossal Uiora de Sus find (5,800 fragments and a high 1,300 kg of bronze) held 93 fragments of swords and only 55 of spearheads (Mozsolics 1985, 23). This find may reflect an early phase of the Late Bronze Age (cf. Nordic Periods III and IV), in which swords are more prominent than spear/lances, the deposits mirroring aristocratic combat (rather than the commoner's).

In fact, a survey of all Danish finds with swords from the Late Bronze Age has yielded 129 specimens from Period IV, 80 from Period IV, but only 8 from Period VI (Jensen 1972); these numbers include, respectively, 44, 53, and 8 swords from wet areas and from hoards on dry land (all sacrifices, no doubt). The numbers of spear-heads from the same Bronze Age periods are, respectively, 37, 62, and nil (finds from wet areas and from hoards on dry land make up 22, 35, and nil specimens, respectively). Again we see that the sword is prominent in Period IV, while the spear is more equally represented in Period V.

From early in Nordic Period VI (contemporaneous with the Early Iron Age or so-called Hallstatt-culture in Central Europe, periods Hallstatt C and D, c. 800-500 BC) and until the Hjortspring find, weapons are, de facto, unknown in Scandinavian finds (cf. the above statistics, and Jensen 1966, for the imported Hallstatt C-swords from Northern Europe). Changes in the character of the ritual finds (and of the burial customs) account for this and mean that the crucial phase when the development towards phalanx warfare in Greece (and Italy) took place, with massed infantry tac-tics in which the shield and the (rather cheap) lance — as in Hjort-spring — are the central and standardized elements, is indeed poorly illuminated as far as military affairs in the Nordic region are concerned. However, we are not completely without means to track the roots of Hjortspring even from earlier southern inspirations than those of the crucial fourth century BC of the sacrifice.

The development in Central Europe during the Hallstatt culture was described above (cf. Chapter 9A). In the eastern Alpine region, as well as in adjacent northeastern Italy, representations on situlae of the sixth (to fifth) century BC depict similarly equipped infantrymen with spear and shield as the main weapons (cf. Fig. 66). Also some cavalry, equipped in the same basic fashion, are seen. Emerging phalanx techniques may also be detected in the western Alpine preference, from the sixth century BC, for the heavy dagger (replacing the earlier sword) and the spear/lance. Indeed, in the same period, similar trends in military equipment and tactics can be traced right to the southern Baltic.

D. Passentin and Beyond

From a stream and bog at Passentin on Lake Mallin (Kreis Waren), central Mecklenburg, North Germany, comes an early and highly interesting military sacrifice made up of 51 iron spearheads, as in Bronze Age hoards without their shafts (Schoknecht 1974) (Fig. 46). No swords were found with the deposits. The spearheads lay within an area of only two sq.m, thus also resembling the circumstances of find of a Bronze Age hoard or sacrifice. The items are dated to about the sixth century BC (similar spearheads were also made in bronze). Unfortunately, only 36 (71%) specimens reached the museum, two broken ones were thrown away, while the whereabouts of the remaining spearheads, despite the find being a fairly recent one, remain unknown.

The spearheads of the Passentin sacrifice are rather similar and therefore difficult to divide into categories. The longer the blade, the greater the width; this relationship is thus unimportant for classification. The length of the blade or, rather, of the entire spearhead and the length of its socket, however, may yield some clues to the composition of the fighting unit of the find.

One fine, powerful specimen has a very long ornamented slit socket with a bronze ring around it. Three or, rather, four (the last one is fragmentary) short (less than 30 cm), but splendid spearheads with long sockets (10 cm and more) resemble the first one;

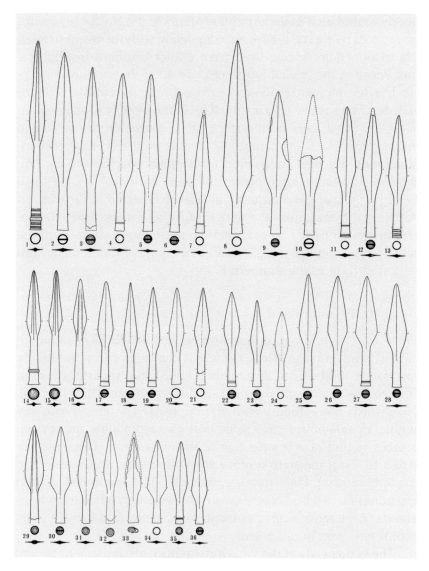

Fig. 46. Iron spearheads from the Passentin hoard/military sacrifice from Mecklenburg, North Germany, dated to (about) the sixth century BC (after Schoknecht 1974).

these five all narrow-bladed spearheads, apt for penetration, may make up a group of their own in which the transition between shaft and head is strengthened at the same time as the shaft, if broken, is easy to replace. The fine specimens, thus, may have been made for particular use. 12 common spearheads are long (up to 48 cm), but have relatively short sockets (nearly all less than 10 cm). The remaining 19 spearheads are short and have short sockets too. We may thus, if simply pairing the spears/lances, have some 19 javelins and about the same number (5 + 12 = 17) of lances.

Thus, at least one, possibly even four or (rather) five, 'commanders' or seniors (perhaps even horsemen; in contemporary Central Europe, they may even have included a charioteer) are detected, along with a group of common infantrymen, perhaps 12-14. (We are here drawing on the models of phalanx-type warfare developed in connection with the above analyses of Hjortspring and Krogsbølle, cf. Figs. 13 & 15, among other.) If the seniors carried lances only (except for one, possibly joining the ordinary warriors), three scenarios are possible: (1) Half the common warriors with lance, possibly the front rank, have two spears (cf. Hjortspring). (2) A group of about six warriors have only spears, thus giving the following numbers of fighters: five seniors + twelve common + six light (probably young) = 23. (3) The number of common warriors, all equally equipped, may have been 15-16. (The original number of warriors is, due to the loss of 29% of the spear-heads, throughout, one third higher.)

At any rate, the strong emphasis on spears/lances in Passentin, even in novel iron, clearly reflects the general development towards hoplite-type weaponry and phalanx-type tactics, however diluted and transformed, in, respectively, the Mediterranean (earlier than Passentin) and Central Europe (more or less parallel with the Mecklenburg find). The lack of shields in the Passentin deposit is possibly due to the circumstances of find, though. Incidentally, the Passentin platoon (with 51 lances and spears in all) was most probably of about the same size (or slightly larger) as the crew of the, albeit somewhat later Hjortspring boat.

Another highly interesting North European, although still not Nordic, indication of the emergence and spread of the phalanx and its weaponry seems to be present in the extraordinary Polish 'face-urns' of the so-called middle phase, also dated to about the sixth century BC (La Baume 1963) (Figs. 47-48), rather earlier than later. These urns come from the region between the middle Oder and the lower-middle Vistula rivers, and are thus not far from the Baltic. More important, the vessels are from the same general region as the famous slightly earlier fortresses of Biskupin type

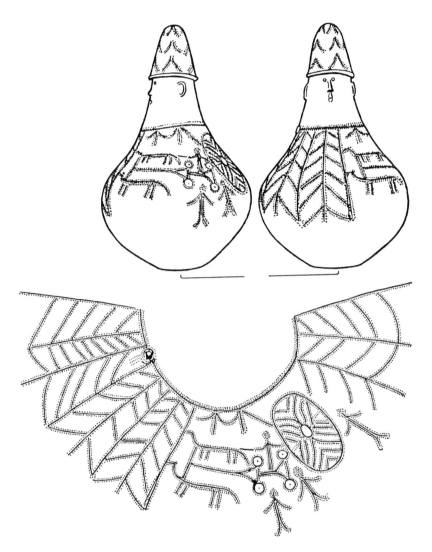

Fig. 47. Face-urn, found at Grabów near Starogard to the south of Gdánsk (German Grabau at Stargard south of Danzig), northern Poland, sixth century BC (after La Baume 1963).

(e.g., Bukowski 1961; Ostoja-Zagórski 1983; Niesiołowska-Wędzka 1989; Jaskanisa 1991; Ważny 1993 for new dendro-dates) (Fig. 49).

More than a few of the 'male' face-urns from the said region display simple representations of horsemen, often carrying spears, seemingly mainly engaged in hunts, and of waggons or chariots

Horseman	13
– with one spear	7
– with two spears	6
Waggon	11
Human with one spear	2
– with two spears	2
One spear	4
Two spears	25
Three spears	2
Sword/dagger	2
Shield/shield-boss	27

Fig. 48. Weapons and related equipment depicted on Polish 'Face-urns' of, about, the sixth century BC (data, La Baume 1963). Concerning transportation, no boats are seen (only horses and waggons). The riders often participate in hunts. The Waggons (with four wheels) comprise horse(s) (and driver). The single weapons (and jewellery, etc.), seemingly, belong to the person represented by the face-urn.

(with four wheels). More common, however, are the items that 'belong' to the face-urn, in casu a symbolic rendering of a human being, whose cremated bones the vessel contains: spears/lances (usually two) with short tips and shields (or shield-bosses); only a few swords/daggers are seen (Fig. 48). The numerical distribution of the weapons and related items on the face-urns thus seems to indicate a local adaptation to the current weaponry of Central and Southern Europe, the centuries around 500 BC indeed making up the very age of infantry lance fighting. However, fighting-scenes are lacking on the Polish urns (the hunts are the nearest thing to fighting), more stress being put on display. Significantly, as regards mobility, no boats are shown, only the waggon and the riding-horse, prime status symbols of Central Europe, in spite of the fact that the many rivers of the region are navigable. Probably the boats in the interior of Poland were small and thus of limited social prestige.

Biskupin itself, with a system of parallel lanes and more than

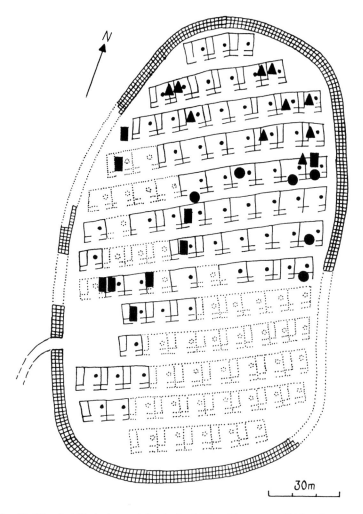

Fig. 49. The fortified planned (or 'colonial') settlement at Biskupin, east-central Poland. Late eighth to seventh century BC. The distribution of activities on the site (in spite of the similarity of size and lay-out of the house-structures) is, incidentally, as follows:

In the early phase, agricultural implements concentrate in the north, refuse from the production of artefacts of antler in the eastern part of the settlement. — In the late phase (plan) items related to agriculture (and horses) are found in all sectors (not shown), those to weaving (rectangles) in the west, to fishing (triangles) in the north, and to bronze-working (dots) in the eastern part of the settlement. (Figure (re)drawn by M. Randsborg; other data extracted from Niesiołowska-Wędzka 1989; Ważny 1993 for new dendro-dates).

100 houses of identical size and lay-out, must be a planned settlement, possibly a 'colony', probably even inspired from planned cities of the Mediterranean, for instance, Greek colonies in southern Italy (Fig. 49). Central Poland is, during this period, linked with eastern Central Europe and even Italy, as exemplified by the northward distibution of Etruscan stick-chains (for hanging pyxides) (Kromer 1986, 23f with Abb. 22-23). A hoard found at faraway Hassle, Glanshammar parish, Närke, in Central Sweden — apart from a couple of Hallstatt C bronze swords — even contained a huge Greek or, rather, Etruscan cauldron, and, among other things, two ribbed situlae from North(eastern) Italy, and 12 circular iron-rimmed discs, perhaps so-called heart armour (or horse-trappings), possibly also from Italy (Stjernquist 1967, etc.).

Incidentally, a surprising number of central Polish and Scythian artefacts have been found within a very limited area on the eastern coast of Jutland (near the town of Vejle). These items, probably arriving by way of the Oder estuary, perhaps even denote a colonization attempt in Denmark (Jensen 1969; cf. Bukowski 1977). In such a social setting, regarded from whichever party, a military organization is a necessity. Indeed, the phalanx seems to be an almost logical extension of the solidarity, uniformity, and planning invested in the creation of the Biskupin fortress and its several sisters from the same region.

10. The Rise of Infantry

I don't like a tall general, swaggering,
proud of his curls, with a fancy shave.
I'd rather have a short man, who looks bow-legged,
with a firm stride, full of heart.
  Archilochos (c. 680-640 BC)

A. After the Bronze Age

From about the year 1300 to the early first millennium BC, the weaponry in both the western part of the Near East, the Aegean and Central and Northern Europe, displays some remarkably similar elements. These came about through elite communication (including trade) and even migrations of armies and supporting populations. Much of this identity in weaponry is functional, but there are also common and rather specific typological traits, in spite of the fact that weapon production was mostly local.

In Europe, common types of (1) flanged sword and dagger blades, in fact Central European types extended to the Aegean and beyond, were accompanied, but, seemingly, only in Central Europe and the Aegean, by: (2) metal and other helmets, often with horns (bronze helmets were a Near Eastern invention adopted by the Aegean in the 14th century BC, in Denmark in the same century thick woolen felted caps of similar shape were worn for protection against blows); (3) small bossed and fluted round bronze-shields (probably at first used in the Aegean, but metal-studded wooden round-shields, and possibly ritual ones covered by gold foil, may have been in use as early as the 14th century BC in, respectively, Central Europe and Denmark (Schauer 1980 (Fig. 41); Randsborg 1967 (cf. a possibly reinterpretation of the studs in the Ørskovhede grave); 1993); (4) bronze cuirasses (perhaps even a Central European invention: the well-known find from the princely Čaka grave, Slovakia, being the best illuminated of several early specimens (Točík & Paulík 1960; cf., e.g., Mozsolics 1985, 25f for a Hungarian find; a metal-studded leather cuirass seems to come from the rich Milavče grave, Bohemia (Kytlicová 1988) (Fig. 42)); and, (5) Bronze greaves, which were known in both the Aegean and in Central Europe (to the south of the Danube) since the early first millennium BC (Schauer 1982). Bronze shields have a wider distribution than the greaves, but the many very thin specimens may primarily have been for ceremonial purposes; in close fighting they are relatively useless. In Scandinavia bronze cuirasses and greaves were apparently unknown, while shields and the very rare metal helmets may have served ritual and display in connection with both parade and combat, the two, or, rather, three activities probably being interlinked, as the rock-carvings would seem to imply.

In the Aegean, this new equipment, however 'aristocratic' it may have seemed to peoples living further north, must be seen in the light of the emergence of a new mobile light infantryman with standard equipment for middle-range fighting. He is, for instance, depicted on the well-known so-called 'Warrior-Vase' of the 12th century BC, wearing a horned helmet and possibly leather armour, and carrying a light shield and a spear, but no sword, although this is common in contemporary finds (Fig. 50). Also from, for instance, Cyprus (Enkomi) come Late Bronze Age representations of such warriors (Müller-Karpe 1980, Taf. 188, B1).

Highly significantly, similar representations are seen on the famous reliefs from Rameses III's (c. 1190-1158 BC) temple at Medinet Habu, Luxor, depicting the victories over intruding 'Peoples of the Sea', perhaps from Cyprus (Fig. 51). The latter attacked Egypt and the eastern Mediterranean by sea and by land from the late 13th century BC on, Egypt, notably, around 1182 BC (e.g., Müller-Karpe 1980, Taf. 71 and, especially, Taf. 72-75; cf. Kemp 1989, 227). The Peoples of the Sea wear horned helmets, carry round rather large but still light shields (manoeuvrable with the hand only), and are equipped with long swords. Their boats, or rather ships, in this very rare depiction of an early battle at sea, have (fighting) platforms at either end each embellished with the large head of a web-footed bird: symbolically uniting the sky and the waters and a favoured idiom of the Central European Late Bronze Age Urnfield Culture and other groupings of the centuries around 1000 BC.

Such relatively similarly equipped Aegean and other shielded light foot-soldiers, carrying spears as the first offensive weapon, but certainly using swords too, may, during the opening stages of battle (on land), have been fighting in a phalanx-like formation (as

Fig. 50. The so-called 'Warrior-Vase' from Mycenae, Greece (after Marinatos 1960). 12th century BC.

might even the ranks of earlier Aegean Bronze Age spear- and swordsmen with their huge shields). The new infantrymen, or, at least, their aristocratic commanders and other wealthy individuals, came to enjoy an ever better protection, at least during the ninth to eighth centuries BC, with further developments of defensive armour, in particular helmet, breast-plates and greaves. Thus, shortly after c. 700 BC, no doubt as a result both of the experience of fierce combat and of the influx of new wealth in society, making defensive armour available for larger groups, the final steps were taken to create the heavily armoured infantryman of the classic Greek Hoplite phalanx.

The organization of this particular type of phalanx was also conditioned by a new set of concepts, indeed probably born in opposition to traditional aristocratic society, namely those of citizenship, of rights, and of obligations towards the state. In the Hoplite formation all warriors enjoyed in principlethe same protection as, or even better than, the aristocratic commanders of the Iron Age,

Fig. 51. 'Sea-Peoples' battling Egyptians in c. 1186 BC. From Medinet Habu, Luxor, Egypt, 12th century BC (figure after Müller-Karpe 1980; supporting interpretations by Kemp 1989, 227). — In these battles the Egyptian soldiers wield spears and have oblong shields (upper end rounded); they are sometimes assisted by mercenaries with horned helmets topped by a disk. The enemy ('Cypriots' or 'Anatolians' (?)) wield spears (even two), long swords, and have round shields. In the naval representation (above) the Egyptians fight Sea-Peoples with horned helmets or feathered head-dresses.

but with the result that individual (and group) mobility was again restricted, and that battles became an ever more intense affair.

In view of the comprehensive literature on the Greek Hoplite, the role of the ship in forming Greek and other Mediterranen military organization is given far too little attention, in particular in studies of warfare and society before the crucial battle of Salamis (against the Persians) in 480 BC. In fact, half the depictions of battle on the ceramics of the Greek Geometric period are of naval encounters: in all, 15 on land (none of siege-warfare) and 13 at sea (Ahlberg 1971).

In most of the Aegean in the early to mid-first millennium BC, the dominant cremation rite and the highly restrictive norms of inclusion of burial gifts (in itself an early encounter with traditional aristocratic norms, although accepted by the Iron Age magnates) prevent the study of the classic Hoplite infantryman based on grave goods. Thus, only in regions marginal to the southern Aegean can we hope to employ this classic archaeological approach to the study of individuals of the past. Weapons, especially defensive, have been noted from sanctuaries, though — for instance in large numbers from Olympia (Fig. 52) (cf. Chapter 6A).

An inhumation cemetery of 177 burials (at least 67 men, 15 boys, 52 women, 13 girls, and 14 infants) on the fringes of the classical world, at Vitsa in the high mountains of northwesternmost Greece (Vokotopoulou 1986), displays a remarkably long sequence of weapon graves, from c. 850 to 300 BC. Here, the iron-tipped spear/lance, in 23 graves included in pairs, is throughout the dominant weapon. In all, 108 (93 closely dated) spears/lances were recorded against some 19 swords only (at least eight double-edged and nine single-edged), mostly found together with spears/lances. Interestingly, spear/lances even dominate at Vitsa in periods prior to the transition to spear-domined warfare (at c. 700 BC) according to the southern Aegean vase-paintings (cf. Fig. 39).

Incidentally, at Vitsa, a substantial amount of Corinthian pottery was imported from the eighth century BC on; Athenian wares dominate after 500 BC. The Vitsa cemetery seems to belong to a semi-nomadic (transhumance) community, using the artefacts of the city-dwellers and farmers to the south and, seemingly, even phalanx tactics of massed fighting. Shields were not found in the cemetery, however; in fact, shields do not figure as grave-goods anywhere in the Aegean (they have been donated to sanctuaries, though). Two items, claimed to be shield-bosses worn as 'caps', are, in fact, tutuli (cf. Fellmann 1984). Thus, in the rich sixth century BC inhumation cemetry of Aghia Paraskevi, near Thessaloniki, in the

BC	800-725	725-650	650-575	575-500
Tripod-Cauldrons	c. 280	c. 240		
Oriental cauldron attaches		58	?	
Conical helmets		31		
Illyrian & Corinthian helmets		47	c. 72	43+
Cuirasses		2	c. 10	1+
Hoplite shields		8	90+	c. 80
Decorated shield armbands			35+	40+

Fig. 52. Patterns of sacrifice of selected artefacts at Olympia, Greece, c. 800-500 BC: cauldrons and defensive weapons (after Snodgrass 1980). (Weapons of attack are comparatively rare and rather difficult to date precisely.)

heart of Macedonia, shields are also missing, while (paired) spears, swords, and helmets are common ((Sismanidis in) Vokotopoulou 1993, 170f).

Italy is a different case from southern Greece. Culturally, the northern part was, until the second quarter of the first millennium BC, a part of Central Europe, rather than of the Mediterranean region. The southern part, with its own cultural traditions, had, probably since the eighth century BC, been settled by Greek traders and colonists or come under their influence. (Phoenician traders arrived even earlier.) In Central Italy, the later Etruscan cities, gradually discarding their cultural membership of the Central European sphere during the earlier Iron Age (parallel with the north Alpine Late Bronze Age), came under heavy, at first Near Eastern (till 650 BC), then Greek, influence. This development is very clearly reflected in the weaponry. New phalanx tactics were no doubt adopted along with the Greek Hoplite weaponry (lance-dominated fighting was an even earlier phenomenon here, as it was in Greece). Still, the Etruscan armies always seem to have preferred mobility to protection when a conflict between the two arose.

In Vetulonia, one of the few Etruscan centres with a longer sequence of weapon-graves, the development is characterized by the following changes (Fig. 54). Possibly, the transition to lance-dominated combat took place, as at Greek Vitsa, already in the early Iron Age (traditional dates 900-700 BC, probably before 1000 to c. 800 (cf. Peroni 1994, 210f), or, the latest Bronze Age in Central Europe). However, the traditional long-sword was only gradually supplanted by the heavy dagger (which, in turn, disappeared in the middle of the seventh century BC), or by the heavy knife (a cousin of the short Hoplite sword). It was the ubiquitous axe, always common in Italy, but unknown in Greek hoplite warfare, which took over from the sword and became the common weapon for close-range fighting in Central Italy from the seventh century BC on.

A very rich or 'princely' tomb (Grave 871) with weapons, including a particularly fine helmet, 64 cm tall, from the Grotta Gramiccia cemetery at Veii in southern Etruria, dated to the eighth century BC, may represent the very last early Iron Age milieu (contemporary with the close of the Late Bronze Age in central Europe) (Müller-Karpe 1974) (Fig. 53). In this grave the foreign imports are still modest, and the weapons stressing the sword cum axe and spear/lance(s) model of fighting of commanders.

The famous Bernardini tomb at Palestrina near Rome, at the very most, only a century later than Grave 871, Veii (from the beginning of the seventh century BC), by contrast, has very rich Near Eastern and other imports. These two graves thus demonstrate the dramatic cultural and economic development during the eighth century BC in Central Italy. In social and military terms, from a commander distinguishing himself to one separating himself from the common people.

The Bernardini tomb is but one of a series of contemporary truly princely graves, many with weapons, conspicuously displaying the new Oriental luxuries acquired through trade (Canciani & von Hase 1979). The grave-goods in Bernardini, the iron being in a very poor shape, comprise three large round decorated bronze shields, three fine daggers (one bronze, two iron), with silver scabbards etc., three (or, perhaps, four) iron sword blades, seven or perhaps eight, or even nine, spear-heads (one bronze, the rest, iron), and two iron axes; this looks like three full archaic sets of shield, fine dagger, sword, and two (or more) spears (etc.). The grave dates to the period just prior to the phase of marked import of, in particular, Greek defensive weaponry. In the latter phase,

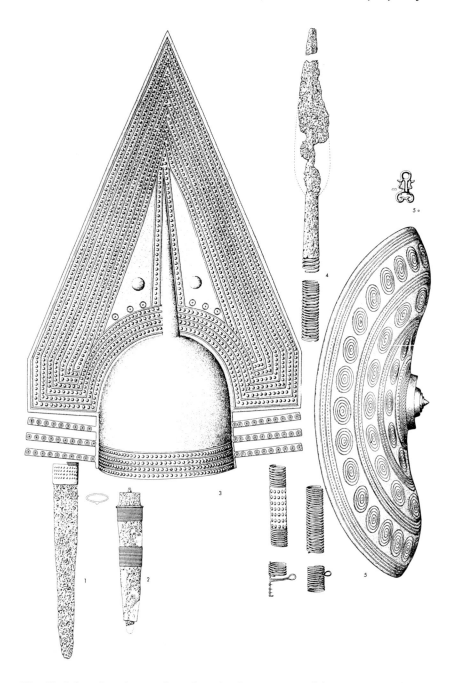

Fig. 53. Selected equipment from the princely Grave 871 of the Grotta Gramiccia grave-field, Veii, Central Italy (after Müller-Karpe 1974). The burial is dated to the (late) eighth century BC *or, rather, somewhat earlier.*

BC	Helmet	Armour	Sword	Dagger	Knife	Axe	Lance	Waggon (Bridle)
IX-VIII (17)	–	–	4	1	1	3	17	–
VIIA (22)	4	4	–	16	3	13	23	7 (18)
VIIB (9)	3	4	–	–	2	10	17	6 (10)

Fig. 54. Numbers of weapons from graves at Vetulonia, Etruria, Italy (data Stary 1981, 46f & 107f). Traditional dates are given (the period IX-VIII centuries BC should be raised to before 1000 to c. 800 BC (cf. Peroni 1994, 210f)). The respective numbers of weapon-graves are indicated in brackets after the date. 12 of the 17 weapon-graves (out of a total of 64 graves) from the period c. 900-700 BC (IX-VIII) only held lances. In the seventh century as many as 31 out of 72 graves held weapons. The term 'Armour' comprises three shields and one breastplate from the period 700-650 BC; from the period 650-600 comes only greaves; in the latter period Greek impact on the weaponry is very clear. (Two of the axes from this period are highly unusual double-axes (weapons?).)

The transition to lance-dominated combat (perhaps, though hardly likely, in formation) apparently took place already in the early Iron Age (Late Bronze Age in Central Europe and Scandinavia). However, the longsword was only gradually supplanted by the dagger and the heavy knife (in turn, the former disappear in the period 650-600 BC). In the early Iron Age, unlike the seventh century BC, axes were still relatively rare.

Etruscan/Central Italian adherence to the norms of 'Greekdom' — thus, polis- organization of the cities and an economy dominated by demand — should even be cast in a reaction against the aristocratic displays of wealth, for instance at burial, during the Orientalizing period.

By contrast, the somewhat earlier, well-known and highly expressive bronze figurines from Sardinia, dating to the early first millennium BC, show warriors equipped with a selection of (horned) helmets (or, perhaps, only leather caps), pectorals, greaves (perhaps also of leather), a rather small shield, sword, heavy daggers, some remarkable long 'war-sticks', bow (and arrow), etc., but, significantly, no spears. These figurines are highly important in showing, probably, full standard weaponries, for once not seen through the ritual 'screens' of burial rites and conventions of sacrifice. The war-stick must have served the normal purposes of lance/staff and long-sword (it occurs with dagger, but not with sword). In short, this appears to be an 'earlier Late Bronze Age' type of weaponry, resembling that of aristocrats (and others) in Central (and Northern) Europe in the period where spears are less prominent (e.g., Lilliu 1987) (Figs. 55-56). However, the common daggers may show that at least some of the figurines are slightly later.

In Spain, the equipment of 'the new infantryman' (and some-times even the warrior himself), again, no doubt a local aristocrat, is depicted on stelae from the province of Extramadura in the south-west, also from around 1000 BC (and later) (Almagro 1966; Burgess 1991) (Fig. 57). Thus, with his sword, a spear, a shield, even a helmet, a metal mirror, and perhaps also a waggon for transport, the local appearance of this warrior is definitely elitish; there are no indications of such warriors massing to march up in phalanges, as they might have done in a wealthier Near Eastern setting.

While southern Greece, even during the Dark Ages, at the close of the second and the beginning of the first millennium BC, was always facing the eastern Mediterranean, the north of Greece, although regularly in contact with the southern Aegean, was rather an extension of the landlocked central parts of Europe, rich in both people, produce and metals (Kilian 1975). Thus, in the northern parts of Greece, the new light, albeit sometimes armoured, infantry-man of the early first millennium BC was equipped with a sword of, for instance, Central European derivation. In the rich graves from Vergina, the traditional royal centre of Macedonia, 21 such swords and 19 spears/lances (of iron) were found in a total of 38 graves. Interestingly, only two of these burials held both a sword and a lance (Rhomiopoulou & Kilian-Dirlmeier 1989). Perhaps we are observing two age-sets: the senior warriors being equipped with swords, the spear/lance (plus shield, etc.) not included; the junior warriors with only their (one) spear/lance (and, again, no shield). Indeed, we may here have a premonition of the much later order of battle both of Hjortspring and the early Roman legion, organization along lines of seniority (cf. Figs. 19-20).

– – –

Also in north Alpine Europe, as in Italy, the number of weapon-graves from the first millennium BC is very high, but the archae

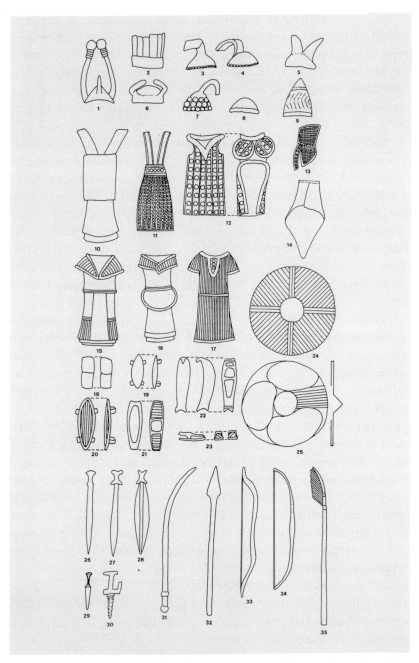

Fig. 55. Early first millennium BC *weapons etc. carried by prominent Sardinian warriors (bronze statuettes) (after Stary 1991).*

Helmet	Armour	Pectoral	Greaves	Shield	War-stick	Sword	Dagger	Bow
84(+)	4	26	36(++)	46	34(+)	58(+)	29(+)	32

Fig. 56. Weapons etc. seen on local early Iron Age (mainly Late Bronze Age in Central Europe) figurines from Sardinia (data, Stary 1991). Notes: 43(+) of the helmets are horned. The 'War-stick' is a club-like weapon; it usually occurs with the dagger, but not with the sword and the shield and never with the bow (which, in turn, is often accompanied by sword). Only one spear is noted.

ological literature is often incomplete and confusing; besides, no one library covers the entire field of information (in a multitude of languages). Furthermore, great regional, chronological and, not least, cultural and ritual differences are detected in the data, making a search for the realities of past warfare and related dimensions very difficult indeed. However unsatisfactory, the following observations nevertheless seem reliable.

In Central Europe, the converging traits in military artefacts after c. 1300 BC should primarily be seen in terms of élite or élite-sponsored warfare. The Late Bronze Age aristocrats here readily accepted and may even have invented elements of the novel weaponry. This applies both to the particular European flange-hilted sword and the cuirass of metal (bronze), the latter a defensive weapon still seriously used in the present century. Nevertheless, the same elites were remarkably slow in adopting iron for weapons (not until the eighth and seventh centuries BC, and then only gradually). Seemingly, the chieftains of Central and adjacent areas of Europe did not readily give up their ancient ways of fighting either. In the early first millennium BC they took a new pride in the sword. Later on, albeit probably under southern inspiration, they revived their old interest in fine waggons, or chariots, studded with metal and now usually with four multi-spoked wheels (Pare 1992). This vehicle was, like the flashy, but thin, protective armour, apt for social display: both in ritualized warfare and in religious rites. Indeed, aristocratic weapon-graves tend to occur in Central Europe either at the beginning of the Late Bronze Age, parallel with the latest Aegean Bronze Age, or, in particular, at the end of the Late Bronze Age and at the beginning of the Iron Age (the Hallstatt C Period).

In eastern Central Europe, by contrast, in particular the Carpathian basin and adjacent regions, which, incidentally, first

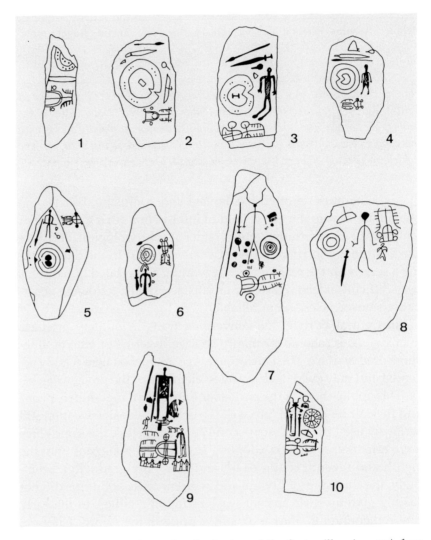

Fig. 57. Late Bronze Age stelae (beginning of the first millennium BC) from various localities in south-western Spain demonstrating the trappings of prominent warriors — including weapons, waggons, etc. (after Almagro 1966).

saw the two-wheeled chariot, the burials render the chieftains as mounted warriors in accordance with the norms of the steppes further to the east. The impact from the southeast European steppes, the corridor of quick contact and communication with Central and even East Asia, made itself felt from about the ninth century BC on. The early period of contact involved, for example, the heavy horse-bits and other trappings usually termed 'Thraco-Kimmerian' (referring to textual information). The later, or so-called Scythian, period, from the sixth century BC on (if not earlier), saw a much wider array of nomad artefact types.

B. Central European Developments

As emphasized above, it was not until the early Iron Age that major alterations in military organization were taking place in Central Europe. These changes were inspired, at least in part, by the Mediterranean phalanx (including the classic Hoplite one), in part by the just-mentioned horsemen of the steppes. The nomads were armed with long-range composite bows, short swords and daggers, axes and even 'clubs'; the scale-armour of heavy Scythian lance cavalry has been found as far west as Hungary (e.g., Kromer 1986, 37f; Bukowski 1977).

In the mid-sixth century BC the Scythians were attracted by the rich Middle Danubian steppe grasslands and perhaps also by the opportunities to acquire slaves. The latter were possibly sold in the Greek cities on the northern Black Sea coast, which flourished in the late Archaic Period around 500 BC, the decennia before the Persian invasion (Randsborg 1994). In southeastern Central Europe, the weapory with which the Scythians were countered initially consisted of oval shields, spears or lances as well as, notably, axes, reminiscent both of Greek and other phalanx tactics and of Etruscan warfare (Stary 1982) (Figs. 58-59). The axe was, as we have noted above, widespread in Italy as well as in the eastern Hallstatt culture. In the sixth century BC, cavalry (in part with steppe trappings) was already common in the regions north-east of Adria, to judge from both grave finds and depictions, for instance on the above well-known situlae (cf. also Fig. 66).

Western Central European 'Galatians', the later 'Celts' or Gauls, are known to have settled in northern Italy from at least c. 500 BC, and may have served as mercenaries in the Etruscan cities from about the same time (Wells 1980). At any rate, the Celts must have been able to follow the development in the Mediterranean region closely. After the formation of the huge royally commanded armies, probably of so-called 'Personenverbandstaat' type — using a term applied to the later AD Migration Period (Steuer 1989; cf. 1992) — in connection with the historically known Celtic expansions, further

	Graves	AXE	SWORD	KNIFE	one LANCE two+		ARMOUR
(A) Ha C	63	81	4	7	3	4	–
(B) Ha C-D	51	85	7	21	10	24	2
(C) Ha C-D, LT	176	281	6	59	37	113	18
(D) LT	54	73	–	20	18	24	–

Fig. 58. Numbers of weapons (a few types omitted) in the common axe-graves from the eastern Alpine region, including Austria, northeastern Italy and Slovenia (data, Stary 1982). The axe-types in question are in the main from Austria (Types (1) & (2)) and Slovenia (Types (3) & (4)).

Type (1) = Winged bronze axes, Hallstatt (Ha) C period; Type (2) = Winged iron Axes, Hallstatt C & D periods; Type (3) = Socketed iron axes, Hallstatt C & D to Early La Tène (LT) periods; Type (4) = One-sides winged (iron) axes, Early (and Middle) La Tène period(s).

The spears/lances are divided into those found alone and those found together with at least one other specimen. From the Early Hallstatt to the Early La Tène periods the increasing number of spears/lances (including pairs etc.) is noted. (Perhaps slightly fewer lances were deposited in the La Tène period.)

new, and decisive, changes in composition and organization of the military came about. These alterations included the third century BC re-introduction of the long slashing sword among the Celts, probably in response to the weaponry and more flexible tactics of the armies of the novel Hellenistic and related kingdoms in the Mediterranean and beyond. These armies, the military successors to the heavy Hoplite phalanges of Archaic and Classical Greece, stressed the use of lightly armoured Hoplites, much cavalry and phalanges both deeper than before and of uneven depth, thus with a greater chance of penetrating the enemy front while holding the line in other places.

A couple of samples of Celtic (La Tène period) weapon graves highlight the development in north-Alpine Central Europe. From the Champagne Region of northern France (to the east of Paris) come some 222 graves of the Early La Tène period with, respectively, lance/spear(s); sword; and sword and lance/spear(s) — shields not being counted (Fig. 60). 131 graves are with lance(s) only, the rest with sword only (30 graves) or both sword and

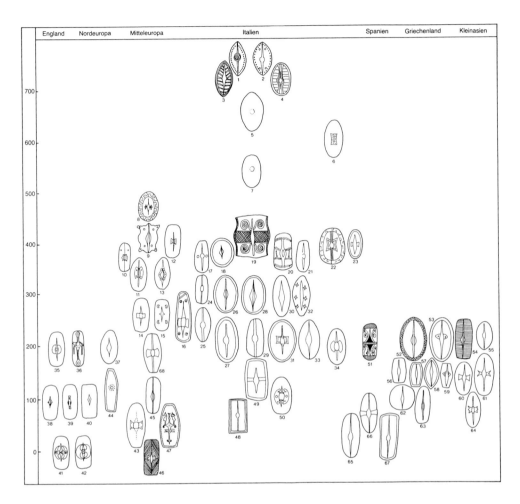

Fig. 59. Iron Age shields with a lenticular boss (after Stary 1981b). Note that the date of Hjortspring (no. 37) is far too low.

lance/spear(s) (61 graves) (cf. Fig. 59). 69 graves of this sample are of the Middle La Tène period, the third century BC on, three quarters of these have a, by then, standardized combination of sword and lance. Thus, in the Champagne graves we seem to observe a clear transition from the spear/lance-dominated Late Hallstatt and Early La Tène periods (to which tradition Hjortspring belongs) — to the Middle La Tène infantry with, usually, one sword and one lance only.

From the Carpathian Basin, Hungary and adjacent regions, come 910 Celtic graves, mainly of the La Tène C period ('third cen-

	EARLY LA TÈNE	MIDDLE LA TÈNE
One lance/(spear)	80	–
More than one lance	51	–
Sword (alone)	30	16
Sword & one lance	30	52
Sword & more than one lance	31	1
No. of Graves	222	69

Fig. 60. Celtic weapon graves of the Champagne region, north(eastern) France (data Lorenz 1978). Among the Early La Tène (Central European La Tène A & B) graves are 36 princely tombs, all with a waggon. These contain 19 swords (always only one to a grave), 78 lances, 7 helmets and 6 pieces of armour (the latter two artefact types are nearly always found together); only one sword-grave is without lances. In the rest of the graves (18) are 55 lances (2 of those found as single specimens, the rest (53) in pairs, or an even higher number). Shields are not listed. (Middle La Tène = Central European La Tène C.)

tury BC'); 166 (18%) of these contain weapons (Bujna 1982). Of the latter burials, 108 graves had a sword (or a scabbard) and 145 a lance or the ferrule of a lance (or, very rarely, from two to even five lances); sword-belts (chains of iron (or bronze)) were, however, found in 152 graves. Shields occurred in 70 graves. Also here the Celtic Middle La Tène equipment, made up of one sword and one lance, seems to be common. The weaponry of the Carpathian graves may, however, have been more 'symbolic' in selection and composition than in the western Champagne region.

In fact, the very rich, in particular western, Central European finds allow for a long sequence of arms and tactics to be closely studied, even from the angle of details of the weapon typology. The latter, far from merely lending data to considerations of style, is deeply rooted in changing circumstances of fighting, dependent, for instance, on the composition and equipment of enemy forces (Rapin 1988):

During the Celtic La Tène A 2 period, before or around 400 BC (Central European LT A and LT B making up the LT I, or Early

LT-period, in the traditional system), swords gradually became more numerous than earlier, and a standardization of the length of the blade to 60 cm was attempted. In the Early La Tène period spears, often paired, were, as stressed, omnipresent, sometimes accompanied by very short swords, as, for instance, among the so-called Celtibrians in northeastern Spain (e.g., Cerdeño & Perez 1993) (Fig. 61). This is the equipment, including shields of organic materials, that was used by the Gauls in, for instance, the attack on Rome in 390/385 BC.

In La Tène B, or before and around 300 (when the Gauls pushed in the direction of the Balkans and Greece, as mercenaries in the Aegean in the 360s BC, plundering Delphi in 280 BC), weapons were already becoming somewhat heavier, facilitating close-range infantry-combat against armoured forces like the late Greek Hoplites. The sword (some were carried in the earliest specimens of the notorious iron-chained belts, sometimes hurled at close quarters) was still short, however, and the shield-bosses bipartite (like those of Hjortspring) (cf. Fig. 62). The recent Carbon-14 dates of the Hjortspring find (mid- to late fourth century BC, cf. Chapter 1) thus seem nicely confirmed by the development of weaponry in Central Europe.

In La Tène C 1 (= early LT II, the Middle LT-period, or c. 250 BC on) the equipment is further standardized with an emphasis on each warrior being equipped with a longer sword (in a very heavy iron-chained belt, a terrible weapon in itself, as the written sources remind us), a lance (with an iron socket or ferrule), and a shield with a heavy iron-plated boss; some lances are longer than others. This is the equipment of the Gauls who in the Second Punic War fought with Carthage against Rome and also migrated to, for example, Asia minor. In La Tène C 2 (around 150 BC) the belt-chains disappear; the lances are now quite long and tipped with narrow bayonet-like spearheads, a development linked with the novel stress on cavalry, which earlier was used with much success by the Macedonians.

Due to drastic changes of the burial rituals, weapons were not included in Celtic funerary rites in La Tène D (= LT III, the latest LT-period, from about 100 BC on). Contemporary weapons are, however, known from other sources: long sabres (for cavalry) appear, along with round shield-bosses. Round shields, with round iron bosses, incidentally, characterize almost the entire barbarian

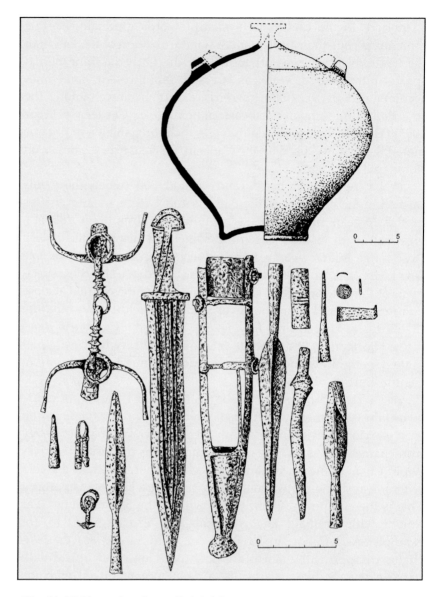

Fig. 61. Richly equipped so-called Celtiberian warrior-grave (cremation in urn) from a cementary at Sigüenza, north-eastern part of central Spain (province of Guadalajara); fourth century BC *(after Cerdeño & Perez 1993).*

scene in the first millennium AD (and beyond), possibly an indication of the continuing great importance of close combat with swords in this period.

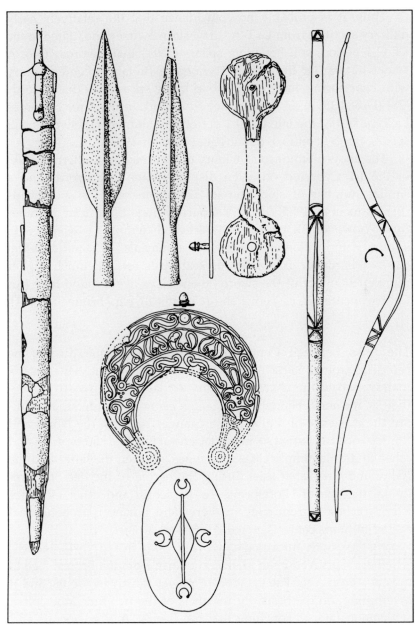

Fig. 62. Warrior grave (with sword, spears and shield) from Etrechy (Marne), northern France; Early La Tène period, fourth century BC (after Brunaux & Lambot 1987).

Thus, it is probably no coincidence that the relatively early military sacrifice from La Tène in western Switzerland, dated to the LT C 1 period, still has more spears (269+) than swords (166). A somewhat earlier find, from Tronoen in Bretagne, contemporary with Hjortspring, has even twice as many spears (60) than swords (28) (Duval 1990). In the sacrifice from Port, in the same region as La Tène but of the late LT D 1 period, the numbers of swords and spears are, by contrast, about equal (Müller 1992).

The abovementioned sanctuary of Gournay in northern France, of the LT C period on, even displays some 256 swords and a similar number of shield-bosses (275), but only 73 spearheads (Bruneaux et al. 1985) (Fig. 37). Gournay may differ from the other finds, however, in being an established 'temple', possibly with another composition of the sacrifices; it may also be significant that 621 scabbards or fragments of scabbards, etc., a much higher number than that of the swords themselves, were found here (for Celtic sanctuaries, cf. above and (Chapter 8), e.g., Bruneaux 1991).

– – –

The links between Central and Northern Europe during the centuries around 500 BC are, as mentioned, often relatively obscure, mainly due to the character of the archaeological record. Nonetheless, the small Hjortspring phalanx cannot be understood without the existence of military interchanges between the North and the advanced stratified societies of Central Europe. Hjortspring, and other finds, also imply close exchanges between the latter and the Italics and Greeks, at least during the period of the rise of Macedonia, the age of Hjortspring. As Passentin and other evidence from Northern Europe suggest, there were, however, probably also earlier military contacts, around 6-500 BC, in fact.

We are poorly informed about leadership in the North, indeed, whether it survived in an aristocratic form from the Bronze Age to the early Iron Age. The symbols of power mostly evade us, and it is tempting, on the basis, for instance, of the rich but rather plain settlement data, to conclude that the Bronze Age aristocrats and their followers were supplanted by a more egalitarial structure, perhaps reminiscent of the Aegean novelty of 'citizenship' in a small region. If so, this gives us an idea of the powers of 'republican' ideas in Europe in the mid-first millennium BC.

When Alexander encountered the Galatians or Celts on the

lower Danube (in 335 BC) and was met with the legendary boast
that they 'feared nothing, but that the sky would fall down', he
was, in fact, witnessing the culmination of a military process which
had ramifications even at the other end of Europe. The long and
multi-phased development in Celtic weaponry and in fighting
tactics and techniques perhaps, by transmission of military knowledge, enabled barbarian Germanic tribal groups, with links to
Scandinavia, to settle in Moldavia around 200 BC. Certainly, it
made possible the migration of the Cimbri and their, however
short-lived, publicity on the centre-stage of the civilized Roman
world a little later. But the Germanic peoples were to win new
reputation for their warrior skills in the millennium to come.

Caesar gives a vivid description of the, broadly speaking, contemporary Celtic armies in Gaul. In connection with the migrating
Helvetians and their allies, a census, 'written in Greek characters',
found by the Romans, is quoted (Caesar, 1.29). Men, women and
children, according to this, made up 368,000 persons, out of which
92,000 named men (or a high 25% of the entire population) were
listed as fit for fighting. This number looks much like a total military force when under attack or on migration, rather than an expeditionary army dominated by young warriors. It may also explain
the huge armies fielded by the Cimbri. To fight the huge armies of
the Mediterranean civilizations, barbarians would have to launch
whole tribes, indeed, start a migration.

11. After Hjortspring

Then Bryhtnoth dressed his band of warriors,
from horseback taught each man his task,
where he should stand, how keep his station.
He bade them brace their linden-boards aright,
fast in finger-grip, and to fear not.
    From 'The Battle of Maldon' (fought AD 991)

A. Germania in the Imperial Age

The post-Hjortspring development of north European Iron Age
warfare must, although weaponry and tactics forever changed, be
seen in the light of the remarkably standardized, and no doubt
well-drilled, Hjortspring phalanx and the similar small 'regimental'
armies across Europe to the north of the Mediterranean. These armies, taken together, represent a major break with the fighting
practices of the Bronze (and Stone) Ages. In turn, the phalanx-type
tactics of the mid-first millennium BC were themselves modified
during the millennium or more of antiquity in the North following
Hjortspring. The introduction of new modes of fighting, for instance employment of massed bowmen and, in particular, major
cavalry forces, and large truly sea-going amphibious forces from
the late first millennium AD on, no doubt compelled the main
infantry, both expeditionary and home militia, constantly to re-
define its tactics and stratagems.

  For the period between Hjortspring and the third century AD,
when major military sacrifices again occur in the region, the military organization, at least in Denmark, must be inferred from the
— fortunately — quite large number of grave-finds with weapons,
although in many 'Germanic' cemeteries and areas weapons are
lacking in the graves (cf. Steuer 1970; in particular, Adler 1993).
Such weapon burials, for instance from Fyn/Funen in the early
Imperial Roman period, are dominated by spears/lances (54),
double- and (mainly) single-edged swords (16), and shields (40)
(Albrectsen 1956; cf. 1971). A few graves (5) with spurs are also
known. We seem to note a distinction between swordsmen and

warriors equipped with spears/lances only. In addition, the existence of élite cavalry is demonstrated.

From the end of the first century AD comes Tacitus' highly interesting description of the Germanic armies and fighting techniques (Tacitus, *Germania*, 6f). The main weapons, according to Tacitus, are: a spear/lance, javelins, and a (brightly colored) shield; only a few warriors carry large lances or swords. Thus, this Germanic equipment is, in composition and function, more reminiscent of Hjortspring than of late Celtic or even contemporary Roman armies. The above grave-finds from Funen also fit quite well into this description. In general such troops would be no match for armoured Roman Legionaries, skilled swordsmen with a very large shield and *pilum*-type javelins to open up the enemy line. Certainly, the weaponry of Germans and Romans is not symmetrical in this period. Both kinds of armies tend, however, to fight in formations looser than the Hoplite phalanx.

Furthermore, Tacitus writes, infantry, including regiments of one hundred selected young warriors from each district marched up to the front, is the main arm of the army; simple cavalry is also utilized. (The young troops at the front may have been elite units (for aggressive effect) or skirmish troops, or both.) The order of battle is in wedge-shaped formations. Initial fighting is more like skirmishing. Only a few warriors have breast-plates and fewer still, helmet. The bodies of fallen warriors are brought back during retreat. It is particularly disgraceful to loose one's shield in battle. (The latter, in particular, sounds a bit like a literary cliché, but may, nevertheless, have been the case.) The (supreme) commanders are chosen for their abilities, but 'Gefolgschaften', of (young), probably both noble and *plebs*, warriors under noble, though elected, command, also exist (cf. Adler 1993).

Incidentally, in *Germania Libera*, to the south of Scandinavia, at Kalkriese very near Osnabrück in northwestern Germany the battle-ground of one of the decisive battles of Europe, the Teutoburger engagement, has recently been convincingly identified (Schlüter 1993). The Teutoburger battle took place in the year AD 9, between Germanic forces led by Prince Arminius against Varus' three élite Roman legions. This is perhaps the most exciting military archaeological find in recent times, indeed a huge prepared ambush- and battle-ground. The Roman army was annihilated, which resulted in the very varied and highly interesting spoils found. The site reminds us of the common Roman descriptions of 'tricky' Germanic tactics, ambushes and faked withdrawals, followed by counter-attacks and full-scale assaults.

A highy important correlation between age and type of wea-pons is noted in the huge, exclusively male, Hamfelde urn ceme-tery, southeastern Holstein, North Germany, also from the first to the second century AD (Bantelmann 1971; cf. Kunst 1978; data re-analyzed by the present author). This graveyard is made up of c. 890 graves, of which 25% are for children (mostly between 6/7 and 14 years) and adolescents, the rest mostly for adults (62%), mainly in their thirties; to these comes 13% mature men, between 40 and 60 years of age (Aner 1971). The 56 weapon graves in Hamfelde (10%), 74 if all burials with spurs are included, are exclusively from the (mid- to) late second century AD, the period of the Marco-mannic Wars, and may, one way or the other, be related to these.

The weapon burials of Hamfelde contain some 20 swords plus several chapes etc. (some without sword), 58 lances (or spears) and 6 javelins (all found together with lances/spears), and, 38 shields (8 found alone); spurs were found in 27 graves, in nine of these (16%) with sword and/or lance, and (except one) shield. The corre-spondence with Tacitus' statements and with the Funen graves is evident.

The swords and chapes of the Hamfelde cemetery, found in 22 graves (39%), are evenly distributed across the different age-groups, but since these are of highly varying size, this main weapon, in fact, clearly clusters in the mature group of warriors. Lances and shields concentrate in the group of teenagers and, as implied, in that of mature men; javelins concentrate in the teenage group. Spurs, though even found with children, probably as a symbol of a particular rank, dominate in the mature group.

This interesting pattern may, in fact, explain the differences in weaponry at Germanic cemeteries from the latest first millennium BC and the early Imperial Roman period. Furthermore, we may hypothesize that, perhaps, (1) merely those who participated in expeditions (or belonged to families that did) were buried with weapons, and that (2) such warriors made up only one-tenth of the male population, including children, or, one out of twenty of the entire community. No doubt, many more men were capable of fighting, in particular if their homes or region were attacked.

The potential ramifications of the above for the Hjortspring find are evident. For instance, the spurs-and-weapons warriors of Hamfelde equal the 'commanders' of Hjortspring, who, in turn, may also have been senior in age. Incidentally, the graves with a shield only, but no weapons, clearly indicate that only parts of the weaponry were included, and that the grave-goods are part real, part symbolic. (This also explains the only rather general treatment of Germanic grave-found weapons here.)

In the context of age-groups, we may also recall the, although much earlier, distinctions of the Roman citizen infantry army of the fourth to third centuries BC, after the famous tactical reforms of Camillius of the early fourth century (cf. Fig. 20). Every soldier wore a helmet and carried a sword of some kind. Soldiers were grouped into: (1) *Velites* (young and poor skirmish troops with light shield and light javelins), (2) *Hastati* (in fact, 'lancers', young fully grown men with heavy shield, two heavy javelins and armour, but no lance), (3) *Principes* ('leaders', family men armed as the Hastati), and (4) *Triarii* (veterans with heavy spear (lance), heavy shield and armour) (Warry 1980, 110f). In the fourth century BC, in spite of the confusion of the terms, probably reflecting the battle order of an even earlier Roman army, the Hastati formed the front ranks, Principes the middle, and the veteran Triarii the rear. The implications for contemporary Hjortspring are manifold. Again we are reminded of the southern mail-coats of the senior 'commanders' in the Alsian find. Indeed, did the fathers or grandfathers of the soldiers in the Hjortspring phalanx actually visit Italy to fight alongside the Celts against the Romans?

– – –

The size and character of the military organization in Denmark during the late Roman and Migration periods are directly reflected in the huge military bog offerings of the era, like Vimose, Illerup, Ejsbøl, Nydam, and Thorsbjerg, which, indirectly, even mirror the equipment of Roman auxiliary and federate units (Engelhardt 1865; Ørsnes 1988; Lønstrup 1988; Ilkjær 1989; 1990; Ørsnes & Ilkjær 1993; etc.). These highly important, very large and, indeed, very well-preserved finds are, incidentally, all from the same, obviously much contested, zone, in which also Hjortspring was found, centered on the Lille Bælt sound between Jutland and the island of Funen.

The late Germanic North European armies, according to the bog sacrifices, were larger than that of Hjortspring, their boats larger too, and especially more apt, both for longer journeys and for carrying a load (Fig. 63). These armies also used bows and arrows plus a little cavalry (including the commanders), and had far more swordsmen than Hjortspring or Krogsbølle (Fig. 64). The sword was now (probably for the first time since the Bronze Age) the main personal and certainly most prestigious weapon. As to the tactics, this implies that battles, after initial shooting of arrows, throwing of javelins and spears, and use of lances (possibly in phalanx-type attacks or defenses), might develop into a prolonged massed duel with large casualties. However, the composition of the weaponry, in particular the increasing number of close combat weapons (sword or axe, with the shield), preserved till late in the fighting, would also make it easier to disengage and flee, at least for the better equipped warriors.

The military organization of these armies in standardized but differently structured units, to judge from the numbers of various types of weapons and other equipment, resembles that of the Hjortspring phalanx but is far more advanced. It is very important, that the better-studied late military bog-finds, through their nearly identical numbers of various types of weapons etc., confirm the hypothesis, stated above in connection with Hjortspring, that the large military sacrifices comprise equipment of whole armies (contra, e.g., Lønstrup 1988; but see Ørsnes 1984).

Thus, at Ejsbøl, southeastern Jutland, in the fourth century AD, some 60 swordsmen (including 12-15 commanders, 9 of whom knights), no doubt also with shield, lance, etc., were supported by a company or two of about 120 infantry with only shield, lance and javelin (Ørsnes 1984). At Nydam, also southeastern Jutland, with its fine and famous boats (Fig. 63), and from the same period, or only slightly earlier, we may reckon a company of swordsmen (also carrying shields and, possibly, lance and javelin), some 240 warriors with lances and javelins only and even a large platoon of bowmen with axes (data, i.a., from the exibition at Gottorp Castle, Slesvig; the interpretation is not final). To this comes a little cavalry, probably merely commanders. The composition and tactics of these armies much resembled those of contemporary Roman troops, especially auxiliary regiments.

Fig. 63. The better preserved boat (of oak) in the military or weapon sacrifice, dated to the (late) fourth century AD, *from Nydam Bog, southeastern Jylland/ Jutland (after Müller 1897; cf. Engelhardt 1865).*

B. The Migration Period and Beyond

The new heavy stress on specialized infantry companies, supported by a little cavalry, is, it seems, also mirrored in the early Anglo-Saxon and Continental weapon-graves of the Migration period and later.

A recent study of circumstances in England (700 graves from around the sixth century AD), has given the following main distribution of arms in the graves, allowing for the (partly) symbolic dimension of the distribution (cf. the graves with shields only) (Härke 1992): Lance(s) alone 46%, lance & shield 29% (shield alone 8%), double-edged sword (with lance, with lance & shield, or even with other weapons) 11%, single-edged sword (including combinations) 4%, axes (including a very few combinations) 2%, arrows (including a very few combinations) 1%.

Interestingly, on the basis of epigenetic traits, the Anglo-Saxon cemeteries demonstrate that 'the weapon-grave custom' was limited to certain families and did not, necessarily, correlate with physical

	ILLERUP A	NYDAM I	EJSBØL NORTH
Briddles	c. 10	7 (7)	9
Saddles			9
Spurs (pairs)			8-9
Belts	148		58
Swords	100+	107 (106)	59-60
Knives		(76/86)	56-60
Shields	350(-)	73 (70+)	175
Lances	366	c. 300	189
Javelins	410	c. 300	200
'Spears'		(552)	
Axes		37 (37)	
Bows		40 (36)	
Arrows		170+	675
Fine weapon-sets	5/(45)		12-15

Fig. 64. Selected equipment from military sacrifices of the late Roman period in Denmark. The main part of Illerup (the deposit of the large Area A) is from about AD 200 (Ilkjær 1989; 1990; Ørsnes & Ilkjær 1993); the numbers of the different types of equipment are not yet released in full. Nydam I is, basically, from the fourth century AD (data in Ilkjær 1990 (determinable specimens only, 193 lances and 194 javelins) and in the museum exibition, Gottorp Castle, Slesvig (the numbers of weapons in the original publication (Engelhardt 1865) are given in brackets)). The best preserved of the Nydam boats has recently been dated by dendrochronology to the first quarter of the fourth century AD. The fully excavated well documented Ejsbøl North is of the fourth century AD (Ørsnes 1984; 1988).

stature, health, etc. (Härke 1992, 179f). 18% of the inhumation graves (but almost none of the cremations) have weapons, which translates into a full third of the supposed male population. Such observations may affect the evaluation of, for example, the above Hamfelde cemetery with its rather small number of warriors.

Also in Anglo-Saxon burials the age at death plays a role in the distribution of the different types of weapons: Boys and teenagers are equipped with a lance, common in all age-groups (the few arrows are only found with boys). The shield, however, is a weapon for 'adults', men in their twenties (or thirties), and 'mature', or middle aged, men, who here make up the vast majority of the weapon-grave occupants. Also the two types of sword and the axe (only a few younger persons have double-edged swords) aremainly for the adults and older men.

In contemporary Frankish graves (more than 500 burials), from around AD 600, there is less stress on the lance (49% of the weapon-burials versus 84% of the Anglo-Saxon ones) and the shield (23% versus 45%) (data, Härke 1992). Two-edged swords are represented by the same percentage (11%), while one-edged swords occur in 23% of the Frankish, but only 4% of the Anglo-Saxon burials. Also axes and arrows are far more common among the Franks (14% & 27% versus 2% & 1%), who furthermore display cavalry-equipment (5%). (Among the Alamans, rich in swords, cavalry equipment is even found in 10% of the graves.)

The Saxons of North Germany (only 57 graves) have an about equal percentage of lance and one-edged sword (56% & 60%) and a smaller, but likewise equal percentage of shield and double-edged sword (18% & 18%); axes and arrows occur in respectively 12% & 40% of the burials. The latter distribution of weapon-types might reflect a division of these armies, also noted at Nydam, into swordsmen, lance-men and axe-men.

Fine weaponry has no doubt always been appreciated, but in the Migration Period particular stress was laid on the ornate and very costly equipment of the elites. Helmets and double-edged swords with golden handles or golden rings on the pommel marked out the princes and the aristocracy (Steuer 1987). At Ejsbøl (South), for instance, a minor fifth century AD military sacrifice near the former one, a very high level of quality of, among other things, the sword belts, from some ten or eleven commanders, is displayed (Ørsnes 1984). But among these, three gilded superbly ornamented silver buckles of princely quality stand out. Indeed, there is far more evidence of social differentiation, even among 'officers', in this find than in the fourth century AD one.

– – –

In the North, decoration was typically with the intricate patterns of the so-called Animal Art, a minimalist and miniature manifestation with monumental effect, highly significant both as an ethnic marker and as a symbol of the qualities, norms and beliefs of the Nordic (and Germanic) elites and their followers. Indeed, on the Continent and in England, Nordic Animal Art seems to be a measure of the political links with the North, the prestigious supposed homeland of the Goths and other important Germanic tribes of the Migration period. The contrast with the deliberately undecorated, almost 'Bauhaus-like', only functional, weapons of the Hjortspring find and most of the armament of the Roman period is evident.

In the late first millennium AD, the Carolingian and later periods, heavy cavalry became crucial in West European warfare. Thus, the aristocratic north German (or 'Saxon') graves of the eighth century AD — due to novel burial rites, weapons were no longer included in the Continental Germanic graves — had a weaponry made up of a heavy slashing sword, a very heavy lance, a heavy shield, and, in the late eighth century BC, metal stirrups (Stein 1967).

In Denmark, burials with weapons re-appear in the tenth century AD after having been almost unknown — again, because of particular burial customs — since the second/third century AD. Many of these late Viking Age warrior-graves are of the new elite horsemen of the ruling Jelling-dynasty and even equipped with heavy stirrups and bits adopted from the Hungarians — allowing a much better command of the steed and thus cavalry combat in formations (Müller-Wille 1976, 129f; Randsborg 1980). Also axes, plus bows and arrows, belong with these highly trained multi-tactic horsemen, veritable fighting-platforms, accompanied by their fierce dogs.

Concerning the armament and composition of Viking Age infantry, the best information may, in fact, come from Norwegian burials, archaic, perhaps, in their insistence on a naturalistic representation of the status and role of the dead, but truly rich in weapons (at least 1,572 swords, for instance, already according to

Petersen 1919). A survey of 264 male graves (out of a total of 400, including 92 female ones) from remote western Norway gave the following number of burials with weapons (Shetelig 1912): 201 graves with swords (145 double-edged and 36 single-edged, in 20 graves both types of sword were represented); 140 graves with lance (rather than spear), 18 of these with more than one; 173 graves with axe, 15 of these with more than one; 72 graves with shield, 13 of these with more than one (the fragile iron shield-boss may be underrepresented); and 68 graves with arrows.

Setting aside the symbolic implications of the selection of weapons for burials, these amphibious foot-soldiers (only a couple of the above graves had stirrups or spurs), alighting from their superb ships, were equipped with a mixture of arms, some for possible, but not very likely, phalanx-type attacks (lance), but most for short-range duels, probably massed (axe, then sword). The weapons are heavy (but of very high quality), stressing force and courage rather than ritual, flexibility and organization. Finally, the strikingly high number of male graves with weapons in this Viking Age sample, compared with Hamfelde, Northern Germany (early first millennium AD), and even Anglo-Saxon England (mid-first millennium AD), seems to denote an intense militarization of Norwegian society. The reputed Viking housewife of the Sagas is, perhaps, a mere product of an unusually high percentage of warriors on expedition.

We are well informed about early Germanic methods of fighting on land, often succesful, from Roman literary sources (cf. Engström 1992). Also early Medieval writers reveal much information, in particular on individual combat and navel warfare. Finally, much data can, as sketched out, be inferred from archaeology (cf. Steuer 1970). In perspective, the auxiliary Germanic Late Roman regiments and the Migration period Germanic armies may be seen as the forerunners of the Carolingian development, which, in turn, set the standards, not least of cavalry warfare, in both the high Middle Ages and later, indeed, till the introduction of effective gunpowder weapons.

However, in the late first millennium AD, the techniques and tactics of battle in the North, as well as on the Continent, in spite of the so-called Carolingian 'renaissance', seem to have lost their last links with classical antiquity. The line of development from Hjortspring cannot be drawn any farther, indeed, merely the late military sacrifices and the different character of late first millennium AD fighting made a conclusion of the present work in the Viking Age, however briefly discussed, reasonable. The risk is always there that by putting an archaeological find 'into context', in particular a long and wide one, one tends to ignore some of its uniqueness. Thus, for instance, true, lance-shield dominated phalanx warfare, in the style of Hjortspring, was, in fact, a short-lived mode of fighting. Still, without perspective, much is lost too, in particular a sense of meaning.

– – –

For no period since the Neolithic is it possible to ignore the role of organized conflict and combat in society, although the military horizon varied substantially from area to area and from period to period. The same did the percentage of warriors in the male population (there is no evidence of true female warriors). The concomitant pressures on the biology and psyche of the men, indeed, a result of the increasing sexual specialization of labour, social roles, and public status ever since the Palaeolithic, must at times have seemed almost unbearable. But, no doubt, such hardships won both benefits and gratitude for the warrior.

Modern history, however, concentrating on economics and life-styles, has removed much of the honour and respect that warfare has previously bestowed on the male of the species. Rooted in the Enlightenment and fortified by both Marxism and the western collective experience during the troublesome twentieth century, the taboos on a serious study of war (as well as on religious practices) may, in fact, distort our perception of what the past really was — in particular of how it perceived itself. It is, i.a., in this light that the present volume has been composed.

PART IV

---

12. Conclusions

> I say someone in another time will remember us.
>   (Sappho, c. 600 BC)

A. Hjortspring

The point of departure of the present study is the famous Hjortspring weapon and boat sacrifice, dated to the Early Iron Age (high quality Carbon-14 dates: mid- to late fourth century BC), from a small bog on the island of Als (off Southern Jutland), Denmark. Next, the intricate development of weaponry and types of warfare in Europe is traced, in reality from the Stone Age to the Vikings and from the Mediterranean to the North. The magnificent and fast boat, a gigantic lime canoe with identical bent double prows (perhaps for mid-ship ramming) manned by some 22 warriors cum paddlers has in particular drawn attention, in part for its beauty and very elegant, although simple, construction, but the weapons found with the vessel, and in particular their composition, deserve further scrutiny than has been granted hitherto (cf. Fig. 13).

The basic military units of the Hjortspring army (or phalanx) were standard boat-loads of probably rather young elite warriors armed with shields for both protection and shoving, throwing-stones, bone- or antler-tipped throwing-spears or javelins — one each for half of the 18 (maximum) common warriors — and iron-tipped throwing-spears for all common warriors (half the spears for precise throwing and penetration, the other half for a general barrage) (Fig. 19). The common warriors also wielded a second spear (or, rather, lance) and a relatively broad rounded-rectangular wooden shield for close combat. The four (maximum) 'commanders' of each boat were equipped with a lance with a powerful penetrating iron head, a one-edged sword (at least one specimen has Mediterranean prototypes), a relatively narrow and more elegant oval wooden shield (probably to ease manoeuvring) plus a mail-coat, probably the earliest specimens in Europe, but most likely not manufactured in the North.

Rather, the surprising mail was aquired in or from Central Europe among the Celts who, incidentally, invaded Italy in the early fourth century BC and in the 360s BC were active as mercenaries in the Aegean. No bows and arrows were found in Hjortspring, probably indicating a 'ritual' or 'combat-ethic' abstention, underlining the urge to seek a quick outcome of the battle in fierce formation-fighting involving similarly equipped warriors. Fighting dogs may have been used for support. Among the other interesting equipment is a number of turned wooded boxes, seemingly copying Attic and other pyxides of the (early) fourth century BC.

Hypothetical combat scenarios for attack and defense, mainly based on the composition and distribution of the weapons and the seating in the boat, stress the drawing up of the warriors (when beached) in a phalanx two ranks deep with the commanders, at the close of the fighting, making up a third rank. Perhaps, like contemporary Roman forces, age-sets applied.

The Hjortspring warriors, who have usually been considered 'primitive' (cf. the antler-tipped spears), must thus be seen in the light of Mediterranean 'regimental', or phalanx, combat of the post-Bronze Age period. The heavily armoured Greek Hoplite (originating in the seventh century BC) is the best known such soldier, although his more lightly equipped companions, including the so-called *Peltasts*, are better parallels to the warriors of Hjortspring. The latter army, furthermore, had the benefit of high mobility (and surprise) without having to waste extra manpower on transportation or supply trains to get the fighters to the battle. On the other hand, the fact that the warriors were also paddlers hampers fighting at sea, which only two or three of the commanders could participate in without loss to the manoeuvrability and speed of the vessel.

Intelligently applied, with full use of the surprise factor and the mobility of the boat, this elite force must have been formidable, in particular against local militias. Still, it lost the Battle of Als and Hjortspring. One of the boats and all the equipment of the army, originally (the find was in part destroyed by peat digging) for as many as six boatloads of warriors, were sacrificed in the tiny bog (it barely holds the one boat) at Hjortspring (equipment for at least three boatloads was excavated). About the fate of the vanquished, perhaps slain, enemies, we know only that they did not end up in the bog. The nameless unlucky elite army originated, to judge from the artefacts, in a province of southernmost Scandinavia or north-western Germany, perhaps the latter-day Hamburg region.

B. European Warfare

A study of the development of weapons and warfare in Europe (with a particular eye to the Aegean, Central Europe, and, especially, the North) will note the fourth millennium BC emergence of battle-axes of stone, in Southeastern Europe also in copper, probably even from the late fifth millennium BC, a result of early experiments with metallurgy. More important, these battle-axes represent a new way of linking violence with social status and organization, thus creating the concept of warfare.

New types of battle-axes, practically all in stone, along with halberds and, especially, daggers (most in flint, but quite a number in copper too), characterize the third millennium BC. These weapons were, like the earlier ones, accompanied by the common polished flint and quite a number of copper (later, bronze) axes. The latter, originating in the fifth millennium BC, at first looked much like the flint axes; flanged, more elegant variants dominate from the third millennium BC on. In this millennium the means of transportation of warriors and their necessities had still not exceeded the ox-drawn vehicle and the dug-out, and combat, apart from initial shooting of arrows, was at close range, when serious.

In the second millennium BC, bronze swords and bronze-tipped spears for middle-range fighting, accompanied by the still very common, albeit more anonymous metal axe, dominate the development; daggers are still common. Fast horse-drawn chariots (with four-spoked wheels), for the first time in history adding mobility to warfare and battle, were known even in the North. These vehicles, like much of the other military equipment of the Bronze Age (in particular the defensive weapons), had a parade or ritual character about them, however deadly the pre-Iron Age weapons also were.

Infantry warfare, involving a *phalanx* of shielded warriors whose first weapon was the lance, may, to judge both from representations and weapon finds, be traced to the latest Bronze Age in the Aegean. It was even earlier in the Near East, where 'regiments' were formed in, for instance, ancient Egypt, although the equipment here was simple and almost of Stone Age character.

At the ancient Macedonian capital of Vergina, spear-graves date from the first two centuries of the first millennium BC, and at Vitsa, also in northern Greece (where richly equipped inhumations, unlike in the southern Aegean, are common) spears, often in pairs, dominate the male graves from the ninth to the fourth century BC. Thus, phalanx warfare with lance and shield seems to have been common (at least in Northern Greece) before the introduction of the full *Hoplite* panoply at 700, or, in the seventh century BC. The latter equipment comprises heavy defensive weapons — large round shield (for both protection and for shoving at close range), closed helmet, breastplates, greaves, etc. — and a short sword for close fighting.

In Etruria, although lances dominate the weaponry (as in contemporary Greece), axes (for close fighting) became very common from the turn of the eighth century BC to the Orientalizing period, accompanied by heavy daggers. Greek Hoplite equipment was imported from the late seventh century BC on, and, no doubt, knowledge of Aegean tactics was widespread. However, Etruria, like most of the rest of Europe, preferred mobility to (costly) protection.

The axe also dominates in eastern Central Europe during the entire early Iron Age, the eighth to the fifth century BC, as the representations on the famous situlae from the eastern Alpine region and northeastern Italy remind us. In western Central Europe, the sword was given up for the lance as the prime weapon at the turn of the seventh century BC (a heavy dagger was included for close fighting). In the sixth century BC, lances (accompanied by the common oval shield) are, indeed, the prime weapon of attack as far away as the lower Vistula (to judge from representations). At about the same time, a weapons sacrifice from Passentin in northern Germany (possibly of the turn of the sixth century BC), made up entirely of spears/lances, heralds the weaponry of the fourth century BC Hjortspring find (cf. Fig. 46).

Among the Celts of Central Europe, the sword regained its former position only towards the end of the first millennium BC, the phase following Hjortspring, but also a lance (and the oval shield) belonged with the standard armament. This change from earlier phalanx techniques, where the sword was less important, probably relates to alterations in Greek and Roman weaponry and tactics during the Hellenistic era, including a greater stress on cavalry. It certainly indicates prolonged and bloody battles ending in massed duels. In the early Imperial Roman period, swords were also becoming increasingly important among Germanic warriors (for the first time since the Late Bronze Age).

In the late Roman period a series of weapons (and boat) sacrifices from Denmark again permits a reconstruction of whole amphibious armies (Fig. 64). In the fourth century AD Ejsbøl find from Southern Jutland, for instance, we reckon some 60 shielded swordsmen with lance and javelin (including 12-15 'commanders', nine of whom cavalry), supported by about 120 infantry with only lances and javelins, plus shields. Similarly equipped armies existed during the Migration and into the Carolingian period in western Central Europe (but sometimes with a heavier stress on cavalry, in particular as the first millennium AD drew to its close).

In the North, this development culminated in the Viking Age with, for instance, heavy cavalry with iron stirrups and heavy bits, lance, battle-axe, heavy double-edged sword, shield and even bow and arrow plus, perhaps, a fierce dog: a veritable fighting-platform, possibly even armoured, for instance with a helmet. At the same time, the ships improved, became truly sea-going, in fact, often ocean-going vessels with impressive capacities.

C. Sacrifice

The second, intertwined, development traced here is that of sacrifice, sanctuary and deities. In the North, low-lying and 'wet' localities in the landscape in particular attained a sacred status. In Hjortspring's Denmark, sacrifices in bogs were as old as the first agricultural population and the battle-axe (early fourth millennium BC). Although there is much variation in types of offerings, from pots and flint axes, over costly, 'chiefly', artefacts, weapons, jewellery, metal vessels, waggons, etc., to weapons and boat sacrifices, and even offerings of humans, these deposits represent the one main ritual activity that we are well informed about during the entire period c. 4000 BC to the middle of the first millennium AD, when it vanishes.

ies. The idea was obviously to create a secluded intimate room, like a house or a grave, indeed, quite the reverse of the 'public' sacrifices and display at, for instance, bogs. In the case of the Danish Stone Age cult-houses, and with contemporary cave-like passage graves in mind, communication between the dead and the living may have been the rationale, perhaps linked with initiation rites. Indeed, the same may be the case in the other cases too, although Sandagergård also has a public side to it. Interestingly, a large, perhaps even chiefly settlement was here lying nearby. Probably the structures mentioned all served a shamanistic purpose and thus differed, at least to some extent, from the places of obvious worship of deities of the Mediterranean, although 'healers' and shamans, in one form or the other, no doubt existed there too.

Incidentally, in the Nordic Early Bronze Age there are also eloquent examples of coffins being placed in house structures and of graves dug into the centre of a common farm-longhouse, which, thereupon, is covered by a mound. The cult of death and, again, communication with the forefathers seem the obvious explanation for the construction of such *'heroons'*.

D. Beliefs

The question of beliefs is perhaps the most difficult one to discuss in archaeology. The forces worshipped in prehistory may, however, be inferred from the locality of the sanctuary and the types of the sacrifices. The rituals, as they figure on representations or, inherently, in the finds themselves, may be deduced from the character of the symbols employed, or from later knowledge (often textual) about the 'gods'. Thus, such material or archaeological approach to beliefs does provide substantial information, although it is not fully satisfactory.

For the North, Viking (and earlier) gods may be paralleled with some of the Roman deities, as was in fact done, for instance, in the naming of the week-days (cf. Fig. 23-24). Tacitus interpreted and translated the Germanic pantheon, as Caesar did 150 years earlier with the Celtic one. This brings the perceived existence of anthropomorphic gods in Central Europe right back to the time of the Druids and the main northern late Celtic sanctuaries (continuing into the Imperial Roman period) with their common weapon sacrifices, obviously connected with a Celtic god of war.

Still, finds like Hjortspring are both earlier and geographically more marginal to Mediterranean impact. The above material approach must consequently be brought to bear.

– – –

The cultic symbols of the Nordic Bronze Age comprise circles (probably for the sun and, perhaps, the moon), ships, and four-spoked chariot-wheels. The latter have often, in a number of cases and contexts seemingly with some right, been interpreted as sun-symbols. Nevertheless, they do go back even to the third millennium BC where such chariots are unknown (Hertz et al. 1994, 40f (J. Jeppesen)). The ship-symbols may have simple prows, but towards the end of the second millennium BC prows with animal heads, at first seemingly horses or stags, in the early first millennium BC in particular web-fooded birds, became common. The ship is interesting both in its recurring in the Iron Age weapon sacrifices, and, for being a symbol intimately connected with the fertility deities, male and female. It may have signified change. In addition, axes and, occasionally, other weapons and various items were employed.

The rock-carvings, the rich pictorial ones apparently mainly of the Late Bronze Age, depict rituals comprising chariot driving, wearing of horned helmets, display of over-sized cultic axes, blowing of paired metal lur trumpets, ritual fighting (perhaps a parallel to Mediterranean games at sanctuaries), etc. Occasionally, even belief 'scenarios' can be inferred, as in the case of the famous model sun-chariot from Trundholm, showing the sun being driven across the sky in an aristocratic chariot, or the Kivik grave, with representations on the inner side of the stone cist (Randsborg 1993).

But all this, unfortunately, brings us only partly into the desired close contact with the religious milieu of Hjortspring. For this we must turn to various other types of sacrifices, contemporary with the boat and weapon sacrifice. Among these finds are the so-called 'bog-bodies', often highly evocative and remarkably well preserved, indeed human sacrifices from the Late Bronze and early Iron Ages. Sacrifices of neck-rings are also known, sometimes with other kinds of rings, as in the large deposit from a bog at Smederup, Eastern Jutland, with more than 350 rings, in all. Incidentally, in hoards of the latest Bronze Age, neck-rings often occur in pairs and as the only type of artefact of the sacrifice, just as in most deposits of neck-rings in the early Iron Age. Further separate categories of sacrifices from this period comprise costly metal vessels, like the famous Gundestrup cauldron, four-wheeled waggons, and, not least, simple pots (with food).

Such clearly separated categories of sacrifices may, indeed, have been to different deities or groups of gods (Fig. 65, also for the following). If so, they demonstrate an even earlier existence of anthropomorphic gods than the texts of Caesar and Tacitus from the turn of the millennium refer to. Hjortspring, for instance, might have been to the gods of war and battle (the later Tyr and, perhaps, even Odin). In fact, the name Tyr is the prefix of two very rare ancient heathen place-names, 'Tyr's pond' and 'Tyr's hill', situated close to each other merely a couple of kilometres from the Hjortspring bog and only 700 m from the open coast of the Baltic (perhaps even the very locality of the Hjortspring battle); incidentally, one of Odin's Viking Age nicknames was '*Hærgæst*', the Army Guest or Guardian.

These two deities, of whom at least Tyr is of the sky, the role of Odin being more versatile (and difficult to define), may, as the context of deposition of the Hjortspring find seems to indicate, have been connected with or, more precisely, accommodated by the gods and goddesses of fertility of the later Vane-race, including Freja. According to mythology, Freja owned a magnificent neck-ring (and the ring-sacrifices may have been devoted to her). Freja's brother, Frej, owned a magical ship. Indeed, Tacitus states that the Germanic tribes worshipped the mother goddess — 'Isis' — who also used a ship as her symbol. The same author's information about the waggon of the fertility goddess of Nerthus, clearly a name of the same root as Njord, the father of Freja and Frej, finds a surprising expression in the sacrifice of the magnificent Dejbjerg waggons of the late pre-Roman Iron Age, found in West Jutland (Petersen 1888).

The deities of fertility probably themselves received the common pot (food) sacrifices, notably from bogs. Finally, the 'bog-bodies' may have been sacrificed to Odin ('Mecury') to whom, according to the ancient authors, human sacrifices were given. Consequently, Hjortspring was probably sacrificed to a predecessor of the Viking Age Tyr (rather than to the one of Odin), in spite of the 'wet' character of the sacrifice which may hold a reference exactly to the versatility and generality of Odin. The wet context is common to very many finds, and of very different kinds.

– – –

The observations pertaining to Hjortspring and the period about 1000 BC to AD 1000 in fact suggest a largely natural, or self-evident, bi- or tripartite division of all ritual deposits of the Danish and neighbouring regions since the beginning of the Neolithic around 4000 BC. The division lends itself to the basic powers and deities of, respectively, the Sky, the Earth (both land and sea), and Water (a dimension perhaps not introduced until the Late Bronze Age). This division explains, for instance, why the Iron Age fertility deities may have both ship and waggon as attributes and, futhermore, opens the possibility that anthropomorphic goods existed, although with different qualities, at least from the Neolithic. Indeed, supposing a human character, although with special abilities, for the powers may be just another way of communicating with them.

The offerings, differing from period to period, may for the powerful sky-powers and deities, probably mainly male, have comprised: (A) axes (of both flint and metal), in particular battle-axes, very long and fine ritual flint-axes, over-sized ritual axes, etc., and other symbols of strength (cf. the club of Hercules and the thundering hammer of the Nordic Thor), for instance horns; (B) weapons (cf., for instance, the many Bronze Age sacrifices of such, Hjortspring, and the late Roman Ejsbøl, the latter finds including military boats); (C) certain materials and items related to the sun and to light (the metals, copper, bronze, gold, etc., perhaps especially when first encountered, amber, the Early Bronze Age Sun-Chariot from Trundholm Bog, etc.); (D) items related to sounds and music (for instance, the ritual horn-shaped Bronze Age lur trumpets, etc.).

The changing earth- and sea-powers of fertility, probably primarily female, may have received: jewellery, for instance, neck-rings; offerings of food and, possibly, drink (in pots); tools related to agriculture and to subsistence in general; things connected with boats/ships and waggons.

Finally, the general, versatile and both life-giving and life-taking powers of water pertain to everything both living and dead. To these powers may have been given costly vessels of gold, silver,

SKY (SUN)	EARTH (LAND-SEA)	WATER
Weapon hoards EBA		
Sun-Chariot EBA		
Kivik N panels EBA	Kivik S panels EBA	Skallerup cauldron EBA
		(Web-footed birds)
Cult axes EBA & LBA	Boat symbols	Various metal vessels
Sandagergård? LBA	EBA & LBA	EBA and (mostly) LBA
Lurs (EBA &) LBA	Jewellery hoards LBA	Golden cups LBA
Shields LBA	Ring hoards LBA	
Viksø helmets LBA		

SKY (SUN)	EARTH (LAND-SEA)	WATER
Hjortspring PIA	Smederup rings PIA	Bog Bodies LBA/PIA
& Krogsbølle PIA	Dejbjerg waggons PIA	Gundestrup cauldron PIA
weapon sacrifices	Bog-pots PIA	
Weapon sacrifices	Nors golden boats	
(III-V AD)		Golden Horns (400+ AD)
		Golden bogeys
Tor's hammers,		
late Viking Age		

Fig. 65. Proposed relationships between the experienced world, the cult, and the perceived deities in Southern Scandinavia ('Denmark'). Hypothetical diagram of:

The main dimensions of nature: (A) the SKY (with, in particular, the Sun, plus the Moon, etc.); (B) the EARTH, indeed the surface of the world, thus, both the Land (etc.) and the Sea; and, (C) the connecting element of WATER, both Rain/Hail/Snow, Spring/ Stream/River, and Bog/Lake/Sea.

Archaeological sacrifices, ritual sites, religious symbols, etc. of (TOP) The Early and the Late Bronze Age and (MIDDLE) The Pre-Roman Iron Age, the Roman Iron Age and later periods (a few examples only). All finds are relative to the above dimensions and forces of nature. One very important find is the famous highly decorated Golden Horns from Gallehus of the Migration period, still not fully understood. (The finds quoted are, if not already discussed, all well known and may be found in, for example, Brøndsted 1957-60.)

(BELOW) are given the suggested (later) classical (Mediterranean) and Nordic deities pertaining to the above (cf. Fig. 23).

Note that the seeming dichotomy, at least for inhabitants of coastal countries, between land and sea is obliterated by the connecting force of water. (BA = Bronze Age; E = Early; L = Late; PIA = Pre-Roman Iron Age.)

SKY (SUN)	EARTH (LAND-SEA)	WATER
Mars/Tyr	Isis & Nerthus/	Mercury/Odin
Jupiter &	The Vanes: Freja &	
Hercules/Tor	Frej; Njord	

Fig. 65 continued.

and bronze, perhaps with a drink (like the Late Bronze Age golden cups, the Bronze and Iron Age bowls, buckets and cauldrons, for instance silvern Gundestrup of the late pre-Roman Iron Age, the famous golden horns of Gallehus of the Migration period, etc.).

It is evident that conceptual overlap (and a great deal of general confusion) will occur if both character, address, and physical context of a sacrifice, plus a measure of temporal and social variation in conceived linkages and preferences, are present. (No doubt, the ancients suffered the same problems.) How are we, for instance, to interpret an offering in a well of a set of female jewellery (cf. the Late Bronze Age Budsene find from Møn, Denmark); is it for the power of water or for a fertility godess? Or, do the golden horns of Gallehus in fact belong with the sacrifices to the forces of water: emphasizing the shape of the horns, perhaps they rather belong with the symbols of strength of the sky-powers?

In the above, the divine addresses are stressed, creating a certain unity out of the character of a find and the supposed deity or power who is receiving and supposedly pleased by it. The physical context is given no priority over the particular type and function of items making up the offering. Very many different deposits and hoards, including weapons, come from 'wet' locations. This does not necessarily mean that they all were to the powers of water, or to the fertility gods. Rather, we may see the realm of fertility accommodating all sacrifices and the realm of water sanctifying even offerings to the sky-powers.

A special problem concerns offerings of living things with red blood in them (plants, fish and, probably, birds too were probably sacrificed indiscriminately). It may be claimed that animal sacrifices were originally to the powers of fertility (who also received food (and drink)). From the writings of Caesar and Tacitus it seems that Freja (in the shape of Nerthus) did receive human sacrifices, at least in the form of slaves cleansing her waggon. However, on a regular basis, human sacrifice was exclusively to the supreme god (Mercury/Odin). The god of war (Mars/Tyr) supposedly received only animal sacrifices.

The above is no claim to a definite solution to some of the old and basic problems of the archaeology of the cult in Nordic antiquity. It merely provides a scheme for interpretation and discussion of the main factors. Also, the model takes into consideration both the character of the finds and allows for further discourse, both concerning the addressees of the offerings, the meaning of the physical context and location of the latter, and their wider social and cultural milieux.

It cannot be overlooked that the offerings, from various periods of antiquity, throughout constitute the finest and most conspicuous archaeological finds, they are, indeed, divine.

E. Ancient Society

Early Iron Age northern Germany and southern Scandinavia, the social and political milieu of Hjortspring, is, in respect of a number of material aspects, quite well known. The farms and various minor structures, the settlements, and the overall structure of the social and economic landscape are elucidated through decades of archaeological investigation.

The history of the common three-aisled farm long-house can been traced from the Early Bronze Age to the Middle Ages (Boas 1991; cf. Karlenby 1994). The house structures of the Early Bronze Age are very long (the two-aisled structures of the Late Neolithic even longer), often exceeding 30 m in length and, notably, more than 10 m in width (300 sq. m or more in area). In the Late Bronze Age, these structures, apparently, become smaller, and certainly smaller still at the end of the Bronze Age and the beginning of the Iron Age (around 500 BC), where a three-aisled long-house of 10 by 5 m (50 sq. m) is not unusually small. At least the latter farms are clearly for a core-family only. Furthermore, the integrated stable demonstrates that the family in question was in personal control of its own livestock. Throughout the remainder of the Iron Age, the long-houses again increase in length and area. In the late Imperial Roman period, large individual farmsteads, the size of small Roman villas, are the norm; in the Viking Age the farmsteads were commonly even larger, often centered on elegant halls.

The reduction in size of the first millennium BC farm long-house is difficult to explain, but probably related to a change in the social structure. In addition, the small family-sized units may have been more effective in the face of the technological and many other improvements of the Late Bronze and early Iron Ages, including large regulated field-systems. In the age of Hjortspring, a village on poor West Jutland soil might look like the fenced complex at Grøntoft (Fig. 14), comprising four long-houses each with more than ten cattle, paired with four farmsteads with less than ten, and some four structures without stables, perhaps dwellings, perhaps just magazines (Becker 1965).

In fact, the question must be asked, whether the 'Hjortspring society' might not have combined (1) private property in, for instance, cattle and relatively limited differences in wealth between families (a social group or -level without cattle may have also been in existence, though) with (2) a high degree of communal organization in areas like cult, burial (in cremation cemeteries), the military sphere, and a number of economic matters, including building and agriculture. To a large extent, such society might actually fit into Tacitus's later picture of the early, but still Iron Age, Germans (Tacitus, *Germania*). In fact, an interesting structural parallel is even seen to 'Iron Age' Greek society of the Archaic and Classical periods, dominated by egalitarian ideas.

This assumption of cultural similarity across wide distances and cultural differences may at first seem presumptuous. However, its rationale is housed in a number of concrete factors, which primarily involve transfer of beliefs, ideology and other information, even indirectly, and even without much obvious material contact. Production, unlike today, was then almost entirely local, or regional, merely luxuries and some raw-materials, not infrequently were of foreign origin; the latter, usually indirectly, often travelled long distances. But commercialism, in the Aegean from the sixth century BC on (Sherratt & Sherratt 1993), only involved the North at a much later age.

Firstly, the demonstrable similarities in weaponry towards the end of the Aegean Bronze Age (or, around 1200 BC) must be called to mind. Almost everywhere, at least in agriculturalist Europe, elites or petty aristocracies were in contact with one another. A wealth of fine bronzes, often of trans-regional general types, have in particular been found as sacrifices. Around the begining of the first millennium BC, rank and wealth were, at least partly, 'hidden' in connection with burial, in so far as grave-goods were relatively few in the common cremation-graves, this rite being the dominating one throughout Europe.

Such attitude towards status and wealth was a new, almost revolutionary phenomenon. Previously, at least since c. 3000 BC, rank and status were seemingly expressed, although not always in a straightforward fashion, in the relative amounts and character of the burial goods. Now, in most regions, in particular eastern ones, merely a 'Neolithic' offer of food and drink dominates the picture of the burial and grave. Indeed, already towards the end of the second millennnium BC, starting in temperate Europe, cremation (often in an urn), perhaps arising in response to new beliefs about the freeing of the soul of the dead (cf. Gräslund 1989), became the dominant way of treating the body of the deceased. It is also likely that the cremation rite in itself contains an element of social egalitarianism, dispatching both body and soul in an equal fashion and making burial gifts a redundancy.

Furthermore, we may see these tendencies — indeed, the 'embarrassment of riches' — in the light of the emergence of a new farmer (in the Aegean, eventually, the citizen), manipulating his own means of production, however limited, and making up the social patchwork of thousands of interlinked societies across Europe.

Around and particularly after 1000 BC, the development in population, settlement, economy and technology created a base which could sustain a true elite. This being one tendency, the farmer, who (a) fed the general economic progression, (b) constituted the social and population basis of expansive colonization — a political and economic characteristic of the era — and (c) supplied the labour for construction of the many fortresses (where existing), etc., may not have been prone to accept a lord. Regardless of how useful military protection and organization, long-distance trading and provision of particular raw-materials, luxury goods and other symbols of status may have seemed, the instinct of freedom (and honour) was doubtlessly also very strong.

As indicated, even the aristocrats, at least in part, ascribed to the new ideas of egality. In much the same way, perhaps, as the kings and noblemen of the late eighteenth and early nineteenth century in Europe dressed up in bourgeois black, or in the uniform of the military. Nevertheless, the leaders of warriors and communities in the latest Bronze Age and in the earliest Iron Age in Central Europe and, not least, the trading western Hallstatt-magnates gave the idea of conspicuous consumption new emphasis. The latter princes were in close contact with the wealthy luxury-indulging Greeks of Magna Graecia and the similarly minded Etruscans. Having returned to inhumation burial with customized grave-goods, the west Central European princes (as earlier, their Slovenian cousins) ultimately broke the norms of modesty, not least with their magnificent graves of the sixth century BC.

In spite of sharply rising wealth, the social experiments in Greece nevertheless continued, culminating in the (late) Archaic period with communities playing on several alternatives to traditional aristocratic power: oligarchy, tyranny, and even democracy. The motor was, as Solon's famous laws from around 600 BC would seem to indicate, the shortage of land. (Interestingly, also affairs and revolts in Republican Rome were often related to questions of land.)

It is against this background that the rise of phalanx warfare (and, in the seventh century BC, the heavily armoured Greek Hoplite), stressing mutual trust and solidarity, must be appraised. Thus, the particular organization of the phalanx army, requiring well-trained warriors, may, firstly, have provided certain political rights for the citizen-warrior (or maintained old ones) and, secondly, made an egalitarian ideology the desirable one. The latter does not imply the introduction of a democracy, though, as the formidable fighting-machine of Sparta reminds us.

Characteristically, in the same period as the political experiments, religion took on a new importance, the cult apparently freeing itself from direct supervision by the elites. Both urban and non-urban Greek sanctuaries and temples were the foci of a very widespread religious practice centered on beliefs in a pantheon of anthropomorphic deities. The cult involved the whole population (also women, slaves and foreigners), thus, effectively, though indirectly, mediating political, military, and other aspects of society.

However, the phase of social experiment was a relatively short one, although the ideas of constitution, legitimacy and citizenship, among others, became an important legacy permeating all later societies, even kingdoms and empires, in and beyond classical antiquity.

In the North, this economic and social development, albeit in cycles and linked with events in Central Europe and the Mediterranean, eventually led to the decline of the traditional Bronze Age aristocracy. The economic and social powers of these chiefs, during, for instance, the wealthy Early Bronze Age (in period parallel with the Mycenean palaces), were based on large farmsteads for extended families, and on exchange.

In Poland and adjacent regions of Germany, Bohemia, Slovakia, etc., the lands of the so-called Lausitz Culture and related complexes, truly huge cremation cemeteries, with an only occasional occurrence of other artefacts than ceramics and a few dress-pins and knives, characterize the Late Bronze Age. Only very sporadically do items of contemporary 'aristocratic' weaponry occur in the east, and then, almost never in graves.

Another important characteristic of this area is the hundreds of hill-forts which, among other things, may have held the community grain-supply, as did West European Iron Age fortified settlements like Danebury in England or Altburg in Germany (Audouze & Buchsenschutz 1989, 303; Roymans 1990, 196). The Late Bronze Age hill-forts of Central Europe in general were surrounded by open settlements and, to judge from the particular quality of the pottery and the testimonies of metal-working, controlled by petty elite groups (cf. Simon 1984). (Alternatively, the modest luxuries reflect the cult celebrated at the hill-forts.)

Collectively, the Lausitz and other forts demonstrate the division of the landscape into small social nuclei. A major settlement like the famous planned and very well preserved fortress-township of Biskupin (less than 1½ ha), along with other similar fortresses in central Poland (all probably 'colonies') founded in the late eighth century BC — and thus of the general era of Solon — is a key site in describing the situation in the latest or early Iron Age phase of the Lausitz culture (Fig. 49). At Biskupin, all homesteads, placed along 12 parallel streets, are of virtually the same size (there is only one gate). No signs of an elite were detected, although the inhabitants of the settlement may well have constituted one in themselves, although materially part of a highly egalitarian society.

In Central Europe, a similar process to the eastern one can be observed, but close economic links with the south, in particular Italy, infused new energy into the 'aristocratic' lifestyle, which, as indicated, bounced back at the close of the Late Bronze Age to culminate in the sixth to fifth centuries BC when Mediterranean commercialism (mercantilism) and urban development created a need for raw-materials, mercenaries, and slaves, obtainable from neighbouring cultures in Central Europe. (Northern Europe was too far away to play a direct role in this, although it did supply, for example, amber, very common in contemporary Italy.)

The contrast between Biskupin and the west Central European magnate farms (Fig. 34) and 'Fürstensitze', for instance the well-excavated Heuneburg in southwestern Germany, is striking indeed. In the latter, massive traces of crafts, Mediterranean, even Near Eastern, imports (mostly dispatched from the Greek colony of Marseilles and mainly entering Central Europe by way of the Rhône Valley), use of Mediterranean architects, and, not least, 'shamelessly' equipped princely tombs, are common.

The general development of west Central European settlement-sites in the early first millennium BC may, perhaps, best be described at the well-known Wasserburg, Buchau settlement in southern Germany (Audouze & Buchsenschutz 1989, 267; Kimmig 1981). In the early phase (early Late Bronze Age), the 38 structures within the palisade fence were all small. In the late phase (the latest Bronze Age), the farms, nine in number, are several times larger (and, incidentally, resemble the ones of the early Iron Age Hallstatt culture). The differences in size between the main structures in the two phases were never great; thus, possible homes of chiefs or leaders did not distinquish themselves. But the creation of larger units is contrary to the development in, for instance, the North.

A fine example of the magnate farms of the early Iron Age is Aiterhofen in Bavaria, which has two main phases (Christlein & Stork 1980; Reichenberger 1994 for interpretation and survey) (Fig. 34). In the first one, two rectangular simple palisades enclose an area of c. 85 by 65 m. In the inner area, substantial two-aisled wooden buildings are seen. In the second phase only the inner fence (and the structures) remain standing, now surrounded by a double ditch, perhaps dated to the eighth or seventh centuries BC; there is an entrance to the south. The first phase is hardly much older than the second one. An ordinary settlement on the same site dating from the end of the Late Bronze Age (late Period Hallstatt B) gives a terminus post quem. The small finds were dominated by drinking-vessels and animal bones.

– – –

An egalitarian ideology embodies the denial of power and status as personal prerogatives. The strength of this ideology at the turn of the second and in the early first millennium BC in eastern Central Europe (and in the North), in particular, is remarkable, especially for such densely populated regions. One reason is probably the relative poverty of the communities. But the question also, and even, arises whether a combination of the Aegean decline of the Bronze Age highly stratified Palace society in combination with the surge of the pan-European development is not the main factor, indeed the knowledge and experience behind the later egalitarian constitutional and other thinking in Greece, including, by implication, the concept of Democracy. In turn, such ideas, institutions and manifestations had an even stronger 'Rückstrom' influence on Europe, as Biskupin, Hjortspring and probably also the character of the Pre-Roman Iron Age settlement in Denmark exemplify.

Characteristically, the strength of the new trading and other aristocracies of the Hallstatt D and early La Tène periods (sixth to fifth centuries BC), highly dependent on external forces, varied greatly both regionally and chronologically, and we observe no stability of development in any one area. A couple of generations before Hjortspring, this 'new' order finally broke down into the tribal kingdoms of the Celtic expansion, taking place, incidentally, during the same period as the political and economic alliances of the Greek societies of the Classical period were transformed.

The most important of these powers, Athens, Sparta and Corinth, had fought the tyranny of Persia, but, weakened by mutual rivalry, were nevertheless conquered by the new Hellenistic kingdoms, many of which employed the Celts in great numbers as mercenaries. Eventually, facing the hammer of Roman expansion, even late Celtic society, dominated by huge tribal oppida centres, gave way to a southward expansion of Germanic tribes and culture, which were bound to face Mediterranean culture across a wide front, thus determining the future of Europe.

Long before this happened, however, the western Celts of the post-aristocratic period of expansion experienced what in terms of organization of society might be called conspicuous 'warrior egalitarianism'. Ironically, this period, the fourth century BC, also marked the end of Celtic almost exclusive employment of shield and lance in phalanx combat; soon after, the sword would grow and regain its former role in face of new military challenges.

Fig. 66. Warriors depicted on a late fifth century BC scabbard from the Hallstatt cemetery (grave 994), Austria (after Moscati 1991/Kromer).

Notably, the fourth century BC was also the age of Hjortspring. The society of the small Hjortspring phalanx, albeit in a context of military leadership, thus linked up with a renewed, and, so far, final outburst of egalitarian ideas, which, in a great number of forms, have greatly influenced European society since the collapse of the Aegean Late Bronze Age. While the Mediterranean, especially in the late Classical to Hellenistic periods, itself discarded many of these ideas for good, they were seemingly upheld in the North to a degree hardly surpassed in other regions, and certainly not in Central Europe.

In more ways than one, Hjortspring thus remains a symbol.

13. Epilogue

He knew a lot of things, but never knew them right.
Unknown (Greek, seventh century BC)

Concerning the theory and method of archaeology, a question that has often been raised in recent decades is how 'best' to approach pre- or early historic society. In the present case, what might be termed a scientific approach has been considered appropriate for the study of the formal, functional and economic properties of, for instance, settlements, although only marginally investigated here. Also for burials, sacrifices, etc., a scientific approach is useful in the study of the formal aspects of material phenomena (as throughout in logic). Certainly, such an approach enables the archaeologist to establish the culture-historical dimensions and other structural properties of the data. These, although no doubt often unknown to ancient societies, are important in our own perception of past human culture, and for any recent, indeed, for all investigation of social matters in the western tradition.

This approach does, however, not necessarily comply with the perceptions that ancient society had about itself, the world, and its phenomena. The scientific approach to archaeology, i.a. for lack of manageable data, and thus by necessity, can illuminate only a few dimensions of ancient values and beliefs. Nevertheless, rich material data allow us to understand the emphasis that was once put on areas like burials and cult, and, therefore, on what must have been 'hardware' reflections of central aspects of ancient systems of cultural and social values, and of ancient beliefs and explanations of the world. Values made ancient society conscious of itself and others, made it mobilize resources, justify or criticize the social order, in short, develop and thereby change. Beliefs created the conceptions enabling man to accept and understand nature, establish his sense of honour, and motivate him to act.

Indeed, to judge from the sheer wealth deposited in such finds, social — or 'political' — affairs and religion may well have been what most occupied the distant past beyond the repetitive carrying out of agricultural, other subsistence duties, and familial activities.

In this perspective, also ancient warfare (being an ultimate and to us even highly interesting and fascinating element of life in ancient societies), with its convergence of social structure, conflict, abrupt changes, etc., calls for renewed attention. No doubt intermittent warfare and, in particular, the threat of war must have shaped the readiness and actions of society, indeed permitted a degree of mobilization and delegation of power not otherwise possible.

The archaeological study of burial and cult may thus make us approach ancient and, perhaps, in particular, prehistoric society more on its own terms than the scientific approach to settlement, economies, etc. However, such kinds of study are not without methodological complications. For instance, in the present case we have applied a rather straightforward approach to cult, using (A) written information from classical authors, of the time around the birth of Christ, on Celtic and Germanic worship, coupled with later data on Nordic mythology; and (B) an independent study of the character and composition of sacrifices, mainly in the North, through the ages. Such an approach is, in part, retrospective, in part structural, but nevertheless attempts a historical reconstruction of conscious behaviour of past societies.

Other archaeological approaches to the beliefs and norms of the past have, on the one hand, been more abstract, on the other, placed more stress on the subconscious (e.g. Hodder 1990). In particular Post-Processual Archaeology has been representing such efforts in academic archaeology. (The Post-Processual label was coined in critique of the so-called New Archaeology, which, in reaction to traditional archaeology, when reconstructing the developmental processes of past societies, stressed the harder facts of economy and society at the expense of 'culture'.)

Post-Processual studies have appealed especially to prehistorians, who are constantly observing patterns in the archaeological record, but often have only vague ideas about what these structures might mean. The problems are particularly acute when the structures cannot be considered within the 'scientific' sphere of biology, subsistence, the functional aspects of settlements, or, for instance, social inequality, as measured in differences of wealth.

Much Post-Processual archaeology has tended to belittle the distinction between cultural data, temporal ordering and archaeological formulations about past society. For instance, the attitude towards events in antiquity, main or trivial, short-term or long-term, has often been too abstract to enable the formulation of sequential processes. In particular, the historical dimension has been missing from much recent theoretically informed discourse in archaeology (cf. Sherratt 1990): vagueness and opaqueness being the obvious results. In addition, much Post-Processual Archaeology has inherited a fossil modernist language, long gone in literature, making reading more of a clan activity than an intellectual experience.

Furthermore, as theoretically informed archaeology — traditional, 'new', or 'post-' — is making conjections about past culture and society, questions from general research, as well as from the changing queries of the global village, are aired and projected onto the picture of antiquity. This is both a strength (in moving horizons) and a weakness (the research process, always a social and highly competitive practice, may be infested by 'viruses'). In the latter case, the study of observable archaeological patterns and the pertenant modelling may give way to mere futurist speculations.

However, the 'archaeology of mind' cannot be evaluated by any one approach alone and has, in fact, concentrated on areas as diverse as social distinctions based on cultural sexuality, astronomy, lay-out of house structures, symbolic implications of grave-goods, and designs of artefacts (cf. Hodder 1990; Renfrew & Zubrow 1994, various papers; Randsborg 1980; Randsborg & Nybo 1984, especially for the present context; etc.). In a series of studies, both well-established patterns of the archaeological record and newly found structures have consistently been accounted for. Transparency, realism, documentation, verification and accountability may be the key-words here.

Finally, cleansing the board of the scribble of the -isms, yet drawing on their experiences, we are tempted to reduce human society (and its individuals) to just four basic, in part intertwined, biological, psychological and cultural dimensions:

Needs

Beliefs   Values

Honour

The Needs (or demands) translate into the human necessities of food, physical protection (clothing) and shelter (housing), tools, materials, transportation, etc. Opposite this is the concept of

Honour, indeed of self-respect and pride (so easily spilling over into conflict and warfare). Along the other axis are the Beliefs (religious and intellectual sensations and perceptions) and the Values (the specifics of culture and of cultual beings, indeed of knowledge). Albeit highly abstract, these four concepts are all embedded in things material and archaeological.

Like latterday gods, archaeologists can, in principle, freely choose how to perform their own research (cf. Yoffee & Sherratt 1993). This is an immense gift. Furthermore, the academic archaeology of today commands more information, more data — by far — and more approaches and methods than ever before. Yet, administrative archaeology, with 'green' interests providing the funds, keeps producing new data at an exponential rate: potential information which is often left undigested and, certainly cannot be appraised by many others than the excavators. (Perhaps future electronic publishing of reports may improve the situation.)

As before in the history of research, theory and narrative are limping after reality — theory being merely the rationalization of experience (Randsborg 1994). A post-Academic archaeology is the likely, and perhaps scaring, result, abandoning the old questions about a proper study of man-kind for the concerns about the cultural heritage, however legitimate. Mysteries entwined.

Appendix
Pre-Roman Iron Age finds from Als

The Danish Cultural-Historical Central Register, The National Museum, Copenhagen, at present (1995), in its truly enormous computer file, holds only the precisely localized finds below, dated to the Early Iron Age/pre-Roman Iron Age from the island of Als, County of Sønderborg (cf. Fig. 2). (Finds not precisely localized are somewhat more numerous.) Hjortspring is situated in Sven(d)strup parish.

The find-lists is made up of earlier recordings by the National Museum, other museums, and similar institutions. The Early Iron Age of Als clearly remains an under-investigated area, in spite of the Hjortspring find.

Recent finds from the archaeological investigations in connection with the work on the cross-country system of main natural gas pipe-lines, running through western, central and northern Als, are found in (Hertz) 1986, 412f, No. 1598f. Among these are a few finds of interest here, which are listed below under their number (preceded by an *) in (Hertz) 1986.

Incidentally, during the period 1864-1920, for the National Museum in very many respects the formative years following upon the basic work of C.J. Thomsen, with an indeed very large acquisition of information, artefacts and finds, main investigations in the field, and intensive recording of archaeological monuments, Als was under Prussian administration. Slugginess from the predominantly Danish population during this period must also be reckoned.

The finds are listed by districts and parishes. SB (followed by a number) is short for 'Sogne-Beskrivelsen', Danish for 'The Parish Register'. An * followed by a number refers to the 'natural-gas' finds in (Herz) 1986 (cf. above). An excerpt from the Cultural-Historical Central Register, the basis for the list below, was kindly provided by H. Jarl Hansen, MA, The National Museum, Copenhagen.

PIA = Pre-Roman Iron Age; RIA = Roman Iron Age; EIA = Early Iron Age (pre-Roman and Roman phases). The large number of finds from Ulkebøl parish is probably accidental (recent visits by an archaeologist).

Two unique place-names relating to the god of Tyr, the ancient heathen god of war, Tisbjerg (Tyr's hill) and Tiskjær (Tyr's pond), are listed below under Egen parish (Prof. J. Kousgaard Sørensen, Copenhagen has kindly provided further information about these locations).

Als, Northern district

Egen parish
The place-names Tiskjær (on the southern side of Nørreskov due north of Elstrup, only c. 2.4 km east-northeast of Hjortspring Bog, Svendstrup parish) and Tisbjerg (at Tiskjær, although the precise location is unknown; there are several earlier Neolithic megalithic tombs, some barrows, and natural hills in the neighbourhood).
SB 309, Stolbro, settlement, early RIA.
SB 310, Stolbro Bæk (Nørregade), settlement, early RIA.

Havnbjerg parish
SB 226, Lunden Bog, vessel, PIA.
SB 261, Brandsbøl, settlement, early PIA.
*1609 Brandsbøl, settlement, early RIA.

Nordborg parish
No finds.

Oksbøl parish
*1612, Oksbøl North, settlement, EIA.

Svendstrup parish
SB 18, Hjortspring Bog, the present weapons and boat sacrifice, early PIA.
SB 127, Magerhøjgård, settlement, early RIA.
*1618, Egebjerg, settlement, EIA.
*1619, Enegård (SB 123), settlement, transition between PIA and RIA.
*1620, Enegård East, settlement, EIA.

Als, Southern district

Asserballe parish
No finds.

Augustenborg town/parish
SB 44, Østerkobbel, settlement, PIA & RIA.

Hørup parish
SB 232, Skivegård, settlement, PIA.
*1626, Lambjerg road (SB 208), settlement, EIA.
*1627, Tomhave, settlement, EIA.

Kegnæs parish
No finds.

Ketting parish
SB 155, Ketting, grave(s), PIA (?).

Lysabild parish
SB 173, Lysabild School, settlement (with structure), PIA.

Notmark parish
No finds.

Sønderborg town/parish(es)
No finds.

Tandslet parish
No finds.

Ulkebøl parish
SB 121, Stenager, settlement, PIA, iron-smelting, PIA, grave, PIA.
SB 337, Ulkebøl Dam, settlement, EIA.
SB 377, Elholms road/Sønderskov, settlement, latest Bronze Age or (early) PIA.
SB 378, Elholms road/Sønderskov, settlement, latest Bronze Age or (early) PIA.
SB 379, The long Bog/Sønderskov, sherds, EIA.
SB 380, Sønderborg Sønderskov, settlement, late PIA/early RIA.
SB 381, Søderborg Sønderskov, settlement, PIA.
SB 382, Sønderborg Sønderskov, settlement, late PIA/early RIA.
SB 383, Sønderborg Sønderskov, settlement, EIA.
SB 384, Sønderborg Sønderskov, settlement, PIA.
SB 385, Sønderborg Sønderskov, settlement, PIA.

Bibliography

Åberg, N. 1937. *Kulturmotsättningar i Danmarks stenålder*. Kungliga Vitterhets Historie och Antikvitets Akademiens Handlingar 42;4. Stockholm (Wahlström & Widstrand).

Adam (Bremensis). c. AD 1070 Gesta Hammaburgensis ecclesiae Pontificum. (Numerous editions and translations, including W. Trillmich (ed.). 1961. *Ausgewählte Quellen zur deutschen Geschichte des Mittelalters* (gen.ed. R. Buchner) XI. Berlin.)

Adler, W. 1993. *Studien zur germanischen Bewaffnung. Waffenmitgabe und Kampfesweise im Niederelbegebiet und im übrigen Freien Germanien um Christi Geburt*. Saarbrücker Beiträge zur Altertumskunde 58. Bonn (Habelt).

Ahlberg, G. 1971. *Fighting on Land and Sea in Greek Geometric Art*. Skrifter utgivna av Svenska institutet i Athen, 4', XVI. Lund (Gleerup).

Ainian, A.J.M. 1983. Early Greek Temples: Their Origin and Function. Hägg 1988. 105ff.

Albrectsen, E. 1956. *Fynske jernaldergrave II. Ældre romersk jernalder*. Copenhagen (Munksgaard).

Albrectsen, E.. 1971. *Fynske jernaldergrave IV;1-2. Gravpladsen på Møllegårdsmarken ved Broholm*. Fynske Studier IX. Odense (Odense Bys Museer).

Albrethsen, S.E. & E.B. Petersen. 1976. Excavation of a Mesolithic Cemetery at Vedbæk, Denmark. *Acta Archaeologica* 47. 1ff.

Almagro (Basch), M. 1966. *Las estelas decoradas del suroeste peninsular*. Bibliotheca Praehistórica Hispana VIII. Madrid.

Almagro (Gorbea), M. 1977. *El Bronce final y el período orientalizante en Extremadura*. Bibliotheca Praehistórica Hispana XIV. Madrid.

Andersen, N.H. 1989. *Sarup. Befæstede kultpladser fra bondestenalderen*. Århus (Jysk Arkæologisk Selskab/Aarhus University Press)

Andersen, S.H., B. Lind & O. Crumlin-Pedersen. 1991. *Gravformer og gravskikke. Bådgravene*. Slusegårdsgravpladsen III. Jysk Arkæologisk Selskabs Skrifter XIV;3. Aarhus (Aarhus University Press).

Anderson, J.K. 1991. Hoplite Weapons and Offensive Arms. Hanson 1991. 15ff.

Aner, E. & K. Kersten. 1973f. *Die Funde der älteren Bronzezeit des nordischen Kreises in Dänemark, Schleswig-Holstein und Niedersachsen If.* Copenhagen/Neumünster (National Museum of Denmark/Karl Wachholtz).

Aner, U. 1971. Die anthropologische Untersuchung der Leichenbrände aus dem Urnenfriedhof Hamfelde, Kreis Herzogtum Lauenburg i.H. Bantelmann 1971, 58ff.

Arnold, B. 1990. *Cortaillod-Est et les villages du lac de Neuchâtel au Bronze final. Structure de l'habitat et protourbanisme*. Archéologie neuchâteloise 6. Saint-Blaise (Ruau).

Ashbee, P. 1963. The Wiltsford Shaft. *Antiquity* XXXVII No. 146 June. 116ff.

Audouze, F. & O. Buchsenschutz. 1989. *Villes, villages et campagnes de l'Europe celtique*. Paris (Hachette).

Aurigemma, S. 1960 & 1965. *Le necropoli di Spina in Valle Trebba*. Scavi di Spina I;1-2. Rome (Bretschneider).

Axboe, M. & A. Kromann. 1994. DN

ODINN P F AUC? Germanic 'Imperial Portraits' on Scandinavian Gold Bracteats. Fischer-Hansen et. al. 1992. 271ff.

Bæksted, A. 1965. *Guder og helte i Norden.* (2nd. ed.) Copenhagen (Politiken).

Bantelmann, N. 1971. *Hamfelde, Kreis Herzogtum Lauenburg. Ein Urnenfeld der römischen Kaiserzeit in Holstein.* Offa-Bücher 24. Neumünster (Wachholtz).

Bartoloni, G. 1989. *La cultura villanoviana. All'inizio della storia etrusca.* Rome (La nuova Italia scientifica).

Becker, C.J. 1948. Die zeitliche Stellung des Hjortspring-Fundes innerhalb der vorrömischen Eisenzeit in Dänemark. *Acta Archaeologica* XIX. 145ff.

Becker, C.J. 1961. *Førromersk jernalder i Syd- og Midtjylland.* Nationalmuseets Skrifter. Større beretninger VI. Copenhagen (National Museum of Denmark).

Becker, C.J. 1964. Neue Hortfunde aus Dänemark mit frühbronzezeitlichen Lanzenspitzen. *Acta Archaeologica* XXXV. 115ff.

Becker, C.J. 1965. Ein früheisenzeitliches Dorf bei Grøntoft, Westjütland. Vorbericht über die Ausgrabungen 1961-63. *Acta Archaeologica* XXXVI. 209ff.

Becker, C.J. 1971. 'Mosepotter' fra Danmarks jernalder. Problemer omkring mosefundne lerkar og deres tolkning. *Aarbøger for Nordisk Oldkyndighed og Historie* 5ff.

Becker, C.J. 1982. Siedlungen der Bronzezeit und der vorrömischen Eisenzeit in Dänemark. *Offa* 39. 53ff.

Becker, C.J. 1993. Cult Houses of the Funnel Beaker Culture. Hvass & Storgaard 1993. 110ff.

Behm-Blancke, G. 1989. Heiligtümer, Kultplätze und Religion. Herrmann 1989. 166ff.

Bennike, P. 1985. *Palaeopathology of Danish Skeletons. A Comparative Study of Demography, Disease and Injury.* Copenhagen (Akademisk Forlag).

Bennike, P. & K. Ebbesen (& L.B. Jørgensen). 1986. The Bog Find from Sigersdal. Human Sacrifice in the Early Neolithic. *Journal of Danish Archaeology* 5. 85ff.

Bergquist, B. 1967. *The Archaic Greek Temenos. A Study of Structure and Function.* Skrifter utgivna av Svenska institutet i Athen. 4°. XIII. Lund (Gleerup).

Bernatsky-Goetze. 1987. *Möringen. Die spätbronzezeitliche Funde.* Antiqua. Veröffentlichungen der Schweizerischen Gesellschaft für Ur- und Frühgeschichte 16. (Basel).

Best, J.G.P. 1969. *Thracian Peltasts and their Influence on Greek Warfare.* Studies of the Dutch Archaeological and Historical Society 1. Groningen (Wolters-Noordhoff).

Bilde, P., T. Engberg-Pedersen, L. Hannestad, J. Zahle & K. Randsborg (eds.). 1993. *Centre and Periphery in the Hellenistic World.* Studies in Hellenistic Civilization IV. Aarhus (Aarhus University Press).

Bittel, K., S. Schiek & D. Müller. 1990. *Die keltische Viereckschanzen.* Atlas archäologischer Geländedenkmäler in Baden-Württemberg 1;1-2. Stuttgart (Theiss).

Blanchet, J.-C. 1984. *Les premiers metallurgistes en Picardie et dans le nord de la France. Chalcolithique, Age de Bronze et début du premier Age du Fer.* Memoires de la Societe Prehistorique Française 17. Paris (Société Préhistorique Française).

Bloemers, J.H.F., L.P. Louwe Kooijmans & H. Safartij (eds.). 1981. *Verleden Land. Archeologische opgravningen in Nederland.* Amsterdam (Meulenhoff Informatief).

Boas, N.A. 1991. Late Neolithic and Bronze Age Settlements at Hemmed Church and Hemmed Plantation, East

Jutland. *Journal of Danish Archaeology* 10. 119ff.

Bokotopoulou, I. 1986. *Vitsa. Ta nekrotapheia mias molossikis konis A-G* (three vols.). Athina (Ekdosi tou tameiou archaiologikon poron kai apallotrioseon).

Bonfante, L. (et al.). 1986. *Etruscan Life and Afterlife. A Handbook of Etruscan Studies.* Detroit (Wayne State University Press).

Bonnamour, L. (ed.). 1990. *Exposition 1990-1991. Du silex à la poudre. 4000 ans d'armement en Val de Saône.* Montagnac (Mergoil).

Borchardt. 1972. *Homerische Helme. Helmformen der Ägäis in ihren Beziehungen zu orientalischen und europäischen Helmen in der Bronze- und frühen Eisenzeit.* Mainz (Römisch-germanisches Zentralmuseum Mainz/Philipp von Zabern).

Boyer, R., 1981 (1992). *Yggdrasill. La religion des anciens Scandinaves.* Paris (Payot).

Bourgeois, E. 1992. Evolution du peuplement humain dans la haute vallée du Doubs à partir des données polliniques. Kaenel & Curdy 1992. 15ff.

Boysen, Aa. & S.W. Andersen. 1983. Trappendal. Barrow and House from the Early Bronze Age. *Journal of Danish Archaeology* 2. 118ff.

Bradley, R. 1990. *The Passage of Arms. An archaeological analysis of prehistoric hoards and votive deposits.* Cambridge (Cambridge University Press).

Broholm, H.C. 1943-49. *Danmarks Bronzealder I-IV.* Copenhagen (Nyt Nordisk Forlag)

Broholm, H.C., W.P. Larsen & G. Skjerne. 1949. *The Lures of the Bronze Age. An Archaeological, Technical and Musicological Investigation.* Copenhagen (Gyldendal)

Brøndsted, J. 1954. *Guldhornene. En oversigt.* Copenhagen (National Museum of Denmark).

Brøndsted, J. 1957-60. *Danmarks Oldtid I-III* (Stenalderen, Bronzealderen, Jernalderen). 2nd.ed. Copenhagen (Gyldendal).

Brunaux, J.-L. 1986. *Les gaulois. Sanctuaires et rites.* Paris (Errance).

Brunaux, J.-L. (ed.). 1991. *Les sanctuaires celtiques et le monde méditerranéen. Actes du colloque de St-Riquier (8 au 11 novembre 1990) organisés par la Direction des Antiquités de Picardie et l'UMR 126 du CNRS.* Archéologie aujourd'hui. Dossiers de protohistoire 3. Paris (Errance).

Brunaux, J.-L. & B. Lambot. 1987. *Guerre et armament chez les Gaulois.* 450-52 av. J.-C. Paris (Errance).

Brunaux, J.-L., P. Meniel & F. Poplin. 1985. *Gournay I. Les fouilles sur le sanctuaire et l'oppidum (1975-1984).* Révue archéologique de Picardie 1985 (Numéro spécial).

Brunaux, J.-L. & A. Repin. See, Rapin, A. & J.-L. Brunaux.

Bujna, J. 1982. Spiegelung der Sozial-struktur auf latènezeitlichen Gräber-feldern im Karpatenbecken. *Památky Archeologické* LXXIII. 312ff.

Buchholz, H.-G. (et al.). 1980. *Kriegswesen 2. Angriffswaffen: Schwert, Dolch, Lanze, Speer, Keule.* Archaeologia Homerica I;E;2. Göttingen (Vandenhoeck & Ruprecht).

Buchholz, H.-G. & J. Wiesner (et al.). 1977. *Kriegswesen 1. Schutzwaffen und Wehrbauten.* Archaeologia Homerica I;E;1. Göttingen (Vandenhoeck & Ruprecht).

Buchsenschutz, O. 1991. Viereckschanzen et sanctuaires en Europe celtique. Brunaux 1991. 106ff.

Bukowski, Z. 1962. Fortified Settlements of Lusatian Culture in Great Poland and Kujawy in the Light of Research Carried out in the years 1945-1960. *Archaeologia Polona* IV. 165ff.

Bukowski, Z. 1974. Besiedlungscharacter

der Lausitzer Kultur in der Hallstattzeit am Beispiel Schlesiens und Grosspolens. Chropovský 1974. 15ff.

Bukowski, Z. 1977. *The Scythian Influence in the Area of Lusatian Culture*. Wrocław, etc. (Polish Academy of Sciences. Institute of the History of Material Culture/Ossolineum).

Burgess, C. 1991. The East and the West: Mediterranean Influence in the Atlantic World in the Later Bronze Age, c. 1500-700 BC. Chevillot & Coffyn 1991. 25ff.

Caesar, Gaius Iulius. (c.) 52 BC. *De belli gallici* ('The Gallic Wars'; numerous translations).

Calligas, P.G. 1988. Hero-cult in Early Iron Age Greece. Hägg 1983. 229ff.

Cambitoglou, A., A. Birchall, J.J. Coulton & J.R. Green. 1988. *Zagora 2. Excavation of a Geometric Town on the Island of Andros*. Excavation Season 1969; *Study Season 1969-1970*. Text & Plates. Bibliothiki tis en Athinais Archaiologikis Etaireias Ar. 105. Athens (Athens Archaeological Society).

Cana, P. Mc. 1983. *Celtic Mythology*. New York (Peter Bedrick).

Canciani, F. & F.-W. von Hase. 1979. *La tomba Bernardini di Palestrina*. Latium Vetus II. Roma (Consiglio nazionale delle ricerche).

Catling, R.W.V. & I.S. Lemos. 1990. *The Pottery. The Protogeometric Building at Toumba*. Part 1. Lefkandi II;1 (M.R. Popham, P.G. Calligas & L.H. Sackett (gen.eds.)). London (The British School of Archaeology at Athens/Thames & Hudson).

Cerdeño (Serrano), M.L. & J.L. Perez (de Ynestrosa) (Pozuelo) (et al.). 1993. *La Necrópolis Celtibérica de Sigüenza: Revisión del conjunto*. Monografias Arqueologicas del Seminario de Arqueologia y Etnologia Turolense. Teruel (Colegio Universitario de Teruel).

Chevillot, C. & A. Coffyn (eds.). 1991. *L'Age du Bronze atlantique. Ses faciès, de l'Écosse à l'Andalousie et leurs relations avec le Bronze continental et la Méditerranée. Actes du 1er colloque du Parc archéologique de Beynac*. Beynac (L'association des musées du Sarladais).

Chochorowski, J. 1974. Bemerkungen über die Chronologie der Pfeilspitzen skythischen Typs im Nordteil von Mitteleuropa. Gedl 1974. 161ff.

Christlein, R. & S. Stork. 1980. Der hallstattzeitliche Tempelbezirk von Aiterhofen, Landkreis Straubing-Bogen, Niederbayern. *Jahresbericht der bayerischen Bodendenkmalpflege* 21. 43ff.

Chropovský, B. (ed.). 1974. *Symposium zu Problemen der jüngeren Hallstattzeit in Mitteleuropa*. Bratislava (Veda).

Coffyn, A. 1985. *Le bronze final atlantique dans la peninsule Ibérique*. Paris.

Coffyn, A., J. Gomez & J.-P. Mohen. 1981. *L'apogée du bronze atlantique. Le dépôt de Vénat*. L'Âge du bronze en France 1. Paris (Picard).

Coles, J. (& L. Bengtsson). 1990. *Images of the past. A guide to the rock carvings and other ancient monuments of Northern Bohuslän*. Vitlycke (Hällristningsmuseet).

Coles, J.M. & A.F. Harding. 1979. *The Bronze Age in Europe. An introduction to the prehistory of Europe c. 2000-700 BC*. London (Methuen).

Collis, J. 1984. *Oppida. Earliest Towns North of the Alps*. Sheffield (Department of Prehistory and Archaeology. University of Sheffield).

Connolly, P. 1981. *Greece and Rome at War*. London (Macdonald).

Coulton & H.W. Catling. 1993. *The Excavation, Architecture and Finds. The Protogeometric Building at Toumba*, 1. Lefkandi II;2 (M.R. Popham, P.G. Calligas & L.H. Sackett (gen.eds.)). London (The British School of Archaeology at Athens).

Crumlin-Pedersen, O. (ed.). 1991A.

Aspects of Maritime Scandinavia AD 200-1200. Proceedings of the Nordic Seminar on Maritime Aspects of Archaeology, Roskilde, 13th-15th March, 1989. Roskilde (Vikingeskibshallen).

Crumlin-Pedersen, O. 1991B. Bådgrave og gravbåde. Andersen et al. 1991. 93ff.

Cunliffe, B. 1983. *Danebury. Anatomy of an Iron Age Hill Fort.* London (Batsford).

Cunliffe, B. & D. Miles (eds.). 1984. *Aspects of the Iron Age in Central Southern Britain. University of Oxford: Committee for Archaeology.* Monograph 2. Oxford (University of Oxford Committee for Archaeology).

Davidson, H.R.E. 1964. *Gods and Myths of Northern Europe.* London (Penguin).

Davidson, H.R.E. 1969. *Scandinavian Mythology.* London (Hamlyn).

Davidson, H.R.E. 1993. *The Lost Beliefs of Northern Europe.* London (Routledge).

Dehn, R. 1967. *Grabfunde der frühen Urnenfelderkultur aus Südwestdeutschland.* Inventaria Archaeologica. Deutschland 14; Blatt D 129-32. Bonn (Habelt).

Dickinson, O. 1994. *The Aegean Bronze Age.* Cambridge (Cambridge University Press).

Diemer, G. 1985. Urnenfelderzeitliche Depotfunde und neue Grabungsfunde vom Bullenheimer Berg: Ein Vorbericht. *Archäologisches Korrespondenzblatt* 15. 55ff.

Dinsmoor, W.B. 1950. *The Architecture of Ancient Greece. An account of its Historic Development.* 3rd ed. London (Batsford).

Djupedal, R. & H.C. Broholm. 1952. Marcus Schnabel og Bronzealderfundet fra Grevensvænge. *Aarbøger for Nordisk Oldkyndighed og Historie* 5ff.

Doumas, C. 1992. *The Wall-Paintings of Thera.* Athens (The Thera Foundation. Petros M. Nomikos).

Duval, A. 1990. Quelques aspects du mobilier metallique en fer anciennement recueilli a Tronoen, en Saint-Jean-Trolimon (Finistère). Duval et al. 1990. 23ff.

Duval, A., J.P. Le Bihan & Y. Menez (eds.). 1990. *Les gaulois d'Armorique. La fin de l'Age du Fer en Europe tempérée. Actes du XIIe colloque de l'A.F.E.A.F. Quimper. Mai 1988.* Revue Archéologique de l'Ouest. Supplément 3.

Ebbesen, K. 1975. *Die jüngere Trichterbecherkultur auf den dänischen Inseln.* Arkæologiske Studier II. Copenhagen (Akademisk Forlag).

Ebbesen, K. 1979. *Stordyssen i Vedsted. Studier over tragtbægerkulturen i Sønderjylland.* Arkæologiske Studier VI. Copenhagen (Akademisk Forlag).

Ebbesen, K. 1986. Offerfundet fra Vejleby. *Fra Holbæk Amt.* 7ff.

Ebbesen, K. 1982. Flint Celts from Single-Grave Burials and Hoards on the Jutlandic Peninsula. *Acta Archaeologica* 53. 119ff.

Ebbesen, K. 1993. Sacrifices to the powers of nature. Hvass & Storgaard 1993. 122ff.

Edlund, I.E.M. 1987. *The Gods and the Place. Location and Function of Sanctuaries in the Countryside of Etruria and Magna Graecia (700-400 BC).* Skrifter utgivna av Svenska institutet i Rom, 4', XLIII. Gothenburg (Åström).

Egg, M. 1986. *Italische Helme. Studien zu den ältereisenzeitlichen Helmen Italiens und der Alpen 1-2.* Römisch-germanisches Zentralmuseum. Monographien 11;1-2. Mainz (Römisch-germanisches Zentralmuseum).

Engelhardt, C. 1865. *Nydam Mosefund 1859-1863.* Kjöbenhavn (Gad).

Engström, J. 1992. Skandinaviskt krigsväsen under mellersta järnåldern. *Meddelande från Arméuseum* 52. 14ff.

Fagerström, K. 1988. *Greek Iron Age Architecture. Developments through*

Changing Times. Studies in Mediterranean Archaeology LXXXI. Gothenburg (Åström).

Fellmann, B. 1984. *Frühe olympische Gürtelschmuckscheiben aus Bronze*. Olympische Forschungen XVI. Berlin (de Gruyter).

Fernández-Miranda, M. & R. Olmos. 1986. *Las ruedas de Toyo y el origin del carro en la Península Ibérica*. Museo Arqueologico Nacional. Catálogos y monografías 9. Madrid (Ministerio de Cultura).

Filip, J. 1970. Keltische Kultplätze und Heiligtümer in Böhmen. Jankuhn 1970. 55ff.

Filip, J. (ed.). 1966. Investigations archéologiques en Tchécoslovaquie. Etat actuel des recherches et leur organisation. *VIIème Congrès international des Sciences préhistoriques et protohistoriques ı Prague, 1966*. Prague (Academia).

Fischer, C. 1979. Moseligene fra Bjældskovdal. Kuml 7ff.

Fischer-Hansen, T., J. Lund, M. Nielsen & A. Rathje (eds.). 1992. *Ancient Portraiture. Image and Message*. Acta Hyperborea 4. Copenhagen (Museum Tusculanum).

Fitzpatrick, A.P. 1984. The Deposition of La Tène Metalwork in Watery Contexts in Southern England. Cunliffe & Miles 1984. 178ff.

French, E.B. & K.A. Wardle (eds.). 1988. *Problems in Greek Prehistory. Papers Presented at the Centenary Conference of the British School of Archaeology at Athens, Manchester April 1986*. Bristol (Bristol Classical Press).

Frey, O.-H. 1969. *Die Entstehung der Situlenkunst*. Römisch-germanische Forschungen XX. Berlin (W. de Gruyer).

Frey, O.-H. . 1973. Bemerkungen zur hallstättischen Bewaffnung im Südostalpenraum. *Arheoloski Vestnik* XXIV. 621ff.

Frizell, B.S. 1991. *Arte militare e architettura Nuragica. Nuragic Architecture in its Military, Territorial and Socio-Economic Context*. Proceedings of the First International Colloquium on Nuragic Architecture at the Swedish Institute in Rome, 7-9 December, 1989. Skrifter utgivna av Svenska institutet i Rom, 4', XLVIII.

Gabrovec, S. 1966. Zur Hallstattzeit in Slovenien. *Germania* 44. 1ff.

Gardner, R. & K.G. Heider. 1968. *Gardens of War. Life and Death in the New Guinea Stone Age*. New York (Random House).

Gediga, B. 1992. *Urgeschichtliche Sanktuarien auf den Gipfeln des Slęża-gebirges in Schlesien*. Schriften für das Vorarlberger Landesmuseum (Bregenz). Reihe A. Landschaftsgeschichte und Archäologie 5. Archäologie in Gebirgen. 113 ff.

Gedl, M. 1974. *Studien zur Lausitzer Kultur*. Zeszyty Naukowe Uniwersytetu Jagiellońskiego CCCLII. Prace Archeologiczne 18. Kraków (Naktadem Uniwersytetu Jagiellońskiego).

Gerdsen, H. 1986. *Studien zu den Schwertgräbern der älteren Hallstattzeit*. Mainz (Philipp von Zabern).

Görman, M. 1987. *Nordisk och keltisk. Sydskandinavisk religion under yngre bronsålder och keltisk järnålder*. Dalby (Görman).

Gräslund, B. 1989. Forntida själstro i arkeologisk belysning. *Kungliga Vitterhets Historie och Antikvitets Akademiens Årsbok*.

Griesa, S. 1989. Früheisenzeitliche Kultplätze. Schlette & Kaufmann 1989. 251ff.

Guibal, J. (ed.). 1990. *Les premiers princes celtes (2000 à 750 ans avant J.-C.). Autour de la tombe de Saint-Romain-de-Jalionas (Isère)*. Grenoble (Musée Dauphinois).

Guida, P.C. 1973. *Le armi difensive dei micenei nelle figurazioni*. Incunabula Graeca LVI. Roma (Ed. dell'Atenco).

Hägg, R. (ed.). 1983. *The Greek Renaissance of the Eighth Century BC: Tradition and Innovation. Proceedings of the Second International Symposium at the Swedish Institute in Athens, 1-5 June, 1981*. Skrifter utgivna av Svenska institutet i Athen, 4', XXX. Lund (Åström).

Hägg, R. & N. Marinatos (eds.). 1981. *Sanctuaries and Cults in the Aegean Bronze Age. Proceedings of the First International Symposium at the Swedish Institute in Athens, 12-13 May, 1980*. Skrifter utgivna av Svenska institutet i Athen, 4', XXVIII. Lund (Åström).

Hägg, R., N. Marinatos & G.C. Nordquist (eds.). 1988. *Early Greek Cult Practice. Proceedings of the Fifth International Symposium at the Swedish Institute at Athens, 26-29 June, 1986*. Skrifter utgivna av Svenska institutet i Athen, 4', XXXVIII. Gothenburg (Åström).

Hansen, S. 1991. *Studien zu den Metalldeponierungen während der Urnenfelderzeit im Rhein-Main-Gebiet*. Universitätsforschungen zur prähistorischen Archäologie 5. Bonn (Habelt).

Hanson, V.D. 1991. Hoplite Technology in Phalanx Battle. Hanson (ed.) 1991. 63ff.

Hanson, V.D. (ed.). 1991. *Hoplites*. The Classical Greek Battle Experience. London (Routledge).

Härke, H. 1992. *Angelsächsische Waffengräber des 5. bis 7. Jahrhunderts*. Zeitschrift für Archäologie des Mittelalters. Beiheft 6. Köln (Rheinland-Verlag).

Hatt, J.-J. 1989. *Mythes et dieux de la Gaule 1. Les grandes divinités masculins*. Paris (Picard).

Hauck, K. 1992. Frühmittelalterliche Bildüberlieferung und der organisierte Kult (Zur Ikonographie der Goldbrakteaten, XLIV). Hauck (ed.) 1992. 433ff.

Hauck, K. 1994. *Altuppsalas Polytheismus exemplarisch erhellt mit Bildzeugnissen des 5.-7. Jahrhunderts* (Zur Ikonologie der Goldbrakteaten, LIII). Uecker 1994. 197ff.

Hauck, K. (ed.). 1992. *Der historische Horizont der Götterbild-Amulette aus der Übergangsepoche von der Spätantike zum Frühmittelalter. Bericht über das Colloquium vom 28.11.-1.12 1988 in der Werner-Reimers-Stiftung, Bad Homburg*. Abhandlungen der Akademie der Wissenschaften in Göttingen. Philologisch-historische Klasse. Dritte Folge 200. Göttingen (Vandenhoeck & Ruprecht).

Hawkes, S.C. (ed.). 1989. *Weapons and Warfare in Anglo-Saxon England*. Oxford University Committee for Archaeology. Monograph 21.

Heidelk-Schacht, S. 1989. Jungbronzezeitliche und früheisenzeitliche Kultfeuerplätze im Norden der DDR. Schlette & Kaufmann 1989. 255ff.

Helms, M.W. 1988. *Ulysses' Sail. An Ethnographic Odyssey of Power, Knowledge, and Geographical Distance*. Princeton (Princeton University Press).

Hencken, H. 1971. *The Earliest European Helmets. Bronze Age and Early Iron Age*. American School of Prehistoric Research. Peabody Museum, Harvard University. Bulletin 28.

Herrmann, J. 1989. Burgen und befestigte Siedlungen der jüngeren Bronzezeit und frühen Eisenzeit. Herrmann 1989. 106ff.

Herrmann, J. (et al.) (ed.). 1989. *Archäologie in der Deutschen Demokratischen Republik. Denkmale und Funde 1. Archäologische Kulturen, geschichtliche Perioden und Volkstämme*. Leipzig/Stuttgart (Urania/Konrad Theiss).

[(Hertz, J. et al. (eds.)]/Rigsantikvarens Arkæologiske Sekretariat. 1987.

Danmarks længste udgravning.
Arkæologi på naturgassens vej 1979-86.
Copenhagen/Herning (National
Museum of Denmark & de danske
naturgasselskaber/Poul Kristensen).

Hertz, J. & S. Nielsen (et al.). 1994. *5000 år
under motorvejen.* Copenhagen
(Vejdirektoratet og Rigsantikvarens
Arkæologiske Sekretariat).

Hiller, S. 1983. Mycenean Traditions in
Early Greek Cult Images. Hägg 1983.
91ff.

Hjortsø, L. 1982. *Romerske guder og helte.*
Copenhagen (Politiken).

Hjortsø, L. 1984. *Græske guder og helte.*
Copenhagen (Politiken).

Hodder, I. 1990. *The Domestication of
Europe. Structure and Contingency in
Neolithic Societies.* Oxford (Blackwell).

Hoddinott, R.F. 1981. *The Thracians.*
London (Thames & Hudson).

Höpfel, F., W. Platzer & K. Spindler
(eds.). 1992. *Der Mann im Eis 1. Bericht
über das Internationale Symposium 1992
in Innsbruck.* Veröffentlichungen der
Universität Innsbruck 187. Innsbruck
(Universität Innsbruck).

Hvass, S. & B. Storgaard (eds.). 1993.
*Digging into the Past. 25 Years of
Archaeology in Denmark.*
Copenhagen/Aarhus (Royal Society of
Northern Antiquities/Jutland
Archaeological Society/(Aarhus Uni-
versity Press)).

Ilkjær, J. 1989. The Weapons Sacrifices
from Illerup Ådal, Denmark.
Randsborg 1989. 54ff.

Ilkjær, J. 1990. *Illerup Ådal 1-2. Die Lanzen
und Speere.* Jutland Archaeological
Society Publications XXV:1-2. Århus
(Aarhus University Press).

Ilkjær, J. 1993. *Illerup Ådal 3-4. Die Gürtel.*
Jutland Archaeological Society
Publications XXV:3-4. Århus (Aarhus
University Press).

Jankuhn, H. (ed.). 1970. *Vorgeschichtliche
Heiligtümer und Opferplätze in Mittel-*

*und Nordeuropa. Bericht über ein
Symposium in Reinhausen bei Göttingen
in der Zeit vom 14. bis. 16. Oktober 1968.*
Abhandlungen der Akademie der
Wissenschaften in Göttingen.
Philologisch-historische Klasse III. 74.
Göttingen (Vandenhoeck & Ruprecht).

Jannot, J.-R. 1991. Armement, tactique et
société. Réflections sur l'exemple de
l'Étrurie archaïque. Frizell 1991. 73ff.

Jansová, L. 1983. Dva fragmenty
kamenných skuptur ze Závisti.
Památky Archeologické LXXIV;2.
350ff.

Jansson S. 1994. Nordsvensk
Hjortspringbåd? *Marinarkæologisk Ny-
hedsbrev fra Roskilde* 2 (Maj 1994). 16ff.

Jaskanisa, J. (ed.). 1991. *Prahistoryczny
gród w Biskupinie. Problematyka osiedli
obronnych na początku epoki żelaza.*
Warszawa (Państwowo Museum
Archeologiczne/Wydawnistwo
Naukowe).

Jensen, J. 1966. Griffzungenschwerter der
späten nordischen Bronzezeit. *Acta
Archaeologica* XXXVII. 25ff.

Jensen, J. 1969. Ein thrako-kimmerischer
Goldfund aus Dänemark. *Acta
Archaeologica* XL. 159ff.

Jensen, J. 1972. Ein neues
Hallstattschwert aus Dänemark.
Beitrag zur Problematik der
jungbronzezeitlichen Votivfunde. *Acta
Archaeologica* XLIII. 115ff.

Jensen, J. 1982. *Nordens guld. En bog om
oldtidens rav, mennesker og myter.*
Copenhagen (Gyldendal).

Jensen, J. 1993. Metal deposits. Hvass &
Storgaard 1993. 152ff.

Jørgensen, E. 1968. Sønder Vilstrup-
fundet. En gravplads fra ældre
jernalder. *Aarbøger for Nordisk
Oldkyndighed og Historie* 32ff.

Jørgensen, L.B. 1971. Et fodbæger i
særegen form fra Stensebygård,
Bodilsker sogn. *Bornholmske Samlinger*
77ff.

Kaenel, G. & P. Curdy (eds.). 1992. *L'Âge du Fer dans le Jura. Actes du 15e colloque de l'Association française pour l'étude de l'Âge du Fer.* Pontarlier (France) et Yverdon-les-Bains (Suisse). Cahiers d'archéologie romande. Bibliothèque historique vaudoise 57.

Karlenby, L. 1994. The Bronze Age house in central Sweden. An evaluation of two recent excavations. *Tor* 26. 5ff.

Kaul, F. 1985. Sandagergård. A Late Bronze Age Cultic Building with Rock Engravings and Menhirs from Northern Zealand, Denmark. *Acta Archaeologica* 56. 31ff.

Kaul, F. 1988. *Da våbnene tav. Hjortspringfundet og dets baggrund.* Copenhagen (National Museum of Denmark/Nyt Nordisk Forlag).

Kaul, F. 1991. *Gundestrupkedlen. Baggrund og billedverden.* Copenhagen (National Museum of Denmark/Nyt Nordisk Forlag).

Kaul, F. 1994. Trivselstegnet. *Skalk* 3. 11ff.

Kaul, F. 1995. The Gundestrup Cauldron. *Acta Archaeologica* 66. (Forthcoming.)

Keegan, J. 1993. *A History of Warfare.* New York (Alfred A. Knopf).

Kemp, B.J. 1989. *Ancient Egypt. Anatomy of a Civilization.* London (Routledge).

Kersten, K. 1936. Das Totenhaus von Grünhof-Tesperhude, Kr. Herzogtum Lauenburg. *Offa* I. 56ff.

Kilian K. 1975. Trachtzubehör der Eisenzeit zwischen Ägäis und Adria. *Prähistorische Zeitschrift* 50. 9ff.

Kilian, K. 1983. Weihungen aus Eisen und Eisenverarbeitung im Heiligtum zu Philia (Thessalien). Hägg 1983. 131ff.

Kilian, K. 1988. Mycenaeans Up To Date, Trends and Changes in Recent Reserach. French & Wardle 1988. 115ff.

Kilian-Dirlmeier, I. 1985. Fremde Weihungen in griechischen Heiligtümern vom 8. bis zum Beginn des 7. Jahrhunderts v. Chr. *Jahrbuch des römisch-germanischen Zentralmuseum Mainz* 32. 215ff.

Kilian-Dirlmeyer, I. 1986. Beobachtungen zu den Schachtgräbern von Mykenai und zu den Schmuckbeigaben mykenischer Männergräber. Untersuchungen zur Sozialstruktur in späthelladischer Zeit. *Jahrbuch des römisch-germanisches Zentralmuseum Mainz* 33;1. 159ff.

Kilian-Dirlmeyer, I. 1993. *Die Schwerter in Griechenland (ausserhalb der Peloponnes), Bulgarien und Albanien.* Prähistorische Bronzefunde IV;12. Stuttgart (Steiner).

Kimmig, W. 1981. Buchau. *Reallexikon der Germanischen Altertumskunde* 4. Berlin (de Gruyter). 37ff.

Kimmig, W. 1983. *Die Heuneburg an der oberen Donau.* Führer zu archäologischen Denkmälern in Baden-Württemberg 1. 2nd.ed. Stuttgart (Theiss).

Klochko, V.I. 1993. *Weapons of the Tribes of the Northern Pontic Zone in the 16th-10th Centuries BC.* Baltic-Pontic Studies 1. Poznań (Institute of Prehistory, The University).

Knorr, F. 1910. *Friedhöfe der älteren Eisenzeit in Schleswig-Holstein.* Kiel (Lipsius & Tischer).

Krämer, W. 1985. *Die Grabfunde von Manching und die latènezeitlichen Flachgräber in Südbayern.* Die Ausgrabungen in Manching 9. Stuttgart (Franz Steiner Wiebaden).

Krause, R. 1988. *Die endneolitischen und frühbronzezeitlichen Grabfunde auf der Nordstadterrasse von Singen am Hohenwiel.* (Grabfunde von Singen am Hohenwiel I). Forschungen und Berichte zur Vor- und Frühgeschichte in Baden-Württemberg 32. Stuttgart (Theiss).

Kremer, B. 1994. *Das Bild der Kelten bis in augusteische Zeit. Studien zur instrumentalisierung eines antiken*

Feindbildes bei griechischen und römischen Autoren. Historia. Einzelschriften 88. Stuttgart (Franz Steiner).

Kromer, K. 1986. Das östliche Mitteleuropa in der frühen Eisenzeit (7.-5. Jh. v.Chr.). Seine Beziehungen zu Steppenvölkern und antiken Hochkulturen. *Jahrbuch des römisch-germanischen Zentralmuseums Mainz* 33;1. 3ff.

Kruta, V., B. Lambot, J.-M. Lardy & A. Rapin. 1984. Les fourreaux d'Epiais-Rhus (Val d'Oise) et de Saint-Germainmont (Ardennes) et l'art celtique du IVe siècle avant J.-C. *Gallia* 42;1. 1ff.

Kunst, M. 1978. *Arm und Reich — Jung und Alt.* (Untersuchungen zu sozialen Gruppierungen auf dem Gräberfeld von Hamfelde, Kreis Herzogtum Lauenburg). *Offa* 35. 86ff.

Kytlicová, O. 1988. K sociální struktuře kultury popelnicových polí. *Památky Archeologické* LXXIX;2. 342ff.

La Baume, W. 1963. *Die pommerellischen Gesichtsurnen.* Römisch-germanisches Zentralmuseum zu Mainz. Kataloge vor- und frühgeschichtlicher Altertümer 17.

Lambot, B., 1991. Quelques aspects funeraires et cultuels chez les Rèmes. Brunaux 1991. 66 ff.

Larsson, T.B. 1986. *The Bronze Age Metalwork in Southern Sweden. Aspects of Social and Spatial Organization 1800-500 BC.* Archaeology and Environment 6. Umeå (University of Umeå, Department of Archaeology).

Lazenby, J. 1991. The Killing Zone. Hanson 1991. 87ff.

Lenerz-de Wilde, M. 1991. *Iberia Celtica. Archäologische Zeugnisse keltischer Kultur auf der Pyrenäenhalbinsel 1-2.* Stuttgart (Franz Steiner).

Levy, J.E. 1984. *Social and Religious Organization in Bronze Age Denmark. An*

Analysis of Ritual Hoard Finds. BAR International Series 124. Oxford (BAR).

Lichardus, J. (ed.). *Die Kupferzeit als historische Epoche 1-2. Symposium Saarbrücken und Otzenhausen 6.-13.11.1988.* Saarbrücker Beiträge zur Altertumskunde 55.

Lilliu, G. 1987. *La civiltà nuragica. Sardegna archeologica.* Studi e Monomenti 1. Sassari (Carlo Delfino).

Lindahl, F. 1988. *Skattefund. Sølv fra Christian IVs tid.* Copenhagen (National Museum of Denmark).

Liversage, D. 1992. *Barkær. Long Barrows and Settlements.* Arkæologiske Studier IX. Copenhagen (Akademisk Forlag).

Lomborg, E. 1956. En højgruppe ved Ballermosen, Jægerspris. *Aarbøger for Nordisk Oldkyndighed og Historie.* 144ff.

Lomborg, B. 1973. En landsby med huse og kultsted fra ældre bronzealder. *Nationalmuseets Arbejdsmark.* 5ff.

Lønborg, B. 1990. Oldtidens drejebænk. *Skalk* 3. 4ff.

Lønstrup, J. 1988. Mosefund af hærudstyr fra jernalderen. Mortensen & Rasmussen. 93ff.

Lorenz, H. 1978. Totenbrauchtum und Tracht. Untersuchungen zur regionalen Gliederung in der frühen Latènezeit. *Berichte der römisch-germanischen Kommission 59.* 1ff.

Lund, A.A. 1993. *De etnografiske kilder til Nordens tidlige historie.* Århus (Aarhus University Press).

Mackeprang, M.B. 1935. Menschendarstellungen aus der Eisenzeit Dänemarks. *Acta Archaeologica* VI. 228ff.

Madsen, T. 1986. Where did all the Hunters go? — an Assessment of an Epoch-making Episode in Danish Prehistory. *Journal of Danish Archaeology* 5. 229ff.

Maier, F. 1990. Das Kultbäumchen von Manching. *Germania* 68;1. 129ff.

Malnati, L. & V. Manfredi. 1991. *Gli*

Etruschi in Val Padana. Milano (Il Saggiatore).

Marinatos, S. (& M. Hirmer). 1960. *Crete and Mycenae.* London (Thames & Hudson).

Martens, J. 1994. Refuge — fortified settlement — central place? Three years of archaeological investigations at the Borremose stronghold (1988-1991), an enclosed settlement from the Pre-Roman Iron Age of Himmerland. *Ethnographisch-archäologische Zeitschrift* 35. 241ff.

Menke, M. 1978-79. Studien zu den frühbronzezeitlichen Metalldepots Bayerns. *Jahresbericht der Bayerischen Bodendenkmalpflege* 19-20. 5ff.

Mordant, C. & D. & J.-Y. Prampart (et al.). 1976. *Le dépôt de bronze de Villethierry (Yonne).* Gallia Préhistoire, suppl. IX. Paris (Editions du CNRS).

Mortensen, P. & B.M. Rasmussen (eds.). 1988. *Jernalderens Stammesamfund.* Fra Stamme til Stat i Danmark 1. Jysk Arkæologisk Selskabs Skrifter XXII. Aarhus (Aarhus Universitetsforlag).

Moscati, S. with O.H. Frey, V. Kruta, B. Raftery & M. Szabó (eds). 1991. *The Celts.* Milano (Bompiani).

Motyková, K., P. Drda & A. Rybová. 1977. The position of Závist in the Early La Tène period in Bohemia. *Památky Archeologické* LXVIII;2. 255f.

Motyková, K., P. Drda & A. Rybová. 1978. *Závist. Keltské hradiště ve středních Cechách.* Památníky naší minulosti 9. Praha (Academia nakladatelství Československé akademie věd).

Motyková, K., P. Drda & A. Rybová. 1984. Opevnění pozdně Halštatského a šasně Laténského hradiště Zavíst. *Památky Archeologické* LXXV;2. 331ff.

Motyková, K., P. Drda & A. Rybová. 1988. Die bauliche Gestalt der Akropolis auf dem Burgwall Závist in der Späthallstatt- und Frühlatènezeit. *Germania* 66;2. 391ff.

Mozsolics, A. 1985. *Bronzefunde aus Ungarn. Depotfundhorizonte von Aranyos, Kurd und Gyermely.* Budapest (Akadémiai Kiadó).

Müller, A. von. 1964. *Die jungbronzezeitliche Siedlung von Berlin-Lichterfelde.* Berliner Beiträge zur Vor- und Frühgeschichte 9. Berlin (Hessling).

Müller, F. 1992. La Tène (canton de Neuchâtel) et Port (canton de Berne): les sites, les trouvailles et leur interprétation. Kaenel & Curdy 1992. 323ff.

Müller, S. 1897. *Vor Oldtid. Danmarks forhistoriske Archæologi.* Copenhagen (Nordisk).

Müller, S. 1900. Et bornholmsk Lerkar af klassisk Form. *Aarbøger for nordisk Oldkyndighed og Historie.* 144ff.

Müller-Brauel, H. 1932. Eine Familien-Grabstätte eines eisenzeitlichen Urnenfriedhofs zu Breddorf, Kr. Zeven. *Mannus* XXIV. 445ff.

Müller-Karpe, H. 1974. *Das Grab 871 von Veji, Grotta Gramiccia.* Prähistorische Bronzefunde XX;1. München (Beck). 89ff.

Müller-Karpe, H. 1980. *Bronzezeit.* Handbuch der Vorgeschichte IV. München (Beck).

Müller-Wille, M. 1976. Das Bootkammergrab von Haithabu. *Berichte über die Ausgrabungen in Haithabu* 8.

Neumann, G. & H. Seemann (eds.). 1992. *Beiträge zum Verständnis der Germania des Tacitus.* Bericht über die Kolloquien der Kommission für die Altertumskunde Nord- und Mitteleuropas im Jahre 1986 und 1987 I-II. Göttingen (Vandenhoeck & Ruprecht).

Nielsen, J.L. 1975. Aspekter af det førromerske våbengravsmiljø i Jylland. *Hikuin* 2. 89ff.

Niesiołowska-Wędzka, A. 1989. *Procesy*

urbanizacyjne w kulturze łużyckiej w świetle oddziaływań kultur Południowych. Polskie Badania Archeologiczne 29. Wrocław etc. (Polska Akademia Nauk.)

Norling-Christensen, H. 1946. The Viksø Helmets. A Bronze-Age Votive Find from Zealand. *Acta Archaeologica* XVII. 99ff.

Orcel, A., C. Orcel & J. Tercier. 1992. L'état des recherches dendrochronologiques concernant l'âge du Fer à Yverdon-les-Bains (canton de Vaud). Kaenel & Curdy 1992. 301ff.

Ordentlich, I. 1972. Contribuţia săpăturilor arheologice de pe 'Dealul Vida' (com. Sălacea, judeţul Bihor) la cunoaşterea culturii Otomani. *Satu Mare-Studii şi Comunicări* 15. 63ff.

Orosius, Paulus. 1936. *Seven Books of History against the Pagans.* (The Apology of Paulus Orosius.) Translated by I.W. Raymond. New York (Columbia University Press).

Ørsnes, M. 1958. Borbjergfundet. Hjemligt og fremmed i et jysk depotfund fra bronzealderens fjerde periode. *Aarbøger for Nordisk Oldkyndighed og Historie.* 1ff.

Ørsnes, M. 1984. *Sejrens pris. Våbenofre i Ejsbøl Mose ved Haderslev.* Haderslev (Haderslev Museum).

Ørsnes, M. 1988. *Ejsbøl I. Waffenopferfunde des 4.-5. Jahrhundert nach Chr.* Nordiske Fortidsminder B, Band 11.

Ørsnes. M. & J. Ilkjær. 1993. Votive deposits. Hvass & Storgaard 1993. 215ff.

Osborne, R. 1987. *Classical Landscape with Figures. The Ancient Greek City and its Countryside.* London (George Philip).

Ostoja-Zagórski, J. 1982. *Przemiany osadnicze, demografíczne i gospodarcze w okresie halsztackim na Pomorzu.* Wrocław, etc. (Polska Akademia Nauk. Instytut Historii Kultury Materialnej).

Ostoja-Zagórski, I. 1983. Aspekte der Siedlungskunde, Demographie und Wirtschaft hallstattzeitlicher Burgen vom Biskupin-Typ. *Prähistorische Zeitschrift* 58. 173ff.

Pare, C.F.E. 1989. From Dupljaja to Delphi: the ceremonial use of the waggon in later prehistory. *Antiquity* 63. No. 238. March. 80ff.

Pare, C.F.B. 1992. *Wagons and Wagon-Graves of the Early Iron Age in Central Europe.* Oxford University Committee for Archaeology. Monograph 35. Oxford (Oxford University Committee for Archaeology).

Parzinger, H & S. Stegmann-Rajtár. 1988. Smolenice-Molpír und der Beginn skythischer Sachkultur in der Südwestslowakei. *Prähistorische Zeitschrift* 63;1. 162ff.

Pascucci, P. 1990. *I depositi votivi paleoveneti. Per un'archeologia del culto.* Archeologia Veneta XIII. Padova (Societá archeologica Veneta).

Pauli, L. 1980. *Die Alpen in Frühzeit und Mittelalter.* München (C.H. Beck).

Pauli, L. 1985. Einige Anmerkungen zum Problem der Hortfunde. *Archäologisches Korrespondenzblatt* 15. 195ff.

Pausanias. c. AD 175/180 *Guide to Greece* (title translated from Greek).

Pedersen, J.-Aa. 1986. A New Early Bronze Age House-Site under a Barrow at Hyllerup, Western Zealand. *Journal of Danish Archaeology* 5. 168ff.

Peroni, R. 1994. *Introduzione alla protostoria italiana.* Roma (Laterza).

Pescheck, C. 1972. Ein reicher Grabfund mit Kesselwagen aus Unterfranken. *Germania* 50. 29ff.

Petersen, H. 1888. *Vognfundene i Dejbjerg Præstegaardsmose ved Ringkjøbing 1881 og 1883. Et Bidrag til Oplysning om den førromerske Jernalder i Danmark.* Copenhagen (C.A. Reitzel).

Petersen, J. 1919. *De norske vikingesverd. En typologisk-kronologisk studie over vikingetidens vaaben.*

Videnskapsselskapets Skrifter II. Hist.-filos. Klasse 1919. No. 1. Oslo (Jacob Dybvad).

Planck, D., J. Biel, G. Süsskind & A. Wais (eds.). 1985. *Der Keltenfürst von Hochdorf. Methoden und Ergebnisse der Landesarchäologie. Katalog zur Ausstellung Stuttgart, Kunstgebäude vom 14. August bis 13. Oktober 1985.* Stuttgart (Landesdenkmalamt Baden-Württemberg/Theiss).

de Polignac, F. 1991. Convergence et compétition: aux origines des sanctuaries de souveraineté territoriale dans le monde grec. Bruneaux 1991. 97ff.

Poulík, J. & J. Nekvasil (eds.). 1969. *Hallstatt a Býčý Skála.* Brno (etc.) (Československá Akademia věd. Archeologický ústav).

Py, M. 1990. *Culture, Économie et société protohistoriques dans la région nimoise 1-2.* Collections de l'École française de Rome 131. Paris/Rome (de Boccard/Bretschneider).

Radt, W. 1974. *Die früheisenzeitliche Hügelnekropole bei Vergina in Makedonien.* Prähistorische Bronzefunde XX;1. München (Beck). 98ff.

Randsborg, K. 1967. 'Aegean' Bronzes in a Grave in Jutland. *Acta Archaeologica* XXXVIII. 1ff.

Randsborg, K. 1990. The Periods of Danish Antiquity. *Acta Archaeologica* 60. 187ff.

Randsborg, K. 1991. Gallemose. A Chariot from the Early Second Millennium BC in Denmark? *Acta Archaeologica* 62. 109ff.

Randsborg, K. 1992. Historical Implications. Chronological Studies in European Archaeology c. 2000-500 BC *Acta Archaeologica* 62. 89ff.

Randsborg, K. 1993A. Greek Peripheries & Barbarian Centres. Economic Realities and Cultural Responses. Bilde et al. 1993. 86ff.

Randsborg, K. 1993B. *Kivik. Archaeology and Iconography.* Acta Archaeologica 64;1. (1ff.)

Randsborg, K. 1994. Ole Worm. An Essay on the Modernization of Antiquity. *Acta Archaeologica* 65.

Randsborg, K. & C. Nybo. 1984. The Coffin and the Sun. Demography and Ideology in Scandinavian Prehistory. *Acta Archaeologica* 55. 161ff.

Randsborg, K. (ed.). 1989. *The Birth of Europe. Archaeology and Social Development in the First Millennium AD.* Analecta Romana Instituti Danici. Supplementum XVI. Rome (Bretschneider).

Randsborg, K. (ed.). Forthcoming. *Kephallénia. Archaeology and History.*

Rapin, A. 1982. Das keltische Heiligtum von Gournay-sur-Aronde. *Antike Welt* 13;2. 39ff.

Rapin, A. 1988. L'armement, fil conducteur des mutations du Second Age de Fer. Duval et al. 1988. 287ff.

Rapin, A. 1991. Weaponry. Moscati (et al.) 1991. 321ff.

Rapin, A. & J.L. Brunaux. 1988. *Gournay II. Boucliers, lances. Dépôt et trophées.* Révue archéologique de Picardie. (Errance.)

Rech, M. 1979. *Studien zu Depotfunden der Trichterbecher- und Einzelgräberkultur des Nordens.* Offa-Bücher 39. Neumünster (Wachholz).

Reichenberger, A. 1994. 'Herrenhöfe' der Urnenfelder- und Hallstattzeit. (Schauer) 1994. 187 ff.

Renfrew, C. 1972. *The Emergence of Civilisation. The Cyclades and the Aegean in the Third Millennium BC.* London (Methuen).

Renfrew, C. 1981. Questions of Minoan and Mycenean Cult. Hägg & Marinatos 1981. 27ff.

Renfrew, C. (et al.). 1985. *The Archaeology of Cult. The Sanctuary at Phylakopi.* The British School of Archaeology at

Athens. Supplement 18. London
(Thames & Hudson).

Renfrew, C. & E.B.W. Zubrow (eds.). 1994.
The ancient mind. Elements of cognitive archaeology. New directions in archaeology. Cambridge (Cambridge University Press).

Rhomiopoulou, K. & I. Kilian-Dirlmeier. 1989. Neue Funde aus der eisenzeitlichen Hügelnekropole von Vergina, Griechisch Makedonien. *Prähistorische Zeitschrift* 64;1. 86ff.

Rich, J. & G. Shipley (eds.). 1993. *War and Society in the Greek World.* London (Routledge).

Rieck, F. 1991. Aspects of coastal defense in Denmark. Crumlin-Pedersen 1991. 83ff.

Rieck, F. 1994. The Iron Age Boats from Hjortspring and Nydam — New Investigations. Westerdahl 1994. 45ff.

Rieck, F. & O. Crumlin-Pedersen. 1988. *Både fra Danmarks oldtid.* Roskilde (Vikingeskibshallen).

Rolley, C. 1983. Les grandes sanctuaires panhelléniques. Hägg 1983. 109ff.

Rosenberg, G. 1937. *Hjortspringfundet.* Nordiske Fortidsminder III;1. Copenhagen (Gyldendal).

Roymans, N. 1990. *Tribal Societies in Northern Gaul. An anthropological perspective.* Cingula 12. Amsterdam (Albert Egges van Giffen Instituut voor Prae- en Protohistorie).

Rusu, M. 1969. Das keltische Fürstengrab von Ciumeşti in Rumänien. *Berichte der römisch-germanischen Kommission 50.* 267ff.

Rutkowski, B. 1986. *The Cult Places of the Aegean.* New Haven (Yale University Press).

Rybová, A. & B. Soudský. 1962. *Libenice. Keltská svatyně v středních Čechách.* Monumenta Archaeologica X. (Praha).

Rychner, V. 1979. *L'age du bronze final a Auvernier (Lac de Neuchatel, Suisse). Typologie et chronologie des anciennes* collections conservées en Suisse. Auvernier 1-2. Cahiers d'Archéologie Romande 15-16. (Lausanne).

Sakellarakis, J.A. & E. Sapouna-Sakellaraki. 1991. *Archanes.* Athens (Ekdotike Athenon).

Salo, U. 1962. Früheisenzeitliche Lanzenspitzen der skandinavischen Halbinsel. *Acta Archaeologica* XXXIII;1. 63ff.

Sanden, W.A.B. van der (ed.). 1990. *Mens en moeras. Veenlijken in Nederland van de bronstijd tot en met de Romeinse tijd.* Archeologische Monografieën van het Drents Museum 1. Assen (Drents Museum).

Schauer, P. 1971. *Die Schwerter in Süddeutschland, Österrreich und der Schweiz I (Griffplatten-, Griffangel- und Griffzungenschwerter).* Prähistorische Bronzefunde IV,2. München (Beck).

Schauer, P. 1980. Der Rundschild der Bronze und frühen Eisenzeit. *Jahrbuch des römisch-germanischen Zentralmuseums Mainz* 27;II. 196ff.

Schauer, P. 1982. Die Beinschienen der späten Bronze- und frühen Eisenzeit. *Jahrbuch des römisch-germanischen Zentralmuseums Mainz* 29. 100ff.

(Schauer, P.) 1994. *Archäologische Untersuchungen zum Übergang von der Bronze- zur Eisenzeit zwischen Nordsee und Kaukasus. Ergebnisse eines Kolloquiums in Regensburg 28.-30. Oktober 1992.* Regensburger Beiträge zur prähistorischen Archäologie 1. Regensburg/Bonn (Universitätsverlag/ Habelt).

Schindler, R. 1960. *Die Bodenaltertümer der freien und Hansestadt Hamburg.* Veröffentlichungen des Museums für hamburgische Geschichte. Abteilung Bodendenkmalpflege I. Hamburg (Hans Christian).

Schlette, F. & D. Kaufmann (eds.). 1989. *Religion und Kult in ur- und frühgeschichtlicher Zeit.* Historiker-

Gesellschaft der DDR. XIII. Tagung der Fachgruppe Ur- und Frühgescgichte vom 4. bis 6. November 1985 in Halle (Saale). Berlin (Akademie-Verlag).

Schlüter, W. (ed.). 1993. *Kalkriese — Römer im Osnabrücker Land. Archäologische Forschungen zur Varusschlacht.* Bramsche (Rasch).

Schoknecht, U. 1973. Ein früheisenzeitlicher Lanzenhort aus dem Malliner Wasser bei Passentin, Kreis Waren. *Bodendenkmalpflege in Mecklenburg. Jahrbuch* 1973. 157ff.

Schubart, H. 1975. *Die Kultur der Bronzezeit im Südwesten der Iberischen Halbinsel.* Madrider Forschungen 9. Madrid (Deutsches archäologisches Institut).

Schüle, W. 1969. *Die Meseta-Kulturen der iberischen Halbinsel. Mediterrane und Eurasische Elemente in Früheisenzeitlichen Kulturen Südwesteuropas.* Madrider Forschungen 3:1-2. Madrid/Berlin (Deutsches archäologisches Institut Madrid/W. de Gruyter).

Schwabedissen, H. 1949. Die Bedeutung der Moorarchäologie für die Urgeschichtforschung. *Offa* 8. 46ff.

Schwantes, G. 1911. *Die ältesten Urnenfriedhöfe bei Uelzen und Lüneburg.* Die Urnenfriedhöfe in Niedersachsen I. Hannover.

Ščukin, M.B. & V.E. Eremenko. 1991. Zur Frage der Datierung keltischer Altertümer in Transkarpatengebiet der Ukraine und einige Probleme der Latène-Chronologie. *Acta Archaeologica Carpathica* XXX. 115ff.

Shaw, I. 1991. *Egyptian Warfare and Weapons.* Princes Risborough (Shire).

Sherratt, A. 1990. The genesis of megeliths: monumentality, ethnicity and social complexity in Neolithic north-west Europe. *World Archaeology* 22;2 (October). 147ff.

Sherratt, S. & A. 1993. The growth of the Mediterranean economy in the early first millennium BC. *World Archaeology* 24;3 (February). 361ff.

Shetelig, H. 1912. *Vestlandske Graver fra Jernalderen.* Bergens Museums Skrifter, n.s. II;1. Bergen.

Sievers, S. 1991. Armes et sanctuaires à Manching. Bruneaux 1991. 146ff.

Simon, K. 1984. Höhensiedlungen der Urnenfelder- und Hallstattzeit in Thüringen. *Alt-Thüringen* 20. 23ff.

Snodgrass, A. 1964. *Early Greek Armour and Weapons. From the End of the Bronze Age to 600 BC.* Edinburgh (Edinburgh University Press).

Snodgrass, A. 1967. *Arms and Armour of the Greeks.* London (Thames and Hudson).

Snodgrass, A. 1980. *Archaic Greece. The Age of Experiment.* London (Dent).

Snorri Sturluson (d. AD1241). Early 13th century/c. AD 1200 (A). The Elder Edda ['The Older Great-Grandmother' (in fact, a handbook for poets); the first part, Gylfaginning ('The Blindness of King Gylfa'), is a survey of the Nordic mythology]. (Several editions and translations (even excerpts in English), including Larsen, M. (ed.). 1943-45. *Den ældre Edda og Eddica minora.* Copenhagen (Gyldendal?).)

Snorri Sturluson. Early 13th century/c. AD 1200 (B). Heimskringla ['The Earth's Disk', The Norwegian Royal Sagas]. (Several editions and translations, including Hødnebø, F. & H. Magerøy (eds.). 1979. *Norges Kongesagaer* 1-5. Oslo (Gyldendal Norsk Forlag).)

Sørensen, J.K. 1992. Haupttypen sakraler Ortsnamen Südskandinaviens. Mit einem Anhang zur Kartierung der exemplarisch erörterten Sakralnahmen Südskandinaviens auf einem Falttafel. Hauck 1992. 228ff.

Soudský, B. 1966. Habitat de la civilisation de Knovíz à Čakovice près de Prague (Bohème). Filip 1966. 159.

Sparkes, B.A. & L. Talcott. 1970. *Black and Plain Pottery of the 6th, 5th and 4th Centuries BC The Athenian Agora XII;1-2.* Princeton (The American School of Classical Studies at Athens).

Spindler, K. (ed.) 1980. *Vorzeit zwischen Main und Donau. Neue archäologische Forschungen und Funde aus Franken und Altbayern.* Erlanger Forschungen Reihe A 26. Erlangen-Nürnberg (Universitätsbund/ Universitätsbibliothek).

Spivey, N. & S. Stoddart. 1990. *Etruscan Italy. An Archaeological History.* London (Batsford).

Stary, P.F. 1979. Foreign Elements in Etruscan Arms and Armour: 8th to 3rd centuries BC. *Proceedings of the Prehistoric Society* 45. 179ff.

Stary, F.P. 1980. Das spätbronzezeitliche Häuptlingsgrab von Hagenau, Kr. Regensburg. Spindler 1980, 47ff.

Stary, F.P. 1981a. *Zur eisenzeitlichen Bewaffnung und Kampfesweise in Mittelitalien (Ca. 9. bis 6. Jh. v. Chr.)* Marburger Studien zur Vor- und Frühgeschichte 3 (Text & Tafeln).

Stary, F.P. 1981b. Ursprung und Ausbreitung der eisenzeitlichen Ovalschilde mit spindelförmigem Schildbuckel. *Germania* 59;2. 287ff.

Stary, F.P. 1982. Zur hallstattzeitlichen Beilbewaffnung des circum-alpinen Raumes. *Bericht der römisch-germanischen Kommission* 63. 17ff.

Stary, F.P. 1991. Arms and Armour of the Nuragic Warrior-Statuettes. Frizell 1991. 119ff.

Stein, F. 1967. *Adelsgräber des achten Jahrhunderts in Deutschland.* Germanische Denkmäler der Völkerwanderungszeit A IX. Berlin (de Gruyter).

Steuer, H. 1970. Historische Phasen der Bewaffnung nach Aussagen der archäologischen Quellen Mittel- und Nordeuropas im ersten Jahrtausends n.Chr. *Frühmittelalterliche Studien* 4. 348ff.

Steuer, H. 1987. Helm und Ringschwert. Prunkbewaffnung und Rangabzeichen germanischer Krieger. Eine Übersicht. *Studien zur Sachsenforschung* 6. 189ff.

Steuer, H. 1989. Archaeology and History. Proposals on the Social Structure of the Merovingian Kingdom. Randsborg 1989. 100ff.

Steuer, H. 1992. Interpretationsmöglichkeiten archäologischer Quellen zum Gefolgschaftsproblem. Neumann & Seemann 1992. 203ff.

Stjernquist, B. 1967. *Ciste a cordoni (Rippenzisten). Produktion — Funktion — Diffusion.* Acta Archaeologica Lundensia Series in 4', No. 6 (two vols.). Bonn/Lund (Habelt/Gleerup).

Strabon. c. AD 18. *Geographica* (Various translations).

Tacitus, Publius Cornelius. c. AD 98 *De origine et situ germanorum* ('Germania'; numerous translations).

Tauber, H. 1987. Danske arkæologiske C-14 dateringer 1987. *Arkæologiske udgravninger i Danmark* 1987. 227ff.

Tauber, H. 1988. Danish radiocarbon datings of archaeological samples. *Arkæologiske udgravninger i Danmark* 1988. 212ff.

Thrane, H. 1974. Hundredvis af energikilder fra yngre broncealder. *Fynske Minder* 1974. 96ff.

Thrane, H. 1975. *Europæiske forbindelser. Bidrag til studiet af fremmede forbindelser i Danmarks yngre broncealder (periode IV-V).* Nationalmuseets skrifter. Arkæologisk-historisk række XVI. Copenhagen (National Museum of Denmark).

Točík, A. & J. Paulík. 1960. Výskum mohyly v. Čake v rokoch 1950-51. *Slovenská Archeológia* 8;1. 59ff.

Torbrügge, W. 1971. Vor- und

frühgeschichtliche Flussfunde. Zur Ordnung und Bestimmung einer Denkmälergruppe. *Bericht der Römisch-Germanischen Kommission* 51-52. 1ff.

Uecker, H. (ed.). 1994. *Studien zum Altgermanisches. Festschrift für Heinrich Beck.* Ergänzungsbände zum Reallexikon der Germanischen Altertumskunde 11. Berlin (de Gruyter).

Vebæk, C.L. 1945. Smederup. An Early Iron Age Sacrificial Bog in East Jutland. *Acta Archaeologica* XVI. 195ff.

Ventris, M. & J. Chadwick. 1956. *Documents in Mycenean Greek. Three Hundred Selected Tablets from Knossos, Pylos and Mycenea with Commentary and Vocabulary.* Cambridge (Cambridge University Press).

Verger, S. 1990. Du dépôt métallique a la tombe fastueuse. Autour de la tombe de Saint-Romanin-de-Jalionas, l'enfouissement des objets de luxe à l'Âge du Bronze final. Guibal 1990. 53ff.

Vladár, J. 1973. Osteuropäische und mediterrane Einflüsse im Gebiet der Slowakei während der Bronzezeit. *Slovenská Archeológia* 21. 253ff.

Vokotopoulou, J. (ed.). 1993. *Greek Civilization. Macedonia. Kingdom of Alexander the Great.* Athens (Kapon).

de Vries, J. 1956-57. *Altgermanische Religionsgescichte I-II.* 2nd ed. Grundriss der germanischen Philologie 12/I-II. Berlin (W. de Gruyter).

Wankel, H. 1882. *Bilder aus der Mährischen Schweiz und ihre Vergangenheit.* Wien.

Warry, J. 1980. *Warfare in the Classical World. An illustrated encyclopedia of weapons, warriors and warfare in the ancient civilizations of Greece and Rome.* London (Salamander).

Ważny, T. 1993. Dendrochronological Dating of the Lusatian Culture Settlement at Biskupin, Poland. First Results. *NewsWARP* 14. 3 ff.

Wees, H. van. 1994. The Homeric Way of War: The Iliad and the Hoplite Phalanx (I) & (II). *Greece & Rome* (2nd Ser.) XLI;1 & 2. April & October 1994. 1ff. & 132ff.

Wegewitz, W. 1961. *Die Urnenfriedhöfe von Dohren und Daensen im Kreise Harburg.* Die Urnenfriedhöfe in Niedersachsen 5.

Wegewitz, W. 1977. *Die Urnenfriedhöfe der jüngeren Bronze-, der frühen und der vorrömischen Eisenzeit in Kreis Harburg.* Die Urnenfriedhöfe in Niedersachsen 13.

Wegewitz, W. 1988. Rund um den Kiekeberg. Vorgeschichte einer Landschaft an der Niederelbe. *Hammaburg* N.F. 8.

Wegner, G. 1976. *Die vorgeschichtlichen Flussfunde aus dem Main und aus dem Rhein bei Mainz.* Materialhefte zur bayerischen Vorgeschichte 30. Kallmünz (Lassleben).

Weigley, R.F. 1993(/1991). *The Age of Battles. The Quest for Decisive Warfare from Breitenfeld to Waterloo.* London (Pimlico).

Wells, P.S. 1980. *Culture contact and culture change. Early Iron Age central Europe and the Mediterranean world.* Cambridge (Cambridge University Press).

Westerdahl, C. (ed.). 1994. *Crossroads in Ancient Shipbuilding. Proceedings of the Sixth International Symposium on Boat and Ship Archaeology Roskilde 1991.* ISBSA 6. Oxbow Monograph 40. Oxford (Oxbow).

Wheeler, E.L. 1991. The General as Hoplite. Hanson 1991. 121ff.

Whittle, A. 1985. *Neolithic Europe. A Survey.* Cambridge (Cambridge University Press).

Willroth, K.-H. 1984. Die Opferhorte der älteren Bronzezeit in Südskandinavien. *Frühmittelalterliche Studien* 18. 48ff.

Willroth, K.-H. 1985. *Die Hortfunde der*

älteren Bronzezeit in Südschweden und auf den dänischen Inseln. Offa-Bücher 55.Neumünster (Wachholt).

Worsaae, J.J.A. 1853. Fund af en Metalarbeiders Forraad fra Broncealderen, tilhørende Hans Majestæt Kongen. *Annaler for Nordisk Oldkyndighed og Historie.* 121ff.

Wright, E. 1990. *The Ferriby Boats. Seacrafts of the Bronze Age.* London (Routledge).

Yoffee, N. & A. Sherratt (eds.). 1993. *Archaeological theory: who sets the agenda?* Cambridge (Cambridge University Press).

Zápotocký, M. 1969. K významu Labe jako spojovací a dopravní. *Památky Archeologické* LX;2. 277ff.

Zápotocký, M. 1991. Frühe Streiaxt-kulturen im mitteleuropäischen Äneolithikum. Lichardus 1991. 465ff.

Zápotcký, M. 1992. *Streitäxte des mitteleuropäischen Äneolithikums.* Quellen und Forschungen zur prähistorischen und provinzialrömischen Archäologie 6. Weinheim (VCH Acta Humaniora).

Zimmermann, W. 1970. Urgeschichtliche Opferfunde aus Flüssen, Mooren, Quellen und Brunnen Südwestdeutschlands. *Neue Ausgrabungen und Forschungen in Niedersachsen 6.* 53ff.

Geographical Index

Illustrations are indicated by italicized page numbers.

Index of Persons

Subject index